Service Innovation
for Sustainable Business
Stimulating, Realizing and Capturing
the Value from Service Innovation

Service Innovation
for Sustainable Business
Stimulating, Realizing and Capturing the Value from Service Innovation

Editors

Per Kristensson
Peter Magnusson
Lars Witell

Karlstad University, Sweden

World Scientific

NEW JERSEY · LONDON · SINGAPORE · BEIJING · SHANGHAI · HONG KONG · TAIPEI · CHENNAI · TOKYO

Published by

World Scientific Publishing Co. Pte. Ltd.

5 Toh Tuck Link, Singapore 596224

USA office: 27 Warren Street, Suite 401-402, Hackensack, NJ 07601

UK office: 57 Shelton Street, Covent Garden, London WC2H 9HE

Library of Congress Cataloging-in-Publication Data
Names: Kristensson, Per, editor. | Magnusson, Peter R., editor. | Witell, Lars, editor.
Title: Service innovation for sustainable business : stimulating, realizing and capturing the value
    from service innovation / edited by Per Kristensson (Karlstad University, Sweden),
    Peter Magnusson (Karlstad University, Sweden) and Lars Witell (Karlstad University, Sweden).
Description: New Jersey : World Scientific, [2019]
Identifiers: LCCN 2018043522 | ISBN 9789813273375 (hc : alk. paper)
Subjects: LCSH: Customer services. | New products. | Service industries.
Classification: LCC HF5415.5 .S465 2019 | DDC 658.8/12--dc23
LC record available at https://lccn.loc.gov/2018043522

British Library Cataloguing-in-Publication Data
A catalogue record for this book is available from the British Library.

For any available supplementary material, please visit
https://www.worldscientific.com/worldscibooks/10.1142/11074#t=suppl

Desk Editors: Dr. Sree Meenakshi Sajani/Alisha Nguyen/Karimah Samsudin

Typeset by Stallion Press
Email: enquiries@stallionpress.com

Printed in Singapore

Foreword

Innovation continues to be high on the agenda of policy makers and business executives, and in times when industry boarders are blending in the context of IoT and Digitalization, the concept of service innovation becomes the intersection point where technology meets new business opportunities and becomes an enabler for value creation.

The concept of service innovation has taken different forms throughout the years, especially in the corporate setting of technology intensive firms. In 2011, as a new Ericsson employee, I had my first interaction with the researchers at CTF. Back then we together struggled to introduce concepts like value co-creation and service-dominant logic. In 2018, service innovation is still of outmost importance for our firms success, however, now it is a natural part of our daily conversations, whether it is in our work to address customer pain points, form new types of eco-systems or transform business models, yet execution is hard.

It is of great importance that we continue to research and explore how to stimulate, realize and capture value in today's transformative world to excel in what we do. Being a business executive or a scholar, this is the book to read to understand what hidden potential lays in service innovation and how the new business logic can be applied to reap the benefits.

Sofi W. Elfving
Research Leader, Ericsson
May 2018

About the Editors

Dr. Per Kristensson is Professor at the Service Research Center (CTF) at Karlstad University, Sweden. Per earned his PhD at Gothenburg University and his research concerns consumer psychology, innovation and typically focuses on how users experience value creation when interacting with organizations. He has received several nominations and rewards for his research and has published in leading refereed journals and peer-reviewed conference proceedings, including *Journal of Product Innovation Management, Journal of Service Research, Journal of Business Research,* and *Technovation.* Per is also a visiting professor at NHH — Norwegian School of Economics and CSI — Center for Service Innovation and has previously been a visiting professor at ASU, WP Carey School of Business and CSL — Center for Service Leadership and at Mälardalen University. Per can be reached at Per.Kristensson@kau.se.

Dr. Peter R. Magnusson is Professor in business administration at the Service Research Center (CTF) attached to Karlstad University, Sweden. He holds an MSc in electrical engineering from Chalmers University, an MBA in executive business administration from the University of Uppsala, and a PhD from the Stockholm School of Economics. He has 20 years experience in research and development (R&D) in the computing and telecommunications industries. His research focuses on new product and service innovation, idea management, user innovation, and servitization. He has received several nominations and rewards for his research, and has published in leading refereed journals and peer-reviewed conference proceedings, including *Journal of Product Innovation Management, Journal of Service Research, Journal of the Academy of Marketing Science*, and *Creativity and Innovation Management.*

Dr. Lars Witell is Professor at the Service Research Center (CTF) at Karlstad University, Sweden. He also holds a position as Professor in business administration at Linköping University, Sweden. He conducts research on service innovation, customer co-creation, and service infusion in manufacturing firms. He has received several nominations and rewards for his research and has published in scholarly journals such as *Journal of Service Research, Industrial Marketing Management*, and *Journal of Business Research*; as well as in the popular press, such as *The Wall Street Journal.* Lars has also been a visiting professor at UQ Business School, Chalmers University of Technology and Queen Mary University of London, as well as a visiting scholar at University of Michigan and Stanford University.

About the Authors

Maria Åkesson holds a PhD at Service Research Center in Karlstad University, Sweden.

Helen Beckman is a Senior Customer Coordinator of Arla Foods in Jönköping.

Linda Bergkvist holds a PhD in information systems and researcher at the Service Research Center (CTF), Karlstad University, Sweden. Linda earned her PhD at Karlstad University in 2014. Her research focuses on service innovation, user experiences, and digitalization with a particular interest in digital transformation. Linda also has many years of experience from research in the field of contract-based business relationships, with a particular focus on outsourcing of system development, IT operations and IT management. Her research is conducted in cooperation with both the private and public sector. Linda Bergkvist can be contacted at linda.bergkvist@kau.se.

Sebastian Dehling is a PhD Candidate at Service Research Center in Karlstad University, Sweden.

Bo Edvardsson is Professor and Founder, Service Research Center and Vice Rector, Karlstad University, Sweden. In 2008, he received the RESER Award "Commendation for lifetime achievement to scholarship" by The European Association for Service Research and, in 2004, The AMA Career Contributions to the Services Discipline Award. In 2013, Bo was appointed Distinguished Faculty Fellow of the Center for Excellence in Service, University of Maryland and Honorary Distinguished Professor of Service Management, EGADE Business School, Monterrey Tech, Mexico. His research includes new service development and innovation, customer experience, complaint management, service eco-systems and transition from product to service in manufacturing. Bo can be contacted at bo.edvardsson@kau.se.

Bo Enquist is Professor at Service Research Center in Karlstad University, Sweden.

Rolf Findsrud is a PhD Candidate at Service Research Center in Karlstad University, Sweden.

Besma Glaa holds a PhD at Service Research Center in Karlstad University, Sweden.

Christiane Hipp is a Professor in Brandenburg University of Technology at Cottbus, Germany.

Maria Möllerskov-Jonzon is Knowledge and Insight leader within Customer Experience at IKEA Group. Building up capabilities supporting the customer centric development of IKEA, and supporting markets across the globe. Her career has always centered on a deep passion to understand customers' needs, and she has been working within Customers Insights, Market Intelligence, Market Research, and Customer Journey Analytics. Maria is responsible for the academic collaborations within Customer Experience and Service Business in IKEA Group. Her managerial interest includes customer journey analytics and shopping behaviors in the context of the rapidly evolving retail environment. Her passion centers on raising the voice of the customer to enable meaningful and sustainable strategic decision making, benefitting both IKEA and their customers. Currently she is part of developing a new voice of the customer program in IKEA, embedding new data and customer feedback processing methods into the business, to secure actionable customer insight supporting the continuous customer centricity of IKEA. Maria holds a cand.merc. in mathematics and economics from Copenhagen Business School and can be contacted at: linkedin.com/in/mariamjonzon.

Johan Kaluza holds a PhD at Service Research Center in Karlstad University, Sweden.

Jenny Karlsson holds a PhD at Service Research Center in Karlstad University, Sweden.

Chaoren Lu is a PhD Candidate at Service Research Center in Karlstad University, Sweden.

Matos Ricardo a PhD scholar, has worked at Tobii's training and knowledge department since August 2008, and is now responsible for Tobii's training programs. He has a PhD in Zoology, from the University of Copenhagen, Denmark, and 10 years of experience in behavioral sciences research. During his time working in Tobii, Ricardo has been deeply involved in the development of training and knowledge materials regarding Eye Trackers and Eye Tracking Systems.

Per Myhrén Ph Lic, is a Business Manager at Paper Province, Sweden.

Johan Netz is an Assistant Professor in business administration at the Service Research Center (CTF) attached to Karlstad University, Sweden. He holds a PhD from Karlstad University. His research focuses on new product and service innovation, idea management (with a special interest in intuitive and rational decision-making in the initial phases of the innovation process), and user innovation. His research has been published in leading refereed journals and peer-reviewed conference proceedings, including e.g., *Journal of Product Innovation Management* and *Technovation*.

Otterbring Tobias, PhD, is Associate Professor at Aarhus University, Denmark. His research focuses on the effects of nonverbal cues (e.g., smiling, physical appearance, and interpersonal touch) on customers' affective states, attitudes, and purchase behavior. Tobias has published articles in journals such as the *Journal of Marketing Research*, the *Journal of Business Research*, and *Psychology & Marketing*. He has been a finalist in Research Grand Prix and Science Slam, which are competitions similar to a TED talk that honor the most interesting, educational, and captivating research presentation. Recently, Tobias won the prestigious Academy of Marketing Science (AMS) Mary Kay Dissertation Award and qualified as a finalist in two additional award competitions for young, talented scholars, linked to the American Marketing Association (AMA) and the Human Behavior and Evolution Society (HBES).

Peter Samuelsson is a PhD Candidate at Service Research Center in Karlstad University, Sweden.

Samuel Petros Sebhatu holds a PhD at Service Research Center in Karlstad University, Sweden.

Shams Poja, PhD, is associate professor at Service Research Center (CTF) in Karlstad University, Sweden. His research has primarily been focused on consumer decision making and visual attention in the retail environment. Contributions are made within marketing with focus on customer experience using eye-tracking and other process tracing methods in the retail environment. With 10 years of experience in eye-tracking research in lab and in field, he has published in several distinguished journals such as *Journal of Business & Retail Management Research, Journal of Business Research*, and *Psychology & Marketing*. His research has been awarded by the Gunnar Sundblad Research Foundation granted by his majesty the King of Sweden.

Alexandre Sukhov is a PhD Candidate at Service Research Center in Karlstad University, Sweden.

Bård Tronvoll is Professor of Marketing at Inland Norway University of Applied Sciences, Norway and at CTF-Service Research Center at Karlstad University, Sweden. He has previously been a senior distinguished researcher at HANKEN School of Economics, Finland. Tronvoll is a member of the editorial advisory board at Journal of

Service Management and his work has been published in journals such as *Journal of the Academy of Marketing Science, Journal of Service Research, Journal of Business Research, European Journal of Marketing Journal of Service Management,* and *Marketing Theory.* His research interests include marketing theory, service innovation, customer complaining behavior/service recovery, and service marketing. Dr. Bård Tronvoll can be contacted at bard@tronvoll.no.

Wästlund Erik is an Associate Professor at Service Research Center in Karlstad University, Sweden.

Lars Witell is a Professor at Service Research Center in Karlstad University, Sweden.

Contents

Chapter 1

Introduction

Per Kristensson*, Peter R. Magnusson* and Lars Witell*,†

*Karlstad University, Sweden
†Linköping University, Sweden

Introduction

In 1977, in her landmark paper, "Breaking Free from Product Marketing" in *Journal of Marketing*, Lynn Shostack suggested that service marketing has to take into account the specific characteristics of services (Shostack, 1977). The emergent recognition of services formed a new research area; that is, service marketing. Even in the late 90s, services (as compared to products) were often described by their characteristics, by being *inseparable, heterogeneous, intangible,* and *perishable*, popularly abbreviated "IHIP". In the beginning of the new millennium, researchers criticized this simplified and flawed classification of services (e.g., Lovelock and Gummesson, 2004). As a result, services and service innovation have finally shaken off their Cinderella status, in the sense of being neglected and marginal, to achieve wider recognition as a field worthy of study (Miles, 2000).

A milestone for taking a new perspective on services was the introduction of the "service-dominant logic" (SDL) coined by Vargo and Lusch (2004). SDL, in turn, built on research ideas emanating from the

Nordic School of Service Marketing (Grönroos, 2016; Gummesson, 1995; Edvardsson, 1996). This perspective on service virtually erased the borderline between physical goods and services, instead claiming the importance of the value gained from using integrated products and services. So far so good. However, ideas on how to innovate new services, which recently has arisen as a relevant and important research area, still rely on traditional service marketing that to a large extent is inherited from studies on product development.

Many early attempts to describe the development of new services were slight adaptations of established new product development (NPD) models. Commonly, these start with an idea and end with a commercialized product. The process is described as a structured rational sequential process with well-defined stages separated by gates (Wheelwright and Clark, 1992). Innovation and development is thus portrayed as a pre-planned and controlled, rational process. Researchers have suggested adaptions of NPD models to services, often called new service development (NSD) models. Examples of this are Scheuing and Johnson (1989), Bowers (1989), Johnson *et al.* (1999), and Alam and Perry (2002). All these suggested models are sequential, encompassing from eight up to fifteen stages. Service innovation is thus regarded as a special case of product development where adjustments are made to capture the particularities of services.

An alternative perspective has developed that comes from empirical studies of service development and innovation (e.g., Fuglsang and Sørensen, 2011; Høyrup, 2012). This perspective instead recognizes that innovation may also be the outcome of *unintended* and *informal* processes. It also pinpoints that service innovations are mostly incremental, and can emanate from different types of innovation activities (e.g., Toivonen and Tuominen, 2009; Fuglsang and Sørensen, 2011; Sundbo, 1997). Gallouj and Weinstein (1997) define "*ad hoc* innovation" where the innovation represents "a solution to a particular problem posed by a given client." A similar perspective on service innovation is referred to as bricolage or tinkering, a type of "do-it-yourself" problem-solving activity that creates structure from resources at hand (Fuglsang and Sørensen, 2011). These innovations are developed without an intention to innovate, but rather by employees finding a solution to an emerging problem, often in the context of their ordinary work.

Research on service innovation is at a relatively early stage of its development; there are recurrent calls for research to improve our understanding of this topic and its underlying mechanisms (e.g., Ordanini and Parasuraman, 2011; Ettlie and Rosenthal, 2011; Lages and Piercy, 2012; Rubalcaba *et al.*, 2012; Ostrom *et al.*, 2010; Snyder *et al.*, 2016). Service innovation is investigated and understood from several perspectives, often referred to as assimilation, demarcation, and synthesis (Coombs and Miles, 2000). All these perspectives are used in service research, providing a rich view of service innovation in the private and public sector (Witell *et al.*, 2016).

Service Research Center in Karlstad, Sweden

The Service Research Center, CTF (in Swedish, Centrum för tjänsteforskning) is one of the world's leading research centers focusing on value creation through service. CTF is a well established international research community that co-creates research together with business and public sector organizations. In 2012, external reviewers on mission for The Knowledge Foundation in Sweden ranked CTF within the top five service research centers in the world. CTF has a widespread reputation for quality research that is both academically rigorous and relevant, addressing issues related to societal problem solving.

Established by Bo Edvardsson in 1986, CTF today has around 70 researchers and doctoral students who are active researchers in business administration, informatics, working life science, psychology, engineering sciences, and sociology of religion. Since CTF was established, PhD candidates have published 46 dissertations and 22 licentiate theses. More than 500 articles have been published in scholarly journals. CTF is involved in research, undergraduate and graduate education, and close cooperation with leading business and public organizations in various areas of service research. In addition, CTF also arranges highly appreciated external seminars and conferences, both for practitioners and academics.

To live up to its excellent reputation as a leading research center, CTF builds on three pillars:

- CTF is a nationally and internationally recognized, excellent research environment at Karlstad University, characterized by high scientific quality.
- CTF's research and education are conducted in close interaction with the surrounding society (that is, public and business organizations).
- CTF is a multidisciplinary research organization.

The overall ambition of CTF is to develop research regarding *value creation through service*. In doing so, CTF will strengthen its position as a national and international research environment characterized by its high scientific quality. With value creation through service as its vision, its mission is to collaborate with external organizations by doing research on complex and challenging issues relating, to some extent, to value-creating processes.

Over the years, CTF's efforts to develop groundbreaking theoretical and actionable knowledge have developed. New service development and new service innovation represents one of the strongest research areas at CTF. During its collaboration and interaction with leading organizations in Sweden, new and challenging research questions have emerged. Studied over many years, research areas include servitization research (presented in Chapters 7–9, 13 and 14 of this book), how new business models emerge (Chapter 15), and how organizations stimulate ideas for innovation (Chapters 2–5) or manage psychological aspects in their surroundings (Chapters 9–10). Research on business models is now part of several ongoing projects at CTF. In this way, new research streams are expected to grow, and also, in combination with that, new research profiles and subjects are expected to be integrated into CTF's activities.

External cooperation constitutes one of the hallmarks of CTF. This is visible through its vision and mission, to do research in collaboration with organizations in order to strengthen their competitiveness in terms of value creation for their users. CTF's extensive interaction and involvement has contributed to developing partner organizations' operations, as well as created favorable conditions for research funding, access to data collection, and access to an alternative labor market for newly graduated PhDs. Collaboration also has contributed to quality improvements within research, such as how CTF seeks, defines, and tackles research problems, and also how CTF communicates research results. External cooperation with business organizations has been present since CTF was founded, and CTF continues to have close research collaborations with business firms.

Service Innovation for Sustainable Business

The research profile *Service Innovation for Sustainable Business* (project financed by KK-stiftelsen) was launched in September 2011 (it continued 2011–2019) to identify the DNA of service innovation. The research profile provides new knowledge on service innovation that can contribute to building sustainable new work practices and businesses for CTF's partners. In addition, the research profile aims to strengthen the position of CTF as a leading research center in service management. Building on its brand and recognition, CTF has taken a leading position in research on service innovation; CTF has participated in EU grant applications and organized research forums, workshops, and research network meetings.

The overall purpose of the research profile is to **describe and understand the DNA of service innovation.** The metaphor of DNA refers to the mechanisms in the development (process) and functioning (output) of service innovation. The research profile will unfold the generic and specific mechanisms of service innovation. DNA is often compared to a set of blueprints, like a recipe or a code, since it contains the instructions needed to put together or take apart living things; here, the living thing is service innovation.

Based on the DNA of service innovation, the research profile will develop theories, models, and methods for the management, organization, and development of service innovations. The research profile's more specific purposes are to develop theoretical and empirically grounded knowledge on the following:

- What is and how can we describe a service innovation (output and process) and the new service development process?
- What is the role of value capture in service innovation; that is, different ways of capturing value such as new business models?
- What is the role of the service ecosystem and what are resource prerequisites for the stimulation, realization, and further development of service innovation?
- What is the role of technology, people, and data in service innovation?
- What is the role of customer and employee integration in new service development, and does integration have an effect on new service development performance?

The research of Service Innovation for Sustainable Business can best be described through a framework of research themes and research contexts. The three research themes are stimulation, realization, and value capture, and they constitute the structure of this book. The two research contexts that are studied in detail through the research profile are retailing and manufacturing. In particular, we work together with our partners Ericsson, Volvo, Valmet, IKEA, ICA, and Löfbergs to increase our knowledge on service innovation (previously Tetra Pak and Stamford also participated). In the book, we present some of the ideas and knowledge created within the research profile and CTF in general.

Some recent reviews of research on service innovation and new service development show that CTF is recognized as a leader in service innovation. In the paper, "Uncovering the structures and maturity of the new service development research field through a bibliometric study (1984–2014)," Mendes *et al.* (2017) identify the largest network of NSD researchers as revolving around CTF and Professor Bo Edvardsson. During the time period of the study, 59 authors coauthored 46 research papers on NSD, focusing on NSD characteristics, customer involvement, service engineering, and product-service systems and on NSD in manufacturing companies. In a similar paper titled "New service development: How the field developed, its current status and recommendations for moving the field forward," Biemans *et al.* (2016) point out the CTF-led research cohort as the largest and most active researchers on new service development. In particular, they conclude that the Scandinavian researchers focus on the relationship with customers, either as providers of market information or as active collaborators in the development of new services.

Purpose of the Book

The main purpose of this book is to discuss and explain service innovation based on contemporary research. The book explains service innovation based on three core activities: *stimulation, realization,* and *value capture.* All three activities need to be considered, and as a result of these considerations, detailed activities have to be carefully implemented to accomplish service innovation that has an impact in organizations.

- *Stimulation.* Organizations focus on the front end of service innovation; that is, the initial activities that spark ideas for new service. The front end deals with structures, cultures, and processes to stimulate and nurture innovation. Idea management is a central part of it, that illuminates the specifics of handling service ideas.
- *Realization.* Companies investigate how to realize service innovations. Compared to traditional physical products, services that lead to value creation induce specific problems when it comes to realization; for instance, how to visualize your service in order to define and communicate the new value. But also, virtually all service innovation implies some kind of organizational change: new organizational processes and structures have to be implemented, employees have to be trained, and customers have to be informed of how to co-create the service. To be successful in developing new services, organizations must adopt a new mindset and new tools.
- *Value capture.* Companies transiting to more service-oriented models need to reconsider old business models in order to capitalize on their new services. Services are often taken for granted and included for free in the price of the product. This chapter addresses the problem of going "from free to fee".

Who Should Read This Book?

The book should be read by managers and academics interested in gaining knowledge about the following:

- A deeper description of special aspects of service innovation. This description should allow both managers and academics to carry out more profound analyses of service innovation processes.
- Managerial advice for service innovation, with case studies from different types of organizations.
- A framework of service innovation consisting of *stimulation, realization,* and *value capture.*

The target group is people who want to understand service innovation based on knowledge anchored in contemporary research. The book is intended for both academic courses as well as management education; the target group includes researchers, undergraduate and graduate students including MBA students, and managers in both business and public organizations.

Outline of the Book

The first part of the book, which focuses on *stimulation*, includes chapters related to how service innovation begins in organizations.

In Chapter 2, Johan Netz and Peter R. Magnusson discuss why companies sooner or later discover that there are huge differences between developing services and developing products. Service development requires tools and methods different from those used primarily for product development. Even so, the latter types are still frequently used when developing new services. In the chapter, different tools and methods focusing on service development are suggested depending on where in the innovation processes the development project is. Reading this chapter will provide practical advice and knowledge relevant to the future development of new services.

In Chapter 3, Alexandre Sukhov, Johan Netz, and Peter R. Magnusson adress the early stages of innovation by defining and introducing a model of an idea for innovation. This model helps in managing idea generation (by analyzing the content of an idea and whether it needs further elaboration), refinement (by directing the attention on the missing elements and helping to identify the competences needed for its development), and evaluation (by reducing cognitive bias through an improvement of the information content and the narrative of the idea description). The chapter provides real examples of ideas for innovation from the industry that show how the model can be used.

In Chapter 4, Peter Samuelsson, Alexandre Sukhov, Johan Kaluza, and Chaoren Lu take a starting point in what stimulates innovation in the public sector. Since market logic does not apply to service innovation practices in the public sector, this chapter describes and illustrates what does and how. Following this aim, the chapter is conceptual in nature, building upon the service innovation and public management literature, informed by practice theory. The chapter presents a model for service innovation in the public sector, where the guiding logic of public management is broken into three parts: traditional administration, new public management, and new public governance. Different guiding logics give social structures that use different innovation practices. The different innovation practices create different outcomes in terms of value constellations, making it important for public organizations to structure and manage their service innovation operations accordingly.

In Chapter 5, Bård Tronvoll and Bo Edvardsson, from CTF, together with Maria Möllerskov-Jonzon from IKEA investigate how IKEA gets feedback and learns from customers, practices that are critical for service innovation. Feedback from customers seldom contributes to innovation processes; the problem is in using the feedback gathered. This chapter therefore explores customer feedback that stimulates and contributes to the service innovation process. This chapter focuses on IKEA's innovation journey using their "Democratic Design" concept. This journey started with customer feedback and has resulted in an easy-assembly furniture system called the click system.

The second part of the book, which focuses on *realization*, includes chapters related to how service innovation is actually happening in organizations.

In Chapter 6, Rolf Findsrud and Sebastian Dehling positions resource integration processes as a microfoundation for service innovation to occur. The focus is on actors' resource integration processes using operant resources, individually or in collaboration, coordinated by institutional arrangements, to co-create value. Actors' resource integration creates opportunities to discover, reshape or create new combinations of resources. Accordingly, resource integration represents the key process from which potentially better ways of realizing value can be found. As a result, service innovation occurs through new or changed practices that are adopted by a wider collective changing in practice at a higher level of aggregation.

In Chapter 7, Besma Glaa, Per Kristensson, and Lars Witell focus on how service teams can integrate knowledge about value creation with in-depth skills in innovating new, technologically advanced solutions. The chapter synthesizes various research articles that have addressed the problem of finding teams that have knowledge about both value-creation and technical solutions, and emphasizes that successful service innovation considers both of these areas of knowledge.

In Chapter 8, Per Myhrén, Lars Witell, and Maria Åkesson discuss how assigning actors different roles is a prerequisite for open service innovation. More specifically, the chapter focuses on the actors' roles and knowledge transfer in the innovation process. The chapter builds on data from an innovator firm and its network partner and describes how the firm's existence has relied solely on the outcomes from an open service innovation network since the early 1970s. We show how actors take on multiple innovator roles in the innovation process of open service innovation, and we introduce a new innovator role, the "Constitutional Monarch".

In Chapter 9, Per Kristensson and Peter R. Magnusson show that while servitization has been an interesting outcome for industrial organizations, many companies in this sector still struggle to make servitization happen. Instead of depicting servitization phases and identifying challenges, Kristensson and Magnusson showcase how manufacturing firms can apply psychological findings to jump-start servitization and reap the benefits that so many researchers talk about.

In Chapter 10, Erik Wästlund, Poja Shams, and Tobias Otterbring introduce "the 3S model: Store, Shelf, Stock" for studying the servicescape of retailing. They build this model on a review of several of their previously published eye-tracking studies. Thus, this chapter gives a short-cut to many scientific findings. Furthermore, they delineate the importance of studying the process underlying customers' service experiences in the retail servicescape and the necessity to include new technological tools in order to understand customer experiences.

In Chapter 11, Samuel Petros and Bo Enquist addressed the idea of a values driven service innovation through sustainability business practices and service research for transformation, value co-creation, and sustainability/CSR-practice to provide "sustainable service business" a broader meaning. We have given a priority to innovation and transformation that includes the global society and the biosphere. This study is based on the service innovation thinking in the value chain of a values-driven family-owned enterprise, which is engaged on re-configuring their engagement at the BoP by innovating "next practice" thinking. This chapter contributes to developing "next practice" as a business model and proposing a managerial and social embeddedness in sustainability service innovation.

In Chapter 12, Linda Bergkvist and Jenny Karlsson investigate the gaps and challenges in implementing innovative ideas. The chapter draws on a qualitative study of service innovation processes in a healthcare context involving users, frontline employees (FLEs), and managers. Conditions for realizing service innovation are identified and related to environment, organization, management, and users/FLEs. Previous implementation frameworks, with a narrow focus on adoption of innovations, have been extended by introducing a practice-based perspective and by illuminating conditions for the realization of service innovation ideas.

The third part of the book, which focuses on *value capture*, includes chapters related to how service innovation is creating value for the organization undertaking the innovation effort.

In Chapter 13, Peter R. Magnusson, Christiane Hipp, and Bo Edvardsson gives an in-depth account for the challenges that manufacturing companies often encounter when integrating services in their businesses. The main challenges being stuck in a mindset, knowledge spillover, and pricing/charging of services. Furthermore, they derive a model where servitization is divided into five different phases which put different demands on the company to succeed. Finally, managerial implications for handling the transition process are given.

In Chapter 14, Lars Witell, Peter R. Magnusson, Bo Edvardsson, and Helen Beckman show why it is important for manufacturing firms to innovate through services in order to develop ongoing business relationships. The products become platforms for services that create value-in-use for the customer. This study identifies two service-based states of business relationships — revitalization and regression — that help explain the dynamics of value creation through service. The chapter contributes by taking an in-depth look at what happens when a business relationship founded on transactions of goods changes into one based on service.

References

Alam, I. and Perry, C. (2002). A customer-oriented new service development process. *Journal of Services Marketing*, **16**, 515–534.

Biemans, W. G., Griffin, A., and Moenaert, R. K. (2016). Perspective: New service development: How the field developed, its current status and recommendations for moving the field forward. *Journal of Product Innovation Management*, **33**(4), 382–397.

Bowers, M. R. (1989). Developing new services: Improving the process makes it better. *Journal of Services Marketing*, **3**, 15–20.

Coombs, R. and Miles, I. (2000). Innovation, measurement and services: the new problematique. In *Innovation Systems in the Service Economy* (pp. 85–103). Springer, Boston, MA.

Ettlie, J. E. and Rosenthal, S. R. (2011). Service versus manufacturing innovation. *Journal of Product Innovation Management*, **28**, 285–299.

Fuglsang, L. and Sørensen, F. (2011). The balance between bricolage and innovation: Management dilemmas in sustainable public innovation. *Service Industries Journal*, **31**, 581–595.

Gallouj, F. and Weinstein, O. (1997). Innovation in services. *Research Policy*, **26**, 537–556.

Grönroos, C. (2016). *Service Management and Marketing: Managing the Service Profit Logic*. John Wiley & Sons.

Gummesson, E. (1995). *Relationsmarknadsföring: från 4 P till 30 R*. Liber ekonomi.

Edvardsson, B. (1996). *Tjänsteutveckling med inbyggd kvalitet*. Witell, L., *et al.* (2016). Defining service innovation: A review and synthesis, *Journal of Business Research*, **69**(8), 2863–2872.

Høyrup, S. (2012). Employee-Driven Innovation. A New Phenomenon, Concept and Mode of Innovation. In: Høyrup, S., Bonnafous-Boucher, M., Hasse, C., Lotz, M., and Møller, K. (eds.), *Employee-Driven Innovation. A New Approach.* Basingstoke: Palgrave Macmillan.

Johnson, S. P., Menor, L. J., Roth, A. V., and Chase, R. B. (1999). A Critical Evaluation of the New Service Development Process: Integrating Service Innovation and Service Design. In: Fitzsimmons, J. A. and Fitzsimmons, M. J. (eds.), *New Service Development: Creating Memorable Experiences.* Thousand Oaks: Sage Publications, Inc.

Lages, C. R. and Piercy, N. F. (2012). Key drivers of frontline employee generation of ideas for customer service improvement. *Journal of Service Research,* **15**, 215–230.

Lovelock, C. H. and Gummesson, E. (2004). Whither services marketing? *Journal of Service Research,* **7**, 20–41.

Mendes, G. H., Oliveira, M. G., Gomide, E. H., and Nantes, J. F. D. (2017). Uncovering the structures and maturity of the new service development research field through a bibliometric study (1984–2014). *Journal of Service Management,* **28**(1), 182–223.

Miles, I. (2000). Services innovation: Coming of age in the knowledge-based economy. *International Journal of Innovation Management,* **4**, 371–389.

Ordanini, A. and Parasuraman, A. (2011). Service innovation viewed through a service-dominant logic lens: A conceptual framework and empirical analysis. *Journal of Service Research,* **14**, 3–23.

Ostrom, A. L., Bitner, M. J., Brown, S. W., Burkhard, K. A., Goul, M., Smith-Daniels, V., Demirkan, H., and Rabinovich, E. (2010). Moving forward and making a difference: Research priorities for the science of service. *Journal of Service Research,* **13**, 4–36.

Rubalcaba, L., Michel, S., Sundbo, J., Brown, S. W., and Reynoso, J. (2012). Shaping, organizing, and rethinking service innovation: A multidimensional framework. *Journal of Service Management,* **23**, 696–715.

Scheuing, E. E. and Johnson, E. M. (1989). A proposed model for new service development. *Journal of Services Marketing,* **3**, 25–34.

Shostack, G. L. (1977). Breaking free from product marketing. *Journal of Marketing,* 73–80.

Snyder, H., Witell, L., Gustafsson, A., Fombelle, P., and Kristensson, P. (2016). Identifying categories of service innovation: A review and synthesis of the literature. *Journal of Business Research,* **69**(7), 2401–2408.

Sundbo, J. (1997). Management of innovation in services. *The Service Industry Journal,* **17**, 432–455.

Toivonen, M. and Tuominen, T. (2009). Emergence of innovations in services. *The Service Industries Journal*, **29**, 887–902.

Vargo, S. L. and Lusch, R. F. (2004). Evolving to a new dominant logic for marketing. *Journal of Marketing*, **68**, 1–17.

Wheelwright, S. C. and Clark, K. B. (1992). *Revolutionizing Product Development: Quantum Leaps in Speed, Efficiency and Quality*. New York: Free Press.

Witell, L., Snyder, H., Gustafsson, A., Fombelle, P., and Kristensson, P. (2016). Defining service innovation: A review and synthesis. *Journal of Business Research*, **69**(8), 2863–2872.

Chapter 2

Methods and Tools for Service Innovation

Johan Netz and Peter R. Magnusson

Karlstad University, Sweden

Key takeaways

1. There is no unified definition of a service innovation process.
2. This chapter presents seven different practical methods and tools applicable when developing and testing a new or existing service.
3. This chapter advises using a service blueprint as a visual and living document on which other methods and tools can generate input data.
4. This is a practical chapter that is relevant to both private and public innovation management practices.
5. This chapter relates to Chapter 3.

Successful development of new services is challenging, since services are process- and experience-based, and often include human interaction during delivery (Bitner *et al.*, 2008; Gustafsson *et al.*, 2012). Hence, emphasizing the use of tools and methods that capture the process, delivery, and experience from the customer or user perspective during new service development is important. However, many companies try to rely on tools and methods designed for the development of physical products when developing new services. These companies will sooner or later discover that there are huge differences in developing services as compared to products.

For example, product-focused development tools do not invoke the special characteristics of services, such as dynamic co-production between customers, employees, and technology (for example, online hotel booking systems). Product-focused tools instead focus on the design of tangible, often static, physical products, leaving out important elements related to human interaction. Since services often have a high degree of human interaction, they are hard to program. The result is that tools used to design and develop physical products are of little help when developing services.

One reason for the omission of customers when developing innovations is that the information needed about customer needs and experience (that is, the customer value-creation process) is often described as being complex and difficult to acquire (Lemon and Verhoef, 2016). A customer's perceived value is described as "sticky information" (von Hippel, 1994), and according to Lüthje *et al.* (2005) is costly to acquire, since the information is tacit. Thus, it can be difficult for firms to understand the value-creational processes that customers experience.

Hence, companies relying on tools and methods designed for product development are likely to fail in their efforts to fully satisfy their customers when developing new services. We argue that these companies have to reconsider how they work and what methods and tools they apply when developing new services. Using designated service development tools for understanding customer needs will increase their chances of generating successful new services (Witell *et al.*, 2011).

In this chapter, we explore a selection of tools and methods that can be helpful. First, we define a generic service development process encompassing four different stages from exploration to testing. The different stages have different challenges when it comes to service development and require different tools. Then, this chapter focuses on methods and tools to be used in the two middle stages; that is, the development and testing phases.

The Service Innovation Process

Summarizing years of research, it becomes clear that there is no, and will probably never be any, "universal service innovation process". Trying to copy an existing product development process and adopt it for service development will not work perfectly. However, the good news is that today, there are tools that fit different stages in the service development process.

Exaggerating slightly, one could say that virtually every existing development process emanates from the seminal work of Booz, Allen, and Hamilton from the late 1960s (Griffin, 1997). They proposed a multi-stage model for developing products, today known as a stage-gate model. Cooper's (1990) stage-gate model is for instance one of the most frequently mentioned models in this regard, with its clear and defined stages, and subsequent gates at which the project is reviewed and evaluated. The goal at each gate is to either grant the project acceptance for continued development or reject it (Kim and Wilemon, 2002).

Most service development processes have similarities with product development processes, and some models are linear whereas others are iterative. A wide range of different setups has been proposed, ranging from two to more than 10 distinctive phases (as described in the introduction of this book). Regardless of how many phases or steps a process contains, these phases or steps can be summarized into four different generic stages. The process starts with the idea creation stage and ends with launching the final innovation (see Figure 1).

The different stages, visualized in Figure 1, can be described in the following way. In the initial (1) *idea creation stage,* a firm explores new opportunities, identifying market trends and customer needs — in other words, the direction of upcoming development. This initial stage is also referred to as Front End Innovation or FEI (Koen *et al.*, 2001). From the

Figure 1.   The service innovation process.

insights gained, the firm creates ideas, and in the final part of this first stage examines these ideas and selects some for further development. In the subsequent (2) *development stage*, the selected ideas are further elaborated and translated into more robust concepts. At this stage, all stakeholders concerned with the final innovation should be involved. At the end of the development stage, the concept is once again assessed and evaluated. If the concept is perceived as feasible, it moves on to the third (3) *testing stage*. Here the concept is tested and validated before it passes on to the final (4) *launch stage*, where the final service innovation is presented and launched.

Depending on where in the development process you are, different tools are suitable. The key is to be open-minded when using different methods and tools, and to understand that most methods can have multiple purposes and usages. The rest of this chapter proposes seven different tools and methods, suitable for the development and testing stages, that address service characteristics.

Categorization of methods

All methods and tools proposed in this chapter are labeled as either *in situ* or *ex situ*. The labeling is connected to the paradigm shift, from seeing services as a category of market offerings to a perspective of value creation (Edvardsson *et al.*, 2012). Traditionally, focus has been on the differences between goods and services, while the service-dominant logic (SDL) focus is on what goods and services can do for the customer or user; that is, the experienced customer value (Vargo and Lusch, 2004). *In situ* literary means "in place"; hence, the information is generated when a customer (or employee) is in and experiences the service situation. In contrast, an *ex situ* technique is used to understand the customer when he or she is not in the service situation (Edvardsson *et al.*, 2012). Hence, *in situ* techniques can be described as concurrent data collection, whereas *ex situ* techniques are based on retrospective data.

From a practical perspective, it is important to categorize methods and tools as either *in situ* or *ex situ* when selecting and using different development methods and tools, to better understand customers' experiences of service and value co-creation. For instance, while *in situ* techniques at first glance seems preferable, they are labor-intensive compared to *ex situ* techniques. As discussed in this chapter, a combination of both perspectives is good for both seeing the holistic picture of the future service and understanding the details in the customer value-creation and service processes. According to Johne and Storey (1998), the service process "is the chain of activities which must occur for the service to function" (p. 207).

Service Blueprinting — A Holistic View of the Service

As described more thoroughly in Chapter 3, all innovation projects start with an idea. While all methods and tools mentioned in this chapter can give rise to new ideas, we depart from a scenario where the idea is already chosen, or where a clear problem and solution description is in place. It is important to visualize the service process in order to see the greater picture and thus grasp what is needed to make the service run smoothly and effectively, for the intended users or customers.

One tool to initially visualize a new service is the service blueprint. A service blueprint, which was introduced by G. Lynn Shostack in the 1980s (Shostack, 1982), allows firms to visualize the service process from a customer perspective by connecting a customer's interaction to the firm's underlying processes that enable the service. A service blueprint can thus be seen as an tool. However, the blueprint can include *in situ* data, based on inputs from other methods and tools.

Bitner *et al.* (2008) describe in detail how a service blueprint can generate a deeper understanding of how customers experience the service process, by showing how customers experience the service, over time, through interactions with the service process via different touchpoints. The visualized blueprint contains five different layers: (1) *the customer actions*, (2) *onstage/visible contact employee actions*, (3) *backstage/invisible contact employee actions*, (4) *support processes*, and (5) *physical evidence* (see Figure 2).

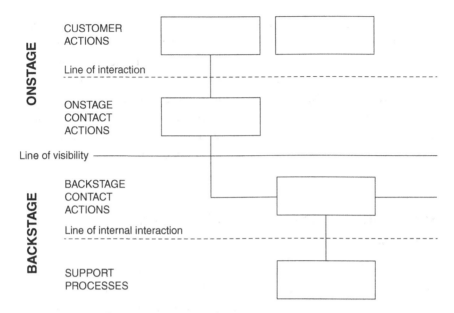

Figure 2.   Service blueprint.

The initial customer actions are described chronologically in the blueprint. The second layer, the onstage/visible contact employee actions, describes the interaction between the customers and the frontline employees (or self-serve technology). The third layer describes the backstage/ invisible contact employee actions, which are hidden from the customers. Thus, these actions can be described as non-visible interactions between the firm and its customers (for example, telephone support), as well as those activities that employees undertake to serve the customers. The fourth layer includes support processes; that is, activities managed by employees not having direct contact with the customers that need to happen for the service to be delivered. Finally, all physical evidence that customers come in contact with is highlighted above the customer actions. Physical evidence includes all "tangibles" that customers are exposed to; for example, a booking confirmation (which could be either printed or digital). Physical evidence can influence customers' quality perceptions of the service.

Every time an interaction occurs between the different layers, the link is highlighted on the blueprint. Hence, a service blueprint can be used to both refine single steps in the customer process (that is, all customer interactions with the service process) and to generate a visual overview of the whole service process.

According to Bitner *et al.* (2008), it is important to start by articulating what type of service process is to be blueprinted, since many firms have different processes based on different customer segments; for example, first-class versus economy passengers. Thus, one type of service might have several different blueprints, depending on what type of customer is the focus. Once type is decided upon, the blueprint built of customer actions is used as a starting point for the visualization, since these actions serve as the foundation to all other activities in the service process. All stakeholders should be involved who make the service process come to life (that is, different departments, partners, etc.), and they should be involved from the beginning of the creation of the service blueprint to get the most out of it and, as early as possible, highlight possible problem areas to be resolved.

While the blueprint is being created, new ideas for how to improve the service might emerge. Idea creation could also occur when different methods and tools are being used to generate input data for the blueprint. Hence, a service blueprint document should be seen as a living document and serve as a base for the development of the service process. The remainder of this chapter describes different methods. To organize them, we use two themes. Initially we focus on methods and tools used to *understand and explore customer needs*. These techniques can be used to test and evaluate already existing services, to test a newly developed service process, and to give rise to new service ideas. In connection to these, we also discuss different methods and tools used to test and simulate new services, from both an *in situ* and an *ex situ* perspective.

Methods and Tools to Understand and Explore Customer Needs

Simply asking your customers about their experience and satisfaction after you have sold them the service is not good enough. By asking right from the beginning, and thus understanding what is important to customers before you develop the idea, you will save money in the long run. Having fresh ideas is a prerequisite for innovation; however, these ideas are in many cases only discussed internally in an organization, regardless of whether an original idea came from a customer or not. In a worst-case scenario, the decision to develop an idea might be based solely on internal convictions about what is "right" for the customer. Since the decision could lead to huge investments, it is important to base it on the right facts and knowledge. Understanding the customer is the key to success. In this section, we discuss three different methods and tools that can be used to explore and understand customer needs.

The first method is *customer-driven service development (in situ)*. Researchers at the Service Research Center at Karlstad University have developed a method for involving users in the ideation process. It is described by Magnusson (2003) as collaborative experimental design (CED). Development teams use submitted user ideas to understand user needs. The method is based on the customers themselves identifying and documenting a problem, solution, idea, or feeling in the moment that it occurs. Using tools such as cameras or smartphones an individual customer can share, express, and visualize his or her inner thoughts immediately with the development team, thus capturing pronounced needs as well as needs that are difficult to articulate. This information can create new ideas for services and can also be used to improve an already existing service, to make it more customer oriented.

Similar to the above, a *service safari (in situ)* is a research method for understanding services by letting employees explore their own service process, or by studying competitors from a customer or user point of view (Stickdorn et al., 2011). By using the service, one will gain a more thorough understanding of how the service works and how it is experienced. The information gathered could later be used to improve the existing service or to be a seed for a new service concept. When carrying out a service safari you should, for instance, consider items like the following: What different people are involved in delivering the service, and what do they do? What objects does the user use or interact with? In contrast with the previous method, here employees take on the customer's role. This is normally cheaper and more convenient than asking customers for help.

However, there is a risk of bias, as the employees' knowledge might be greater than that of a regular customer, which can make the cognitive experience different.

Based on the inputs of the first two methods, a *customer journey (ex situ)* can be used to help visualize the feelings and experiences among customers using the service (Richardson, 2010; Stickdorn *et al.*, 2011). A customer journey describes the journey of a customer, or user, by representing the different touchpoints of the customer's interaction with the service (including interactions with both physical objects and front-end staff). The experience of the service is described step by step as the customer progresses forward in the offering process; this description helps the service provider gain a deeper understanding of the customers' interactions through the whole service process from start to finish. These three methods can thus be used to capture customer needs, and the analyzed data can be incorporated in service development (or the improvement of existing services).

Methods Used to Test and Simulate the Service Process

In the latter part of the development process, the original idea has been implemented and transformed into a robust concept ready to be finalized. The methods presented in this section could be used as a last check before going live with the service.

With every new service, it is important to achieve a competitive advantage, to make a profit. One way to differentiate a service is through creating an attractive service environment that improves the customer experience (Reimer and Kuehn, 2005). According to researchers (Edvardsson *et al.*, 2005, 2010), six design dimensions form the service environment or "experience room" in which the service takes place: physical artifacts, intangible artifacts, technology, customer placement, customer involvement, and interaction with employees. These six dimensions, which affect a customer's experience of a service, can be tested using various *in situ* and *ex situ* techniques; in the following section, three different methods and tools are proposed and briefly described.

Service prototyping (in situ) can be seen as an umbrella technique that includes several underlying methods and tools used to simulate a service experience (Blomkvist and Holmlid, 2012), ranging from pure role play to hand-sketched screens and mock-ups of the service experience room (where the service takes place). The idea behind this method of working is to gain profound knowledge and experience of the service idea from customers, stakeholders, and other parties. By using this technique, a best practice for the future service can already be created when the service is developed, and costly mistakes and redesigns of the service can be reduced.

An example method under the prototyping umbrella is *service staging (in situ)*. A service staging is essentially a role play, using real people; it is like a rehearsal before the grand opening or implementation of the service. When staging the service, different actors, preferably customers, can be invited to test the service, together with both front-line employees and those who work in the back office (Stickdorn *et al.*, 2011). When doing a service staging, the development team can choose to work with the whole service experience from start to finish or to focus on a smaller part of the service.

An example of an *ex situ* method that can be used to test a new service process is the *desktop walkthrough method (ex situ)*. A desktop walkthrough is essentially a quick and cheap way of testing a service at a small scale (Segelström and Holmlid, 2011), and the focus is often a simulated interaction between humans, using small figures (for example, Lego props). The basic setup makes it easy to quickly change, for example, the layout of the service environment (or experience room) at a low cost. Inputs from the walkthrough can hence be used as a design test both before a full mock-up is built and during the testing of a service; for example, a service staging.

How do you start?

After reading this chapter, you may be eager to get started with your service development endeavors. But, where do you start? If you pick only one tool to learn and use from this chapter, pick the service blueprint. Why? It helps you both to better understand your customers' experiences of your services and to actually design and organize the service system. At the heart of adopting services is taking a customer perspective on your operation. In other words, you must understand how the customers benefit from interacting with your services. The service blueprint is the most sufficient tool to elucidate the customers' involvement and touchpoints in the service encounter. Due to its simplicity, it also forms a basis for describing and communicating your service both internally and externally. And, it enables employees to identify and understand their role in the total service offering, among other advantages.

As you work with the blueprint, you will most likely discover that you need more information regarding the customers. Then pick one of the tools in the "Methods and tools to understand and explore customer needs" section. When the blueprint seems ready to implement, take a breath; do not make the mistake of believing that it is ready. Before you go ahead and launch your service, you should simulate the process, to find final issues you have missed. We have mentioned some methods that you can use for this purpose in the "Methods used to test and simulate the service process" section. After testing, do not get dejected if your blueprint was not faultless; be happy that you found out before your customers.

References

Bitner, M. J., Ostrom, A. L., and Morgan, F. N. (2008). Service blueprinting: A practical technique for service innovation. *California Management Review*, **50**(3), 66–94.

Blomkvist, J. and Holmlid, S. (2012). Service Prototyping according to Service Design Practitioners. Paper presented at the *Conference Proceedings; ServDes. 2010; Exchanging Knowledge;* Linköping; Sweden; 1–3 December 2010.

Cooper, R. G. (1990). Stage-gate systems: A new tool for managing new products. *Business Horizons*, **33**(3), 44–54.

Edvardsson, B., Enquist, B., and Johnston, B. (2005). Co-creating customer value through hyperrelality in the pre-purchase service experience. *Journal of Service Research*, **8**(2), 149–161.

Edvardsson, B., Enquist, B., and Johnston, R. (2010). Design dimensions of experience rooms for service test drives: Case studies in several service contexts. *Managing Service Quality*, **20**(4), 312–327.

Edvardsson, B., Kristensson, P., Magnusson, P., and Sundström, E. (2012). Customer integration within service development — A review of methods and an analysis of *in situ* and *ex situ* contributions. *Technovation*, **32**(7–8), 419–429.

Griffin, A. (1997). PDMA research on new product development practices: Updating trends and benchmarking best practices. *Journal of Product Innovation Management*, **14**(6), 429–458.

Gustafsson, A., Kristensson, P., and Witell, L. (2012). Customer co-creation in service innovation: A matter of communication? *Journal of Service Management*, **23**(3), 311–327.

Johne, A. and Storey, C. (1998). New service development: A review of the literature and annotated bibliography. *European Journal of Marketing*, **32**(3/4), 184–251.

Kim, J. and Wilemon, D. (2002). Focusing the fuzzy front-end in new product development. *R&D Management*, **32**(4), 269–279.

Koen, P., Ajamian, G., Burkart, R., Clamen, A., Davidson, J., D'Amore, R., Elkins, C., Kathy, H., Incorvia, M., Johnson, A., Karol, R., Seibert, R., Slavejkov, A., and Wagner, K. (2001). Providing clarity and a common language to the fuzzy front end". *Research Technology Management*, **44**(2), 46–55.

Lemon, K. N. and Verhoef, P. C. (2016). Understanding customer experience throughout the customer journey. *Journal of Marketing*, **80**(6), 69–96.

Lüthje, C., Herstatt, C., and von Hippel, E. (2005). User-innovators and "local" information: The case of mountain biking. *Research Policy*, **34**(6), 951–965.

Magnusson, P. R. (2003). User involvement and experimentation in collaborative research. In N. Adler, A. B. R. Shani, and A. Styhre (eds.), *Collaborative Research in Organizations*, pp. 215–236: SAGE.

Reimer, A. and Kuehn, R. (2005). The impact of servicescape on quality perception. *European Journal of Marketing*, **39**(7/8), 785–808.

Richardson, A. 2010. Using customer journey maps to improve customer experience. *Harvard Business Review*, **15**(1), 2–5.

Segelström, F. and Holmlid, S. (2011). Service design visualisations meet service theory: Strengths, weaknesses and perspectives. Paper presented at the Art & Science of Service Conference; Service Science in Developing Countries; San Jose; California; 8–10 June 2011.

Shostack, G. L. (1982). How to design a service. *European Journal of Marketing*, **16**(1), 49–63.

Stickdorn, M., Schneider, J., Andrews, K., and Lawrence, A. (2011). *This is Service Design Thinking: Basics, Tools, Cases*: Wiley Hoboken, NJ.

Vargo, S. L. and Lusch, R. F. (2004). Evolving to a new dominant logic for marketing. *Journal of Marketing*, **68**(1), 1–17.

von Hippel, E. (1994). "Sticky information" and the locus of problem solving: Implications for innovation. *Management Science*, **40**(4), 429–439.

Witell, L., Kristensson, P., Gustafsson, A., and Löfgren, M. (2011). Idea generation: Customer co-creation versus traditional market research techniques. *Journal of Service Management*, **22**(2), 140–159.

Chapter 3

What is an Idea for Innovation?

Alexandre Sukhov, Peter R. Magnusson and Johan Netz

Karlstad University, Sweden

Key takeaways

1. There is no unified model for what an idea for innovation is.
2. This chapter provides a model for describing the anatomy of an idea and also defines the boundary conditions to be fulfilled for realizing it.
3. An idea is defined as a short contextual narrative consisting of a solution to a certain problem. Ideas have a dual purpose: they provide a description for a certain plan of action, but also trigger new associations and give rise to new ideas. A checklist for managing idea development is provided.
4. This is a conceptual chapter that is relevant for both private and public innovation management practices.
5. This chapter relates to Chapters 2 and 4.

Introduction

Every innovation starts with an idea. It might be big or small; have a technical or social focus; deal with products, services, processes, or policies; or simply suggest new ways of creating value for an interested party.

But what is an *idea* for innovation? Understanding what an idea is can improve our knowledge about managing idea generation, evaluation, refinement, and selection activities, which are essential in the early phases of the innovation process (Koen *et al.*, 2001). By understanding how an idea is created, constructed, and interpreted, we increase our chances of finding good ideas, and reduce the risk of implementing bad ones.

The purpose of this chapter is to propose a model for the anatomy of an idea for innovation, describing the building blocks, which helps in illuminating potential challenges linked to the innovation process. This is accomplished through a conceptualization of an idea within the innovation context, based on a literature overview of creativity and innovation management, accompanied by a few examples from real innovation management projects. The model can be used as a tool for managers to help create, screen, and develop ideas in an organized manner, and to improve the idea's quality.

The Front End of Innovation

According to Koen *et al.* (2001), the innovation process consists of four main stages: idea creation (that is, the front end of innovation), development, testing, and launch (see Chapter 2 for further details). The front end of innovation deals with obtaining and selecting ideas for future products, services, and processes. At this early stage of the process, it is still not known what type of innovation the idea will lead to, yet a decision for selecting some promising ideas needs to be made. Upon selecting an idea, the organization will allocate resources to further develop it into a concept or prototype, and then commercialize and try to diffuse it onto a market (or institutionalize it as a practice within or outside of the organization; see Chapter 4 for further details). All organizations want to obtain good ideas, so that their innovations are novel and bring high value to the end user, since this helps in creating an attractive offer and creating competitive advantage, or simply allows an improved use of resources when performing certain functions (Björk and Magnusson, 2009).

Despite the existing body of literature on the front end of innovation, there is surprisingly little written about the definition of an idea; it is only implicitly or indirectly mentioned by researchers (see e.g., Basadur *et al.*, 2000; Osborn, 1957; Florén and Frishammar, 2012). Accordingly, neither researchers nor practitioners have a consensus about how to define an idea. Some refer to ideas as words written on post-it notes or as suggestions spoken out loud during brainstorming (Osborn, 1957), some refer to ideas as developed scenarios in the form of schematic drawings (Onarheim and Christensen, 2012; Kudrowitz and Wallace, 2013), and some refer to ideas as thematic stories (Froehlich *et al.*, 2016). Therefore, this chapter explicitly outlines what an idea is, through an analysis of previous research, and aids researchers and practitioners in their idea management endeavors.

The Components of an Idea

An idea for innovation is most commonly described as a short narrative created by people who are suggesting an improvement to a certain situation and that leads to a new and useful outcome (Dean *et al.*, 2006; Florén and Frishammar, 2012; Osborn, 1957). Traditionally, the creativity literature has framed idea generation as a session of active problem solving where a group of individuals are asked to find solutions to a stated problem or some sort of challenge (Osborn, 1957). It is also common that participants in idea generation are provided with a certain theme, where they have to identify and redefine different types of problems to solve (Kudrowitz and Wallace, 2013; Dorst and Cross, 2001). In order to identify the problem, the participants have to actively analyze a given environment or situation, and be engaged in the search process of appropriate and realizable solutions that fit the problem (Mumford *et al.*, 1991; Basadur *et al.*, 2000; Florén and Frishammar, 2012; Koen *et al.*, 2001).

Normally, idea generation is followed by idea screening, where participants are asked to rate and select the best ideas by using different criteria. There is, however, a complication with the evaluation that occurs during idea screening. Hatchuel and Weil (2009) describe ideas as objects that are not completely defined. They write that early-stage ideas are fuzzy and incomplete, yet indicate a certain direction for possible improvement. This description implies that substantial efforts are still required to refine ideas into more concrete forms that actually contain a comprehensible problem and solution description, so that an informed decision about the idea can be made (Sukhov, 2018). Sukhov (2018) showed that when ideas lack explicit descriptions explaining the problem and solution, people perceive them as inferior to those that contain explicit descriptions. People also tend to fill the gaps in the narrative of the idea, which means that the decision regarding idea quality is not always based on the information provided in the description, but rather on people's own interpretations of the problem, and how a solution might work.

What is a problem?

According to Smith (1988), a "problem" is defined as the "disharmony between reality and a person's preferences for the reality." Pounds (1969) describes it as "the difference between some existing situation and some desired situation." These definitions suggest that a problem signifies the dissatisfaction caused by the difference between a certain situation and someone's expectations for that situation. It is also clear that the dissatisfaction is a subjective component; many people may experience the same situation without finding it dissatisfactory or problematic. When explaining the notion of service quality, Parasuraman *et al.* (1988) takes up an example of situations that can be perceived differently by different people in the organization due to their knowledge and understanding of that situation. The upper management can, for instance, be blind to the problems that the customers of a service are experiencing, or not perceive them as problems, due to a lack of user-related knowledge. The presence of use knowledge ("an understanding of users' needs and wants and how service creates value for the customer" in Magnusson (2009, p. 580) has also been identified as a key component in the generation of successful ideas (Lilien *et al.*, 2002).

Dean *et al.* (2006) proposed that an idea should explicitly clarify the contextual background and provide a clear and coherent description of a problem and solution, in order to reduce uncertainty in communication and the evaluation of ideas. Thus, in order to explain a problem, one needs to provide information on What is happening, Who is experiencing it, and Why it is important (Sukhov, 2018; Dean *et al.*, 2006; Frishammar *et al.*, 2011). Magnusson (2009) and Sukhov (2018) suggest that the problem description of an idea closely relates to its use value, that is, how valuable the resolution of a given problem would be for its intended user; this description is also found to be the dominant predictor of the holistic impression for the idea (Sukhov, 2018). These results imply that if the problem is clearly communicated and considered relevant for the intended user, the perceived overall quality of the idea will be higher.

Example 1

Here is a real example of an idea for a service innovation from a study by Magnusson *et al.* (2016). In the idea, a person who is experiencing a problem is describing an application of mobile telephony to resolve it:

> *When you are riding the train, sub-way or waiting for a flight, you daydream, sleep or simply not pay attention on where you are. It would be good if a mobile phone could receive a silent SMS; that activates your alarm or puts a direct reminder from e-mail/organizer. A possibility to solve this could be use of NFC (near field communication) that tags the station you would like to get of at, and sets of the alarm automatically.*

In this example, the problem is a commuter missing his stop. The solution is to have a mobile phone automatically sound an alarm to alert the person. The idea is to have the commuter tag his destination and then use NFC to set off the alarm. The problem is shown clearly and shown to be important. Thus, a problem describes a situation and someone's dissatisfaction with that situation. Since a problem is a subjective construct (Smith, 1988), in order to be understood by others there needs to be a clear description of the situation and who experiences it, and an indication of why this situation is important to solve in order to be relevant (Dean *et al.*, 2006).

What is a solution?

A solution is a specification of how a certain problem can be resolved. According to Smith (1988), in order to come up with a solution, the idea creator needs to possess both factual and procedural knowledge related to the problem and the context that are being addressed. This means that a solution can be defined as a description of a method for satisfying a given problem.

Books on engineering design usually focus on the systematic development of solutions to posed and well-defined problems, where designing solutions occurs in stages: identification of the customer needs, translation of the needs into functional requirements, design of parameters that would resolve the functional requirements, and analysis of technical details that are required (Suh, 2001). From this technical perspective, the best and simplest solution design is either (1) the one that contains the least technical uncertainty (identifies unique functional requirements, and seeks out a solution that satisfies as many functional requirements as possible), thus focusing on the simplest method to resolve the problem (the principles of axiomatic design; see Suh (2001) and Liu *et al.* (2014)), or (2) the one that satisfies the problem and its functional requirements through the least amount of resources spent (the Theory of Inventive Problem Solving or TRIZ; see Terninko *et al.* (1998) and Liu *et al.* (2014)).

Another approach to problem solving has been outlined by Hatchuel and Weil (2009) in what they call the C–K theory (C stands for concept, K stands for knowledge) in which knowledge about the problem is used to generate a concept(s) or metaphor(s) that is used in the idea description (K→C). Different types of knowledge adds new properties to the concept and can trigger new associations (C→C′), and subsequently the required knowledge is identified in conjunction with the concept (C′→K′). Thus, this approach focuses on reframing and seeking out the knowledge needed to problem-solve, so that after a number of iterations, a final concept can lead to the creation of new knowledge and solve a problem in a novel way. A key element of this approach is the technological knowledge that is essential for finding a workable solution.

Creating solutions is also associated with handling constraints (Simon, 1996), such as fitting solutions within the cultural and legal boundaries in the social context (e.g., Le Masson and Magnusson, 2002, 2005), and also obeying the laws of physics in the technical context (Hatchuel and Weil, 2009). In contrast to the traditional approaches to engineering design, Simon (1996) introduced a different notion to finding solutions, namely *satisficing*, or accepting an available option as satisfactory, since in real world design situations it may be difficult to find an optimal solution to a well-defined problem. Due to the complexity of a certain problem, or failure to have a highly specific problem definition, sometimes finding satisfactory solutions is greatly desired. This approach has gained popularity in service design (Dorst, 2011) due to the multifaceted nature of user-related problems. It is also useful when the priority is to shorten the search for a solution, and to rely on the resources at hand instead of identifying and pursuing new knowledge needed for an optimized solution (Simon, 1996; Hatchuel and Weil, 2009).

In order for a solution to be implementable and present a viable market opportunity, an organization must have the ability to create the solution (Holmén *et al.*, 2007); this includes having (1) the necessary resources and (2) the ability to reconfigure the resources into a feasible solution. In addition, the organization must be willing to create the solution. The idea must therefore fit the organization's intentional and strategic scope.

An idea's characteristics

Since ideas are not material entities, in the sense that they are projections of someone's imagination that take the form of early descriptions (Hatchuel and Weil, 2009), they may be interpreted differently by people with different perceptions due to their background knowledge and interpersonal differences (Weick, 1995; Runco and Smith, 1991; Gregan-Paxton and Roedder John, 1997). Ideas are also said to be thematic and highly *contextual* (Froehlich *et al.*, 2016). This means that without the shared knowledge of the situation, it is difficult to interpret the idea in the same way as it was intended by its creator. Although the context relates to the situation that the idea addresses, it also expands beyond this situation and encompasses the social and cultural elements that may be mutually understood by both the creator and the idea judge/interpreter (Liu *et al.*, 2014). Accordingly, if the context is not well outlined and the person reading/listening/seeing the idea has a different perception/experience of the context, a misunderstanding of the idea's intended meaning can result (Yus, 1999).

The context in which an idea is conceived also sets social, cultural, and physical boundaries that are sometimes difficult to overcome during idea generation. Generating new ideas may prove itself difficult if the idea creator is indoctrinated into certain practices and ways-of-doing (see e.g., functional fixedness by Duncker and Lees (1945)). This phenomenon was also reported by Kristensson and Magnusson (2010) in their investigation of idea generation by ordinary users, guided users, and experts: ordinary users were able to generate highly original ideas, while experts struggled with originality but were able to generate highly producible ideas. Guided users, who were given technical education during the experiment, were able to generate ideas that both were technically producible and carried a high use value. Therefore, the background knowledge of all three groups constrained them into their own interpretative schemes, which reflected on the type of ideas they produced.

An example of breaking these social boundaries to come up with an unconventional but effective solution is given by Weick (1993) in his analysis of the Mann-Gulch disaster. There, in order to survive a huge natural fire, one of the firefighters set fire to the ground he was standing on in order to burn off the grass/fuel before the larger fire approached. At that instant, his fellow firefighters did not understand his act and assumed he had lost his mind, yet his act provided a solution to the very serious problem of the approaching natural fire. Another example of breaking these boundaries is described by Tanggaard (2012) in her paper on socio-material creativity. She emphasizes that creativity could lurk in the symbolic meaning of objects and things in our everyday life, and by reframing, re-contextualizing, and remaking social practices new, novel and useful meanings could be created. Therefore, contact or resistance with the materials with which we work creates a background, understanding, and a trigger for new ideas to arise.

Dorst (2011) writes that frame creation (contextualization) is a core design practice where designers may actively reframe the problem, so that they can search the broader context of the problem for clues when designing a solution. This is also the underlying principle of TRIZ, to (1) view the problem at hand, (2) step away from the physical context and its boundaries in order to figure out the general problem (abstraction), (3) come up with the most effective general solution for the problem, and (4) return to the specific context and develop a specific application given the available resources (Terninko *et al.*, 1998).

Based on the characteristics of an idea mentioned above, an idea has a dual function: it aims to communicate a certain course of action in relation to a specific situation and provide information on how to do that course of action (which requires that the idea description contains the necessary information to improve its comprehension), but it also triggers associations for the person to whom the idea is communicated (which requires that the person who is interpreting the idea possesses the appropriate background knowledge to help enrich the idea with further information that can improve its quality).

Conceptual Model

Based on the literature overview, we propose a conceptual model of an idea for innovation (see Figure 1). The model consists of three basic parts: a context in which the idea occurs, a problem that is being experienced by someone, and a solution that proposes a way to resolve this problem. The problem and solution can be further divided into four components: (1) a specific situation, (2) someone's dissatisfaction with the

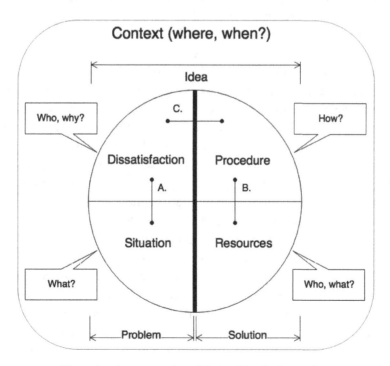

Figure 1.   A conceptual model of an idea for innovation.

situation, (3) a procedure or method on how to take action, and (4) the resources required to implement the action. These components represent the dimensions proposed by Dean *et al.* (2006) but also clarify the structure and relation between the what, why, who, where, when, and how of the idea. This model has been used by Sukhov (2018) to classify the information content in ideas and determine their completeness, which influenced the comprehension of the idea content, which in turn had a significant effect on the perception of idea quality.

Since an early idea can be easily misunderstood, we propose that before an idea is evaluated, it needs to explain the relevance of the problem (link A in the model). The situation and dissatisfaction components need to establish a common ground that both the idea creator and the idea assessor can relate to, and explain why the problem is important to resolve. A lack of background description and a failure to indicate who experiences the problem will make it difficult to assess whether this problem is important and has value for the user. Link B illustrates the relationship between the resources needed to resolve the problem and the procedure that describes how to use those resources. This relationship constitutes the solution part of an idea. These components relate to idea readiness. If the idea provides detailed information about what and how a problem can be resolved, it is easier to assess whether the solution is feasible and whether resources are available, or if the solution requires new resources that have to be obtained to implement the idea. Link C in the model illustrates the match between the problem and solution. Since the same problem could be resolved in different ways, there could be different paths toward an efficient (optimal use of resources), effective (optimal resolution of the problem), or simply satisfactory solution depending on the context, resources available, and strategic intent.

According to Figure 1, apart from the idea components, the links (A, B, C) correspond to the motivations that could be outlined in the idea description; that is, Why is this problem important? Are there existing methods to resolve it and resources to do that? Is this solution viable? Is the idea appropriate in a certain social context? Via the links, the model takes into account both the functional characteristics of an idea and their appropriateness. It signifies the subjective components of someone's dissatisfaction and the situation that the idea attempts to improve. The model also provides practical tools for refining and developing an idea in order to reduce communication gaps and improve its quality. Following is an example of the checklist of questions that can aid in the development of an idea for innovation:

- **Context:** Where? When?
- **Problem:** Situation (What?), Dissatisfaction (Who? Why?)
- **Solution:** Procedure (How?), Resources (Who? What?)

Example 2

The following example describes an idea generated as part of an R&D project from a Swedish telecommunications company (Magnusson *et al.*, 2016).

> *Approve your Credit Card Shopping's with a SMS.*
>
> *… my girlfriend happened to lose her Credit Card at home. A few weeks later, she received a notification from the Credit Card provider, stating that she had filled her car tank with gas for €1800 during that period. The funny part was that she didn't even have a driving license :-) What if, upon credit card [sic] shopping or withdrawal above a pre-defined limit, [sic] a SMS approval is required. In this case, when you are at home watching TV and you receive an SMS requesting an approval of €1000, you have the opportunity to decline :-). With this service, she could have declined the purchase right from the start.*

The idea provides an explicit background description of where and when a certain situation (what) occurred: a girlfriend lost her credit card and received an invoice for money that she did not spend. This is an example of the unlawful use of the credit card that is the point of dissatisfaction with the existing [at the time] credit card service, and explains why and to whom this is important. The situation is personal but at the same time relatable, since anyone could lose a credit card or have its details stolen; therefore, there is a clear sense of common ground. However, this particular example includes greater personalization due to the specificity of the sum of money taken, making it very clear to whom the solution in the form of SMS approval is valuable, and what risks the solution can eliminate. The solution is described in terms of the procedure (how), such as the threshold at which additional approval is needed. However, there is no additional explanation on what is required and who can implement this service, which makes this idea's solution implicit and incomplete according to the completeness criteria used by Dean *et al.* (2006) and Sukhov (2018).

Since the idea was submitted into the idea management system of a telecommunications company, where experts with substantial technological knowledge were evaluating ideas, some of the technical aspects of the idea could be implicit without a risk of being misinterpreted and misjudged. Thus, depending on the shared contextual knowledge between the idea creator and the person assessing it, an idea can be more or less explicit in its description. Nevertheless, idea incompleteness can contribute to larger interpretational differences. These differences are desired if the idea's purpose is to trigger new discussions, since increased ambiguity can improve creative output (Luo and Toubia, 2015; Lin and Chen, 2004), but these differences can also reduce the quality of the idea during its evaluation (Sukhov, 2018; Dean *et al.*, 2006).

Based on the existing literature, we define an *idea* for innovation as *a scenario in a specific context that is deemed unsatisfactory by an actor who explains how this scenario can be improved by applying appropriate resources.* In the early stages of an innovation process, an idea is thus a combination of a problem and solution that is communicated as a narrative between the idea creator and the idea assessor.

Discussion

This chapter describes the anatomy of an idea and illuminates some key components needed for successful management of the front end of innovation activities. The model in Figure 1 presents the idea with two main elements (problem and solution) that exist in a medium (context). The problem element can be broken up into a description of a situation and someone's dissatisfaction with that situation; hence, the definition of a problem is experiential and subjective. Since subjectivity is bounded by someone's existing knowledge, experience, and comprehension of the situation, it is possible to reinterpret the problem in light of a different perspective, suggesting that the framing of the problem can be changed (Tanggaard, 2012). This changeable framing is one of the main principles of design practice (Dorst, 2011; Dorst and Cross, 2001). This possibility of changeable framing also suggests that in order to understand the problem and evaluate its importance, idea assessors need not only a clear articulation of the situation and the storyline (Dean *et al.*, 2006) but also the appropriate use knowledge (Yus, 1999; von Hippel, 1994).

Solution seeking requires a formulation of a problem since this formulation determines the boundaries and constraints (Suh, 2001); however, if the problem changes, so can the solution in an iterative process (Dorst and Cross, 2001; Hatchuel and Weil, 2009). As identified in the model, a solution requires factual and procedural knowledge that is relevant to the idea's domain. Depending on the knowledge, there may be different types of solution to a given problem, and there may be different approaches to the solution. When it is possible to define the problem, the principles of engineering design suggest ways to find the simplest solutions through reducing the technical uncertainty (axiomatic design) or involving the fewest resources (TRIZ). But, in situations when the problem cannot be fully defined, or a long search process for the solution is conducted, satisficing could be used as a viable approach (Simon, 1996): a solution deemed as acceptably satisfying a problem is appropriate.

The front end of innovation includes different phases for finding new ideas, such as idea generation, idea refinement, and idea screening (Florén and Frishammar, 2012). The phases are not always sequential and have distinct scopes, but it is possible to use the model in Figure 1 to aid managers in these phases.

Idea generation is characterized by creating as many ideas as possible, removing judgement, and encouraging a wide range of ideas (Osborn, 1957; Cooper, 1994, 2014; Diehl and Stroebe, 1987). Generation is all about diversity, so that new thoughts and associations are provoked. Usually the ideas produced during this activity are short and spontaneous (see e.g., Sukhov, 2018). Some of the solutions that are generated can also give rise to new problems, which in turn inspire new associations and new solutions (Dorst and Cross, 2001).

According to Diehl and Stroebe (1987), idea generation is best done first individually and later in a group. This way, it is easier to bring the individual perspective and personal experiences to the table, while the group is more selective and may require some form of consensus, which may hinder the generation of new ideas (Schirr, 2012).

The model in Figure 1 helps us to understand that problems deal with individual experiences and that the same situation may be viewed and experienced differently by different people. The model also proposes the questions that help to better define the context and identify who is the beneficiary, what is going on, and why fixing it is important. Thus, the model acts as a template where problem statements are developed, and initial solutions are proposed.

Idea refinement is about improving ideas through developing missing elements or producing spinoff ideas that may help to align the idea concept. This is done by actively working on improving the idea's completeness, removing uncertainty, and improving its clarity through higher detailing (Florén and Frishammar, 2012), but also recontextualizing/reframing the idea so that a new combination of a problem and solution is formed (Dorst and Cross, 2001; Le Masson and Magnusson, 2002). Refinement can be both a formal and an informal process, as long as it helps the ideas to develop into more specific concepts for innovation (Schulze and Hoegl, 2008). During this phase, the model in Figure 1 is most relevant, since the model helps idea refiners systematically work with ideas and identify key elements and competences so that the narrative in which an idea is presented becomes more communicable.

Idea screening is about deciding which ideas should be further developed into concepts and continue into, for example, the new product development process and commercialization (Koen *et al.*, 2002; Eling *et al.*, 2015). As was observed by a number of researchers, idea screening and evaluation are exposed to cognitive biases (Licuanan *et al.*, 2007; Sukhov, 2018; Moreau *et al.*, 2001; Gregan-Paxton and Roedder John, 1997; Onarheim and Christensen, 2012; Schwarz, 2004). Therefore, in order to make an informed decision, the idea assessor needs to understand the intended meaning of the idea, and possess enough use and technology knowledge to make a decision about whether the idea is good or bad. The model in Figure 1 could be used to analyze the information content of an idea and see whether it actually contains the description of a method and indication of resources that would be required, but also a contextual description of the idea and its relevance. If the idea does not satisfy the completeness requirements, it could be sent back for further refinement, while at the same time identifying the type of knowledge required to fill in the gaps in its narrative. This way the potential misunderstandings during screening can be minimized, and the flow of ideas in an organization can become more structured.

Practical Implications

The model (Figure 1) can guide idea development practices. It makes an idea more tangible and assists in tracing its development. Applying the model to an idea helps with analyzing its content and can inform idea managers on whether the idea is complete or is still lacking vital pieces in its description. The model is also useful during the idea refinement stages to direct attention to the parts of the idea that need to be further elaborated. If the problem element is related to use knowledge, and the solution element to technology knowledge, it becomes possible to identify the type of people that could be asked to refine the idea depending on its missing pieces.

Since ideas for service innovation may deal with complex social phenomena and propose ways to create or co-create value, the contextual subjective elements need to be specified in order to understand who the beneficiary of the situation is, and whether the use of resources in the solution is proportional and appropriate to the problem. Thus, the model helps in shaping the narrative in which ideas could be documented in order to reduce ambiguity, consequently improving informed decision making during the selection of new ideas for innovation.

References

Basadur, M., Runco, M. A., and Vega, L. A. (2000). Understanding how creative thinking skills, attitudes and behaviors work together: A causal process model. *Journal of Creative Behavior*, **34**, 77–100.

Björk, J. and Magnusson, M. (2009). Where do good innovation ideas come from? Exploring the influence of network connectivity on innovation idea quality. *Journal of Product Innovation Management*, **26**, 662–670.

Cooper, R. G. (1994). Third-generation new product process. *Journal of Product Innovation Management*, **11**, 3–14.

Cooper, R. G. (2014). What's Next? *Research-Technology Management*, **57**, 20–31.

Dean, D. L., Hender, J. M., Rodgers, T. L., and Santanen, E. L. (2006). Identifying quality, novel, and creative ideas: Constructs and scales for idea evaluation. *Journal of the Association for Information Systems*, **7**, 646–698.

Diehl, M. and Stroebe, W. (1987). Productivity loss in brainstorming groups — Toward the solution of a riddle. *Journal of Personality and Social Psychology*, **53**, 497–509.

Dorst, K. (2011). The core of 'design thinking' and its application. *Design Studies*, **32**, 521–532.

Dorst, K. and Cross, N. (2001). Creativity in the design process: Co-evolution of problem-solution. *Design Studies*, **22**, 425–437.

Duncker, K. and Lees, L. S. T. (1945). On problem-solving. *Psychological Monographs*, **58**, 85–100.

Eling, K., Langerak, F., and Griffin, A. (2015). The performance effects of combining rationality and intuition in making early new product idea evaluation decisions. *Creativity and Innovation Management*, **24**, 464–477.

Florén, H. and Frishammar, J. (2012). From preliminary ideas to corroborated product definitions: Managing the front end of new product development. *California Management Review*, **54**, 20–43.

Frishammar, J., Floren, H., and Wincent, J. (2011). Beyond managing uncertainty: Insights from studying equivocality in the fuzzy front end of product and process innovation projects. *IEEE Transactions on Engineering Management*, **58**, 551–563.

Froehlich, J. K., Hoegl, M., and Gibbert, M. (2016). Idea selection in suggestion systems: A thematic similarity perspective. *R & D Management*, **46**, 887–899.

Gregan-Paxton, J. and Roedder John, D. (1997). Consumer learning by analogy: A model of internal knowledge transfer. *Journal of Consumer Research*, **24**, 266–284.

Hatchuel, A. and Weil, B. (2009). C–K design theory: An advanced formulation. *Research in Engineering Design*, **19**, 181–192.

Holmén, M., Magnusson, M., and Mckelvey, M. (2007). What are innovative opportunities? *Industry and Innovation*, **14**, 27–45.

Koen, P., Ajamian, G., Burkart, R., Clamen, A., Davidson, J., D'Amore, R., Elkins, C., Kathy, H., Incorvia, M., Johnson, A., Karol, R., Seibert, R., Slavejkov, A., and Wagner, K. (2001). Providing clarity and a common language to the "fuzzy front end". *Research Technology Management*, **44**, 46–55.

Koen, P. A., Ajamian, G., Boyce, S., Clamen, A., Fisher, E., Fountoulakis, S., Johnson, A., Puri, P., and Seibert, R. (2002). Fuzzy front end: Effective methods, tools and techniques. *In:* Belliveau, P., Griffin, A., and Somermeyer, S. (eds.), *The PDMA Toolbook for New Product Development*. 2nd Ed. New York: John Wiley & Sons.

Kristensson, P. and Magnusson, P. R. (2010). Tuning Users' Innovativeness During Ideation. *Creativity and Innovation Management*, **19**, 147–159.

Kudrowitz, B. M. and Wallace, D. (2013). Assessing the quality of ideas from profilic, early-stage product ideation. *Journal of Enginering Design*, **24**, 120–139.

Le Masson, P. and Magnusson, P. R. (2002). Towards an Understanding of User Involvement Contribution to the Design of Mobile Telecommunications Services. *The 9th International Product Development Management Conference*, May 27–28, 2002, Sofia Antipolis, France.

Le Masson, P. and Magnusson, P. R. (2005). Involving users in ripping off the blinkers induced by dominant designs. *Conference Paper presented at the Academy of Management Conference, August 5–10, 2005*. Honolulu, Hawaii, USA.

Licuanan, B., Dailey, L., and Mumford, M. (2007). Idea evaluation: Error in evaluating highly original ideas. *Journal of Creative Behavior*, **41**, 1–27.

Lilien, G. L., Morrison, P. D., Searls, K., Sonnack, M., and Von Hippel, E. (2002). Performance assessment of the lead user idea-generation process for new product development. *Management Science*, **48**, 1042–1059.

Lin, C.-T. and Chen, C.-T. (2004). New product go/no-go evaluation at the front end: A fuzzy linguistic approach. *IEEE Transactions on Engineering Management*, **51**, 197–207.

Liu, A., Lu, S., and Wei, W. (2014). A new framework of ideation-orientated customer involvement. *24th CIRP Design Conference*. Milano, Italy.

Luo, L. and Toubia, O. (2015). Improving online idea generation platforms and customizing the task structure on the basis of consumers' domain-specific knowledge. *Journal of Marketing*, **79**, 100–114.

Magnusson, P. R. (2009). Exploring the contributions of involving ordinary users in ideation of technology-based services. *Journal of Product Innovation Management*, **26**, 578–593.

Magnusson, P. R., Wästlund, E., and Netz, J. (2016). Exploring users' appropriatness as a proxy for experts when screening new product/service ideas. *Journal of Product Innovation Management*, **33**, 4–18.

Moreau, P., Lehmann, D., and Markman, A. (2001). Entrenched knowledge structures and consumer responce to new products. *Journal of Marketing Research*, **38**, 14–29.

Mumford, M. D., Mobley, M. I., Reiter-Palmon, R., Uhlman, C. E., and Doares, L. M. (1991). Process analytic models of creative capacities. *Creativity Research Journal*, **4**, 91–122.

Onarheim, B. and Christensen, B. T. (2012). Distributed idea screening in stage–gate development processes. *Journal of Engineering Design*, **23**, 660–673.

Osborn, A. F. (1957). *Applied Imagination: Principles and Procedures of Creative Thinking*, New York, Scribner.

Parasuraman, A., Zeithaml, V., and Berry, L. (1988). SERVQUAL: A multiple-item scale for measuring customer perceptions of service quality. *Journal of Retailing*, **64**, 12–40.

Pounds, W. F. (1969). The process of problem finding. *IMR; Industrial Management Review (pre-1986)*, **11**, 1.

Runco, M. A. and Smith, W. R. (1991). Interpersonal and intrapersonal evaluations of creative ideas. *Personality and Individual Differences*, **13**, 295–302.

Schirr, G. R. (2012). Flawed tools: The efficacy of group research methods to generate customer ideas. *Journal of Product Innovation Management*, **29**, 473–488.

Schulze, A. and Hoegl, M. (2008). Organizational knowledge creation and the generation of new product ideas: A behavioural approach. *Research Policy*, **37**, 1742–1750.

Schwarz, N. (2004). Metacognitive experiences in consumer judgment and decision making. *Journal of Consumer Psychology*, **14**, 332–348.

Simon, H. A. (1996). *The Sciences of the Artificial*, MIT Press (MA).

Smith, G. F. (1988). Towards a heuristic theory of problem structuring. *Management Science*, **34**, 1489–1506.

Suh, N. P. (2001). *Axiomatic Design: Advances and Applications*, New York, Oxford University Press.

Sukhov, A. (2018). The role of perceived comprehension in idea evaluation. *Creativity and Innovation Management*, **27**, 185–193.

Tanggaard, L. (2012). The sociomateriality of creativity in everyday life. *Culture & Psychology*, **19**, 20–32.

Terninko, J., Zusman, A., and Zlotin, B. (1998). *Systematic Innovation: An Introduction to TRIZ*, USA, CRC Press LLC.

Von Hippel, E. (1994). "Sticky Information" and the locus of problem solving: Implications for innovation. *Management Science*, **40**, 429–439.

Weick, K. E. (1993). The collapse of sensemaking in organizations: The Mann Gulch disaster. *Administrative Science Quarterly*, **38**, 628–652.

Weick, K. E. (1995). *Sensemaking in Organizations*, Thousand Oaks, Sage Publications.

Yus, F. (1999). Misunderstandings and explicit/implicit communication. *Pragmatics*, **9**, 487–517.

Chapter 4

Public Management Logics for Service Innovation

**Peter Samuelsson, Alexandre Sukhov,
Chaoren Lu and Johan Kaluza**

Karlstad University, Sweden

Key takeaways

1. Market logic should not be seen as a guiding innovation in the public sector.
2. Public management logics guide service innovation in the public sector and these guiding logics transform over time. Three types of logics have guided public-sector management: traditional public administration (TPA), new public management (NPM), and new public governance (NPG).
3. Service innovation can be described as social practices, which enables understanding how actors action arc rclatcd to the rationale of a context.
4. Each of the three public management logics has its own rationale for how service innovation should be done properly.

5. This chapter is conceptual and based upon the public management literature, with empirical mini cases from the public sector.
6. Those interested in this chapter may also find Chapters 3 and 12 interesting.

Introduction

The modern government faces new demands for services from its citizens, such as an increase in individualized services and digitalization. To address these government challenges, practitioners and scholars have turned to the innovation literature. However, the literature on innovation is for the most part based on a market logic, leading to a provider-orientated bias for the concept of innovation in the public sector (Gallouj and Zanfei, 2013; Tether, 2005). The public sector has hence been seen as a passive receiver of innovations from the private sector (Djellal *et al.*, 2013), such as the diffusion of new technology in public services (see e.g., Barras, 1986). Viewing the public sector as a passive receiver of innovations is problematic because the mission of the public sector is to carefully balance different values and provide service offerings to its citizens by reallocating resources (Pollitt and Bouckaert, 2011), instead of increasing profits. Therefore, the public sector needs to have an active role in managing innovational activities in the interest of the public.

As mentioned in the introduction of this book, the underlying concept of service innovation has been viewed from several perspectives. Service innovation has gone from being understood as either an outcome or a process to also being understood as a practice (see e.g., Skålén *et al.*, 2015; Vargo *et al.*, 2015; Koskela-Huotari *et al.*, 2016). Conceptualizing service innovation as a practice refers to a change in ways of integrating resources, providing new types of value outcomes (Lusch and Nambisan, 2015; Koskela-Huotari *et al.*, 2016; Rubalcaba *et al.*, 2012; Vargo *et al.*, 2015). As an example, when the public sector introduces digital primary care, open 24/7 from wherever the citizens are situated, this conceptualization contrasts the traditional view of innovation as *the work of a lonely entrepreneur, diffused into a market for profit* (Koskela-Huotari *et al.*, 2016), whereas in the same case of digital primary care this conceptualization would emphasize the technical solution diffused by a private operator to county councils, rather than the service it provides the citizens. The traditional view is based upon market logics, where service innovation is often presented as a facilitator for competitive advantage (see e.g., Edvardsson *et al.*, 2013; Salunke *et al.*, 2013; Voss, 1992). The practice perspective extends the concept of service innovation, making service innovation better for targeting public-sector services since the purpose is to reallocate resources for the public good. Considering public service organizations as active actors of service innovation necessitates understanding the prerequisites of managing innovation activities (following Brown and Osborne, 2013). This raises the question: if market logic does not guide service innovation practices, what does?

The public management literature has presented three different management logics that guide the practices of public-sector organizations (Bryson *et al.*, 2014; Denhardt and Denhardt, 2000, 2007; Osborne *et al.*, 2015; Pollitt and Bouckaert, 2011). These guiding logics transform over time and create new social structures, forcing management procedures to follow the logics. Current research has presented a prevailing rationality of social structures within the guiding logics (Bryson *et al.*, 2014) and shown that the logics guide different service innovation trajectories (Gallouj and Zanfei, 2013). However, research on how management logics of the public sector relate to service innovation practices has been overlooked.

This chapter presents a framework illustrating how public management logics guide service innovation practices and shows a pattern of transformation of public management logics. The chapter is conceptual, building upon a review of the service innovation and public management literature. The framework is informed by practice theory, describing how the guiding logics and service innovation relate to each other. The chapter follows Vaara and Whittington's (2012) recommendations for using practice theory a meta-theoretical approach, linking theoretical constructs into a coherent whole and identifying new frameworks (see also MacInnis, 2011; Tsoukas, 1994; Whittington, 2006). The chapter uses two "mini cases" to illustrate the framework in an empirical setting.

The contribution of this chapter is two-fold. First, the chapter will make researchers and practitioners aware of the social structures guiding public service innovation, which makes it possible to see potential constraints and the possibilities for service innovation in the public sector. The chapter also presents a model that illustrates how service innovation activities are interlinked with higher levels of guiding logics, which is of great relevance for service innovation management in both the public and private sectors, since it helps to simplify the complex relationships between the public wants and how innovation activities are carried out. Second, the chapter contributes to public service management by describing some of the social prerequisites for conducting service innovation activities, such as their dependence on the contemporary norms found in the different guiding logics.

Applying a Practice View to Service Innovation

Service innovation as a practice

Service innovation from a practice perspective has been described as *the institutionalization of new resource integration practices among actors in a network, creating new value constellations* (Lusch and Nambisan, 2015; Koskela-Huotari *et al.*, 2016; Rubalcaba *et al.*, 2012; Vargo *et al.*, 2015). Since the conceptualization of service innovation as a practice entails a shift in focus away from more traditional innovation conceptualizations, such as tangible outcomes or technological breakthroughs (Skålén *et al.*, 2015), the conceptualization might seem overly complex and hard to grasp. However, broken down to its components, it makes sense. Institutionalization of new resource integration practices means that, in order to create or deliver a new outcome (for example, digital primary care units), the actors involved need to set a new way of combining resources (using a digital platform for the interaction between doctors and patients), and since not one actor has all the resources herself, this process happens among actors in networks (private firms delivering the technology for the digital platform and public service providers offering the service for the citizens; see Lusch and Nambisan, 2015). A practice can be defined as the shared routines of actors' behavior, including traditions, norms, and procedures for thinking, acting, and using "things" (Reckwitz, 2002). The routinized act of doing (*institutionalization of new resource integration practices among actors in a network*) can thus be seen as a practice. Having a practice view of service innovation emphasizes the social aspects of the actors' shared routines for service innovation. The usefulness of seeing the social aspects lies in understanding how actors are enabled and constrained by the prevailing organizational and societal social structures (Vaara and Whittington, 2012).

Actors of public service innovation practices

In a practice perspective, actors become practitioners, making, shaping, and executing the practices (Whittington, 2006). Service innovation in the public sector involves several practitioners or (from now on) actors, both public and private (see e.g., Thakur *et al.*, 2012; Windrum and Garcia-Goni, 2008; Gallouj *et al.*, 2013; Djellal *et al.*, 2013). Windrum and Garcia-Goni (2008) present a multi-actor framework, encompassing policymakers, public-sector service providers, consumers, and private firms. Previously, policymakers have been overlooked in the innovation literature, since they are not directly involved in service innovation practices; they do, however, promote innovative public services, and should hence be considered a separate actor in service innovation practices (Windrum and Garcia-Goni, 2008). Policymakers have the mission to promote public values, which means that for policymakers, the goal of public-sector innovation is to reallocate resources so that changes in public services reflect the citizens' current values.

The consumer's role in service innovation practices has, over the years, been elevated from being the receiver of innovation outcomes to being actively involved in value co-creation (Hartley, 2005). However, the role of consumers is more complex in public services, since the consumers in this case are citizens. Having a consumerization view of citizenship has some fundamental issues; the relationship between the citizen and the state is different from the one between a consumer and a service provider (Windrum and Garcia-Goni, 2008). Consumers are free-choosing individuals that with perfect information can select their service provider on an open market while looking for their own value creation. Citizens are bound to the supply provided by the state and often cannot choose which service or service provider they want.

Private firms are perhaps the most traditional type of actor in service innovation, where the focus on survival, profits, and competitive advantage drives the private operators in their service innovation practices (see e.g., Edvardsson *et al.*, 2013; Salunke *et al.*, 2013; Voss, 1992). The role of private firms in service innovation in a public context is wide and not easily pinpointed. The role can span from providing new tangible tools for the back-office (as in the example of digital primary units, providing the technical platform) to contracting the service delivery process to private operators, where intangible competences can be added for new value constellations (for example, using service design firms to develop new payment systems in public transport services).

Public-sector service providers have a central position in service innovation practices, since they are often the ones facilitating the services. The absence of a profit interest in public service providers limits their service offerings to the sum of their expenses (Gallouj and Zanfei, 2013). This makes the innovation of public service providers focus on efficiency rather than effectiveness (Gallouj and Zanfei, 2013).

The levels, recursiveness, and transformation of social practices

Multiple levels of social practices

The actors' routinized procedures for thinking, acting, and using "things," are usually expressed as micro-level practices (see Table 1, Level (3); Reckwitz, 2002); however, it is also important to recognize that higher order of practices exist to see what guides the actors' routinized behavior (Vaara and Whittington, 2012). To describe how public management logics guide public management innovation practices, we suggest viewing public service innovation over multiple levels.

Research has presented different levels of analysis on social practices, particularly significant in organizations with a high level of formalization (Whittington, 2006; Vaara and Whittington, 2012), such as public service organizations. As put forward by Whittington (2006),

Table 1. Levels of social practice and structure guiding organizations.

Level of social practices	Description	Core references	Actors
(1) Guiding logics	Extra-organizational practices are a high societal level of practice, where norms create a discourse to guide organizations	Fligstein (1990), Djelic (1998), Barry and Elmes (1997), Maguire *et al.* (2004)	Citizens and policymakers
(2) Management procedures	Intra-organizational practices are characterized by the operating processes, shaping modes of behaviors	Martin (2001), Nelson and Winter (1982)	Top and middle management
(3) Innovation praxis	Micro-level practices are the routinized behaviors of the actors who actually perform the activities	Spender and Grant (1996), Whittington (2006), Reckwitz (2002)	Middle managers, employees of both private and public organizations, consultants, and consumers

social practices can be described on three different levels: (1) on high levels (extra-organizational level) in terms of the *guiding logics*; (2) on mid-levels (intra-organizational level), expressed in terms of modes of behaviors, or simply *management procedures*; and (3) on the lowest level, referring to the activities that the actors actually do, which is *praxis* (micro-activity level).

At the (1) extra-organizational level of social practices, the *guiding logics* can be described as larger societal fields, norms of appropriate behavior, or legitimized recipes for contextual success (Fligstein, 1990; Djelic, 1998). The guiding logics are diffused across fields in time and space as a discourse (Bourdieu, 1990), informing ways of organizational operations (Barry and Elmes, 1997; Maguire *et al.*, 2004). On the (2) intra-organizational level, social practices can refer to *management procedures*, which is characterized by the operating processes that are shaping modes of behaviors (Martin, 2001; Nelson and Winter, 1982). Note that at this level, management procedures tend to change during the different guiding logics. Management procedures not only come from internally generated routines but also from ideas outside of the organization (see Røvik, 1998; Czarniawska and Joerges, 1996), where the guiding logics determines the conditions and rationale for operations at this middle level (Whittington, 2006). On a (3) micro-level, social practices refer to what people actually do (for example, in innovation, idea brainstorming, prototyping, and conceptualizing new products and services) and this is placed at the lowest level, referring to the actors' actual activities or the *innovation praxis* (Reckwitz, 2002) and regulated by the management procedures.

The recursiveness and transformation of practices

Social structure is the medium that actors base their practices upon (Giddens, 1984), a social frame of what constitutes good or correct behavior within a context (Reckwitz, 2002). The human actors are never acting as individuals detached from context, since their possibilities for actions are bound to the shared routines that they are bound in (Vaara and Whittington, 2012). The shared routines of the actors, that is, the practices within the context, also provide the outcome of the social structure, working as a self-sufficient reproductive system (Giddens, 1984). The social practices explain how the social structure and human agency link together (Vaara and Whittington, 2012); hence, by studying the social practices, one can unravel the bounds between the social structure and agency.

Agency is actors' ability for action and change, where actors' agency is bound to the social structure of reality as they interpret it (Giddens, 1984). The social structure in the case of innovation praxis (see Table 1, Level 3) is bound to the management procedures (see Table 1, Level 2). Hence, seeing service innovation out of a practice perspective makes it possible to attribute actors' innovation praxis as a manifestation of the social structure that gives agency to their actions. In other words, the actors cannot act without submitting to the social structure in order to get agency for their actions. Since the actors' management procedures are a manifestation of the prevailing guiding logic, these management procedures will at the same time inform the guiding logic and help to keep the norms of appropriate behavior or legitimized recipes for contextual success. The social practices at different levels will hence not only be an outcome of the social structure, but an active constituting process; this condition has been referred to as recursiveness (Giddens, 1984).

Even though the social structure is explained as recursive, over time systems of social structures dissolve and transform. Giddens (1984) explains this transformation by the negotiable nature of social practices, where deliberate change happens, meaning that new social structures can replace the old ones by actors shaping their own norms of appropriate behavior (see Jarzabkowski, 2008). We argue though that due to the high level of formalization within the public context, the actors innovation praxis is strongly linked to the management procedures and guiding logics (Whittington, 2006; Vaara and Whittington, 2012). That is because the social structures in the public sector are design to regulate themselves to the politics and the people, leaving no actors with agency for changing the system bottom–up. The guiding logics are however not bound only to the management practices recursively, but also to a wider discourse, where values and norms of society are informing the guiding logics. Eventually, the social structures will therefore need to transform in order to stay coherent to the higher levels of norms and values requested by the society. Often, this takes place when the social system is in a crisis of routines (Reckwitz, 2002), where the transformation of guiding logics is caused by conflict between the public values outlined by the government and the values of its citizens (see e.g., Skålén *et al.*, 2015).

Public Management Logics for Service Innovation

The public sector has undergone transformations to tackle governmental challenges and stay coherent with public values. The transformations are characterized into three major episodes of public management: traditional public administration (TPA), new public management (NPM), and new public governance (NPG) (Denhardt and Denhardt, 2000; Pollitt and Bouckaert, 2011). Each of these episodes can be viewed as a guiding logic for public management, and defined as sets of institutionalized principles creating rationality within a specific context. These guiding logics reflect both previous and present rationalities, which have guided innovation management and how it has been developed over time (Bryson *et al.*, 2014; Hartley, 2005). These guiding logics will therefore be presented chronologically, starting with TPA (see Table 2).

TPA is based on a logic of rational-legal authority, which forms the basis for bureaucracy (Pollitt and Bouckaert, 2011). Through public policy, compliance, and predetermined procedures, a hierarchical chain of command governed the public sector. This rational-legal type of governing aims to create an objective handling of errands to guarantee fair and equal decisions in an efficient manner. Thus, public administration is seen as the process of transforming political intentions and policy into praxis. The view of the public sector as a bureaucratic machine administrating the public values contradicted the traditional concept of innovation at the time, making the term "innovation" taboo (Gallouj and Zanfei, 2013). The management procedures consist of internal processes governing public administrators through rule-based and standardized procedures (Hyndman and Liguori, 2016), often referred to as "change" or "modernization" (Gallouj and Zanfei, 2013). Thus, this episode developed different types of bureaucratic and technical management tools to create compliance among public administrators to handle errands consistently. Innovation is therefore connected to the policy level, with progressive policy changes or governing mechanisms implemented by public organizations, and to internal processes, described as bureaucratic and technical control (Edwards, 1982; Callaghan and Thompson, 2001).

Under the TPA, the role of government is to provide political goals, and then decides how innovation is to be implemented by public servants, while monitoring the progress via bureaucratic and elected officials' oversight (Denhardt and Denhardt, 2000, 2007; Hartley, 2005). The public managers are the "clerks and martyrs" who ensure that rules and appropriate procedures are followed (Kelly *et al.*, 2002; Stoker, 2006). The public manager, under the guiding logic of TPA, has limited discretion. The public here refers to voters or constituents (Stoker, 2006). Innovation practices rely heavily on politicians' and experts' interpretation of public interest.

Under TPA, the population is assumed to be largely homogeneous, and the needs and problems of the population are defined by the professionals in the public administration (Hartley, 2005). Thus, the process of service innovation in the public sector during this episode was largely a top–down process (Hartley, 2005). Some examples of innovations from the TPA episode include the establishment of the publically founded national healthcare system (NHS), the 1944 Education Act, the nationalization of major industries, and the establishment of new towns. One of the main characteristics of innovation praxis during TPA was the large scale of the changes and the deployment of legislative, financial, and staffing resources, which led to immediate change that was objectively evident to a range of stakeholders. However, according to Hartley (2005), this top–down approach addresses the users of public services as clients, and does not have a large capacity for continuous improvement or adaptation.

The second major guiding logic is NPM, and was articulated by Hood (1991, 1995) in the early 90s. Market thinking and economic rationality provides the legitimized recipe for contextual success in this guiding logic. Hood (1991) and others (see e.g., Denhardt and Denhardt, 2000; Pollitt and Bouckaert, 2011; Pache and Santos, 2013) argue that markets as governing mechanisms inspire NPM, and that public organizations can implement management tools inspired by private corporations and economic theory. This change in guiding logic aims to solve the problem of growing and costly public organizations that does not manage administrative tasks in a fair and equal manner as promised (Hood, 1991). Market-oriented tools like Lean management and total quality management (TQM) replaces bureaucratic management tools. Organizations are restructured into decentralized units accountable for their output, and different kinds of internal markets are created to raise competition (Lapsley, 2009). Under this episode, innovation becomes a topic in the public sector, with a focus mainly on adopting innovations from the private sector. The management procedures, which manage these innovation praxis, are thus market-oriented and focus on increasing the effectiveness of service provision and service delivery by adopting market mechanisms (Hartley, 2005). Such innovation praxis reposition the role of the citizen in the delivery of public services from passive recipient to self-interested consumer (Fishenden and Thompson, 2012).

Under the NPM logic, the role of government is to steer management procedures (Denhardt and Denhardt, 2000, 2007). The government provides political goals, whereas the public managers manage the inputs and outputs that ensure a strong economy and responsiveness to consumers. The public managers are responsible for defining and meeting the agreed-upon performance targets (Stoker, 2006). With the absence of profit, the innovation goals often target efficiency rather than effectiveness (Gallouj and Zanfei, 2013). Meanwhile, public managers also have wide discretion to achieve entrepreneurial goals, and oftentimes employees are promoted for entrepreneurial ventures. The role of the citizens is as customers who make choices to use certain public services by an economic rational (Kelly *et al.*, 2002; Stoker, 2006). The politicians or public managers gauge the public interest based on the evidence of customer choices.

The latest edition of public management is NPG, and this reflects a networking practice where different types of actors contribute to public service delivery (Liddle *et al.*, 2012). The market facing governing mechanisms is still present in NPG due to the multitude of actors, both private and public, but the aim has shifted toward delivering value to citizens (Denhardt and Denhardt, 2000) through coproduction (see e.g., Osborne *et al.*, 2014). Thus, it has been debated whether this is a new episode of public management in itself (see e.g., Pollitt and Bouckaert, 2011) or if NPG rather should be considered an extension of NPM (Lapsley, 2009; Hyndman and Liguori, 2016) that aims to refocus NPM by adding additional layers. However, the guiding logic of NPG differs from NPM. The logic of NPG can be characterized as cooperative, serving the needs of individual citizens, and trying to re-establish a democratic perspective by acknowledging multiple interests through public value (Osborne, 2010; Bryson *et al.*, 2014). This public value is defined by citizens (as individuals and parts of larger groups) and other actors are active coproducers in the public service provision (Hartley, 2014). The practice governing innovation praxis within the public sector is thus positioning the citizen at the center, with a focus on creating public value through coproduction among multiple actors (Hartley, 2005; Zito and Schout, 2009).

Under the NPG logic, the role of government is to serve the innovation praxis (Denhardt and Denhardt, 2000, 2007). The government and

Table 2. Literature review of three guiding logics for public management.

(a)

Public management logics	Traditional public administration (TPA)	New public management (NPM)	New public governance (NPG)
Basic idea	A hierarchical chain of command	A market-based governance mechanism	A network-based governance mechanism
Origin	Political theory	Economic theory	Democratic theory
Core references	Pollitt and Bouckaert (2011)	Hood (1991, 1995)	Osborne et al. (2014, 2015)
Drivers for service innovation	Synoptic rationality	Economic rationality	Strategic rationality
Focus/Interest	Interpretation, a focus on how different innovation outcomes can be interpreted and categorized and on finding their drivers	Management, how organizations can manage processes and structures for creating new services	Institutionalization, the focal point of study is the process of social change needed to establish service innovations
Value conflict crisis — facilitator for transformation	Too stiff and bureaucratic, above all too costly and inefficient (see e.g., Pollitt and Bouckaert, 2011)	Too target-oriented, implying that the logic is steering away from the main purpose of bringing valuable services to the citizens (see e.g., Fishenden and Thompson, 2012)	Network-based reforms to organizational structure are both potentially powerful and simultaneously impotent (see e.g., Martin et al., 2009)

(Continued)

Table 2.   (*Continued*)

(b)

Public innovation management practices	Policy change, R&D units	Quality management, entrepreneurship	Coproduction, public–private innovation networks
Basic idea	Efficiency and effectiveness can be gained by managing and restructuring organizations. Also by giving resources for predetermined objectives, as for research and the development of democratizing services	Continuous improvements can be achieved by incremental process changes that enhance the efficiency of services. Larger technology changes ensure effectiveness. However, these technology changes should be provided and diffused by private operators	Services can be altered or created by using coproducing practices. Design methods and practices provide essential tools for co-creation, creating more valuable services for citizens
Actors and their roles	Policymakers having a commanding position of what different units within public service organizations should do. The public service organizations set the terms and conditions for what their internal units should do in terms of service innovation, and for what to buy from private operators, providing a balanced set of values for the citizens and public service consumers	Building upon Schumpeterian argumentation and market logics, innovations should be commercialized in order to provide economic value. This makes private operators a key actor in the innovation praxis. Public service providers are more passive receivers of service innovations. However, driven by policymakers' goals in terms of efficiency, public service providers also conduct incremental improvements	Building upon service logics, public service organizations act as a facilitator of networks, inviting both consumers and private operators to co-create service innovations

	Policymakers	Private operators, top management in public service organizations	Public service organizations and citizens
Power-players of the innovation management praxis			
Archetypes of innovation praxis	Restructuring of public service organizations, research and development	Innovation hubs, technical diffusion from entrepreneurs	Embedded service design labs, public–private innovation networks
Focus/Interest	Managing and allocating public resources to administrate public values in the service innovation praxis	Fostering a service innovation agenda inside public service organizations and outside the public sector where outside entrepreneurs raise the efficiency of the public sector by introducing new technology	Finding new ways to co-create value with citizens to be able to offer more valuable services

public managers aim to create public value by effectively addressing what the public most cares about and putting in place what creates value for the individual citizens. Here, the public manager has an active role in steering networks of deliberation and delivery and maintaining the overall capacity of the governance system (Kelly *et al.*, 2002). The public is referred to as coproducers and problem-solvers (Kelly *et al.*, 2002; Stoker, 2006). The public could also actively interact and have open dialogues with public managers (Stoker, 2006), and the innovation practices are based on shared values.

Presenting a Model for Public Management Logics for Innovation

Based on the theoretical framework, we now present a multi-level model of service innovation practices in the public sector (Figure 1). We will describe the model with the help of the public-sector management literature and the two mini cases provided in Table 3. The aim of the mini cases is not to describe the most typical service innovation practices during the different episodes of public management logic but to illustrate the shifts in innovation praxis under the different management procedures.

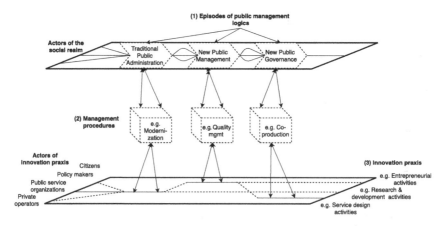

Figure 1.   A multi-level practice model of service innovation in the public sector (in parts influenced by Whittington, 2006).

Table 3. Empirical mini cases.

Mini cases of service innovation practices in the public sector	TPA logic	NPM logic	NPG logic
The Chinese transport sector	**Village Bus Services.** Based on considerations of social equality and economic development in rural areas, the national government launched a political goal of extending bus service to every village. This type of new service is not profitable for public transport operators. However, it resolves the problem of travel difficulty for people who live in the countryside. It represents the government's will of enhancing the accessibility of public transport services to a large scope of citizens.	**Super Bus Services.** In order to deal with residential areas or other areas with less travel demand, ChangZhou Transit Group created a tender to various bus vehicle manufactures to bid for a new bus design that was suitable for the narrow roads of valley transport. The new bus vehicles were named super buses because of the small body with high capacity. The super buses earned 10 utility design patents, such as for the automatic temperature control system and sliding plug door system. All the innovations were focused on incremental changes to enhance the passengers' travel experiences from the daily operation practices. The main actors in all the innovations were external partners, such as vehicle manufacturers.	**Customized Bus Services.** The bus operators (e.g., BeiJing Transit Group) created online platforms (e.g., web based and mobile app based) for citizens to fit bus service to their individual needs in terms of place of departure and destination. Based on the collective needs, the bus operators design and operate customized bus routes suitable for people traveling to work as a "one-stop" service. The citizens are hence actively coproducing the public bus transport service.

(*Continued*)

Table 3.   (*Continued*)

Mini cases of service innovation practices in the public sector	TPA logic	NPM logic	NPG logic
Swedish public healthcare	***Center of Clinical Research.*** In the Swedish county councils, healthcare has a long tradition of research and development, where research and evidence guide the operations. The county council of Värmland offers a place called the Center of Clinical Research, which is a meeting place for all researchers employed by the county council that have a clinical approach to their research. The center offers financial support along with tutoring, data, courses, IT hardware and software, and a place to sit. The center grants access to funding and other resources if management considers the research to be plausibly impactful on the care provided by the county council.	***The Innovation Hub Vivan.*** In the Swedish county council of Värmland, the public healthcare and a regional business partner launched an innovation hub called Vivan, where the main focus was to promote entrepreneurial behavior among employees and patients. Vivan's aim was to contribute to a higher level of quality care within the county by helping entrepreneurs develop their ideas into new products and services. The main rationale for the innovation hub is that continuous improvement thinking can lead to new ideas, born out of the practical problems found in practice. And, that finding solutions that can improve the day-to-day operation of different entities of healthcare can be highly effective. The innovation hub provides support and advice on how to develop an idea to a finished product or service that can be commercialized and diffused onto the healthcare market by the idea holder, and thus be used by more healthcare units and patients around the world.	***Experio Lab.*** This is another healthcare innovation initiative started in the county council of Värmland. Experio Lab's agenda is to improve patient care experiences. The lab's primary function is to open up collaboration among employees, patients, and relatives with the use of service design to coproduce new or altered services that enhance the patient's experience. The method has been proven effective, and, in a couple of years, over 10 new services were deployed. The concept of Experio Lab has spread and been deployed at several other county councils in Sweden.

Figure 1 illustrates the three different levels of social practices in the public sector: (1) public management logics, (2) innovation management procedures, and (3) innovation praxis. The (1) public management logics are illustrated as the higher plane in the model. In the review, we found that TPA, NPM, and NPG are higher-order social practices that prevail in the social structure for innovation management procedures during their respective episodes. At the mid level, different concepts of (2) management procedures were seen as recipes, or modes of operation, for service innovation success during the respective episodes. In the model, these concepts are represented as the boxes between the planes. In the mini case of Chinese public transport (see Table 3), the social structures of TPA create agency for a policy change to create better access to cities for citizens living in rural areas. The public service providers restructured their operations to launch a new bus service targeting the democratic values initiated by policymakers.

In Figure 1, we can follow the transformation of public management logics; these are illustrated as the dissolving and restructuring of actors' social structures over time, forming new social structures in line with their values. This is illustrated by the horizontal lines going from left to right between the dotted arrows of the different episodes of (1) public management logics. In the literature review, we found that this happened based on the critique of the shortcomings of the contemporary public management logics. When an NPM logic is established, the new logic provides a social structure for a new innovation management practice. In the Chinese transport mini case, under the NPM logic, the launch of a new service is instead carried out by targeting various private operators to manufacture and operate a new type of bus that could raise the efficiency of transporting people living in rural mountain areas. In the Swedish public healthcare mini case, innovation hubs are set up for employees and others to start new business ventures in order to increase efficiency. The different (2) management procedures led to different (3) innovation praxis, as in the shift in the Swedish county council from research and development to entrepreneurial activities of private operators. In Figure 1, this is shown by the recursive arrows going back and forth from the boxes to the lower plane of service innovation praxis. In Figure 1, the innovation praxes examples is placed on the right side of the model due to a lack of space; the examples should be positioned below the boxes in the model.

Discussion and Implications

The main point of the new frameworks and illustrative models is to enhance readers' understanding of a complex phenomena. They can provide a groundwork on which others can theorize and base their empirical analyses. By developing the present framework, we contribute to service innovation theory and practice in two ways. First, we illustrate that service innovation practice is a multi-level concept, guided by the social structures of public management logics that are constructed and resolved over time. Second, by conducting a literature review and giving empirical examples, we describe and demonstrate the social structures that guide service innovation practices in the public sector.

By viewing service innovation as a practice, we can describe service innovation in relation to social structures. For instance, service innovation researchers can move beyond the output and process perspective, and target the prerequisite of actors' ability to act within different social structures. The literature and the mini cases imply that different actors gain agency under different public management logics. For example, in the mini case of Swedish public healthcare, under an NPG logic, agency for service innovation praxis is given to actors, who can participate in the co-creation practices; this requires access not generally given to all private actors.

Applying the practice perspective highlights the different service innovation praxes in relation to outcomes. The outcomes of service innovation, or new value constellations, seem to differ for the different management procedures. Consistent with Miles's (2008) suggestion to study the service innovation outcome and process together, we propose that researchers should study the practices of service innovation together with its outcomes. Such a study would capture actors' social prerequisites for service innovation praxis and provide an understanding of what kind of new value constellations different service innovation praxis drives. As shown in the mini cases, the value constellations seem consistent with the values governed in the public management logics; for example, in the Swedish healthcare mini case, the goal of operations efficiency is targeted by adopting quality innovation management practices, such as the continuous improvement activities.

Paradoxically, in order to innovate in the public sector and gain agency for innovation praxes, one needs to submit to the existing ways of doing things. This suggests that the service innovation praxis becomes homogenous and confirms the existing norms. If actors only can gain agency for the service innovation praxis that represents current public values, it could be problematic. First, the public does not always know what it wants in terms of service innovation. Second, public values might not be properly balanced; for example, the public might call for new services addressing their individual value co-creation processes, but there might be a more urgent need for new value constellations targeting the efficiency of the public sector (or vice versa).

This chapter highlights that public management logics transform and are informed by social realms outside of public management. However, two issues must not be forgotten. First, even though the public management logics transform over time and create new management procedures, old management procedures seem to linger. Management procedures crystallize and gain momentum within organizations and legitimize the way of conducting the innovation praxis. However, following Jarzabkowski (2008), the innovation management practices are also incrementally adjusting to the praxis by the actors, due to behavior regularity. Second, there are bottom–up social forces that influence how policymakers and managers create social structures for public management logics; even though we have emphasized that the shift happens on a high societal level of practice. The bottom–up social forces are the citizens values that regulate the behavior of public management. Thus, to shift current public management logic requires some friction between citizens and governing bodies; it is in this conflict that new opportunities and new social structures for innovation praxis are realized (see e.g., Skålén *et al.*, 2015).

References

Barras, R. (1986). Towards a theory of innovation in services. *Research Policy*, **15**(4), 161–173.

Barry, D. and Elmes, M. (1997). Strategy retold: Toward a narrative view of strategic discourse. *Academy of Management Review*, **22**(2), 429–452.

Bourdieu, P. (1990). *The Logic of Practice*. Palo Alto, CA: Stanford University Press.

Brown, L. and Osborne, S. P. (2013). Risk and innovation: Towards a framework for risk governance in public services. *Public Management Review*, **15**(2), 186–208.

Bryson, J. M., Crosby, B. C., and Bloomberg, L. (2014). Public value governance: Moving beyond traditional public administration and the new public management. *Public Administration Review*, **74**(4), 445–456.

Callaghan, G. and Thompson, P. (2001). Edwards revisited: Technical control and call centres. *Economic and Industrial Democracy*, **22**(1), 13–37.

Czarniawska, B. and Joerges, B. (1996). *Travels of Ideas*. Gothenburg, Sweden: Göteborg University — School of Economics and Commercial Law, Gothenburg Research Institute, pp. 13–48.

Denhardt, R. B. and Denhardt, J. V. (2000). The new public service: Serving rather than steering. *Public Administration Review*, **60**(6), 549–559.

Denhardt, J. V. and Denhardt, R. B. (2007). *The New Public Service: Serving, Not Steering*. Armonk, North Castle, NY: ME Sharpe.

Djelic, M. L. (1998). *The Export of the American Model*. Oxford: Oxford University Press.

Djellal, F., Gallouj, F., and Miles, I. (2013). Two decades of research on innovation in services: Which place for public services? *Structural Change and Economic Dynamics*, **27**, 98–117.

Edvardsson, B., Meiren, T., Schäfer, A., and Witell, L. (2013). Having a strategy for new service development — does it really matter? *Journal of Service Management*, **24**(1), 25–44.

Edwards, R. (1982). Contested terrain: The transformation of the workplace in the twentieth century. *Science and Society*, **46**(2), 237–240.

Fishenden, J. and Thompson, M. (2012). Digital government, open architecture, and innovation: Why public sector IT will never be the same again. *Journal of Public Administration Research and Theory*, **23**(4), 977–1004.

Fligstein, N. (1990). *The Transformation of Corporate Capital*. Cambridge, MA: Cambridge University Press.

Gallouj, F., Rubalcaba, L., and Windrum, P. (Eds.). (2013). *Public–Private Innovation Networks in Services*. Cheltenham, UK: Edward Elgar Publishing.

Gallouj, F. and Zanfei, A. (2013). Innovation in public services: Filling a gap in the literature. *Structural Change and Economic Dynamics*, **27**, 89–97.

Giddens, A. (1984). *The Constitution of Society*. Cambridge: Polity Press.

Hartley, J. (2005). Innovation in governance and public services: Past and present. *Public Money and Management*, **25**(1), 27–34.

Hartley, J. (2014). New development: Eight and a half propositions to stimulate frugal innovation. *Public Money & Management*, **34**(3), 227–232.

Hood, C. (1991). A public management for all seasons? *Public Administration*, **69**(1), 3–19.

Hood, C. (1995). The "New Public Management" in the 1980s: Variations on a theme. *Accounting, Organizations and Society*, **20**(2–3), 93–109.

Hyndman, N. and Liguori, M. (2016). Public sector reforms: Changing contours on an NPM landscape. *Financial Accountability & Management*, **32**(1), 5–32.

Jarzabkowski, P. (2008). Shaping strategy as a structuration process. *Academy of Management Journal*, **51**(4), 621–650.

Kelly, G., Mulgan, G. and Muers, S. (2002). *Creating Public Value: An Analytical Framework for Public Service Reform*. London: Strategy Unit, Cabinet Office.

Koskela-Huotari, K., Edvardsson, B., Jonas, J. M., Sörhammar, D. and Witell, L. (2016). Innovation in service ecosystems — Breaking, making, and maintaining institutionalized rules of resource integration. *Journal of Business Research*, **69**(8), 2964–2971.

Koskela-Huotari, K. (2018). *The Evolution of Markets — A Service Ecosystems Perspective* (doctoral dissertation). Karlstad, Sweden: Karlstad University Press.

Kristensson, P., Gustafsson, A. and Archer, T. (2004). Harnessing the creative potential among users. *Journal of Product Innovation Management*, **21**(1), 4–14.

Lapsley, I. (2009). New public management: The cruellest invention of the human spirit? *Abacus*, **45**(1), 1–21.

Liddle, J., McElwee, G. and Disney, J. (2012). Rural transport and social inclusion: The DalesBus Initiative. *Local Economy*, **27**(1), 3–18.

Lusch, R. F. and Nambisan, S. (2015). Service innovation: A service-dominant logic perspective. *Mis Quarterly*, **39**(1), 155–175.

MacInnis, D. J. (2011). A framework for conceptual contributions in marketing. *Journal of Marketing*, **75**(4), 136–154.

Maguire, S., Hardy, C., and Lawrence, T. B. (2004). Institutional entrepreneurship in emerging fields: HIV/AIDS treatment advocacy in Canada. *Academy of Management Journal*, **47**(5), 657–679.

Martin, G. P., Currie, G., and Finn, R. (2009). Leadership, service reform, and public-service networks: The case of cancer-genetics pilots in the English NHS. *Journal of Public Administration Research and Theory*, **19**(4), 769–794.

Martin, J. (2001). *Organizational Culture: Mapping the Terrain*. Thousand Oaks, CA: SAGE Publications.

Miles, I. (2008). Patterns of innovation in service industries. *IBM Systems Journal*, **47**(1), 115–128.

Nelson, R. R. and Winter, S. G. (1982). *An Evolutionary Theory of Economic Change*. Cambridge, MA, and London: Belknap Press of Harvard University Press.

Osborne, S. P., Radnor, Z., Kinder, T., and Vidal, I. (2015). The Service Framework: A public-service-dominant approach to sustainable public services. *British Journal of Management*, **26**(3), 424–438.

Osborne, S. P. (Ed.). (2010). *The New Public Governance: Emerging Perspectives on the Theory and Practice of Public Governance*. Abingdon, UK: Routledge.

Osborne, S., Radnor, Z., Kinder, T., and Vidal, I. (2014). Sustainable public service organisations: A public service-dominant approach. *Society and Economy*, **36**(3), 313–338.

Pache, A. C. and Santos, F. (2013). Inside the hybrid organization: Selective coupling as a response to competing institutional logics. *Academy of Management Journal*, **56**(4), 972–1001.

Pollitt, C. and Bouckaert, G. (2011). *Public Management Reform: A Comparative Analysis — New Public Management, Governance, and the Neo-Weberian State*. Oxford: Oxford University Press.

Reckwitz, A. (2002). Toward a theory of social practices: A development in culturalist theorizing. *European Journal of Social Theory*, **5**(2), 243–263.

Røvik, K. A. (1998). Moderne organisasjoner: Trender i organisasjonstenkningen ved tusenårsskiftet. Bergen-Sandviken: Fagbokforlaget.

Rubalcaba, L., Michel, S., Sundbo, J., Brown, S. W., and Reynoso, J. (2012). Shaping, organizing, and rethinking service innovation: A multidimensional framework. *Journal of Service Management*, **23**(5), 696–715.

Salunke, S., Weerawardena, J., and McColl-Kennedy, J. R. (2013). Competing through service innovation: The role of bricolage and entrepreneurship in project-oriented firms. *Journal of Business Research*, **66**(8), 1085–1097.

Skålén, P., Gummerus, J., von Koskull, C., and Magnusson, P. R. (2015). Exploring value propositions and service innovation: A service-dominant logic study. *Journal of the Academy of Marketing Science*, **43**(2), 137–158.

Spender, J. C. and Grant, R. M. (1996). Knowledge and the firm: overview. *Strategic management Journal*, 5–9.

Stoker, G. (2006). Public value management: A new narrative for networked governance? *The American Review of Public Administration*, **36**(1), 41–57.

Tether, B. S. (2005). Do services innovate (differently)? Insights from the European innobarometer survey. *Industry & Innovation*, **12**(2), 153–184.

Thakur, R., Hsu, S. H., and Fontenot, G. (2012). Innovation in healthcare: Issues and future trends. *Journal of Business Research*, **65**(4), 562–569.

Tsoukas, H. (1994). What is management? An outline of a metatheory. *British Journal of Management*, **5**(4), 289–301.

Vaara, E. and Whittington, R. (2012). Strategy-as-practice: Taking social practices seriously. *Academy of Management Annals*, **6**(1), 285–336.

Vargo, S. L., Wieland, H. and Akaka, M. A. (2015). Innovation through institutionalization: A service ecosystems perspective. *Industrial Marketing Management*, **44**, 63–72.

Voss, C. (1992). Successful innovation and implementation of new processes. *Business Strategy Review*, **3**(1), 29–44.

Whittington, R. (2006). Completing the practice turn in strategy research. *Organization Studies*, **27**(5), 613–634.

Windrum, P. and Garcia-Goni, M. (2008). A neo-Schumpeterian model of health services innovation. *Research Policy*, **37**(4), 649–672.

Zito, A. R. and Schout, A. (2009). Learning theory reconsidered: EU integration theories and learning. *Journal of European Public Policy*, **16**(8), 1103–1123.

Chapter 5

From Customer Feedback to Innovation: The IKEA Innovation Journey from Screws to Click

Bård Tronvoll, Bo Edvardsson and Maria Möllerskov-Jonzon

Högskolen i Innlandet, Karlstad University, IKEA, Sweden

Key takeaways

1. Few studies have focused on linking customer feedback to innovation, although customer feedback includes vital information that a firm can use in the innovation process.
2. This chapter explores customer feedback that stimulates and realizes the service innovation process.
3. Firms should develop initiatives enabling a better understanding of the customer journey and brand experience. Identifying challenges and opportunities across channels and touchpoints provides priorities to foster a firm's service innovation efforts.
4. All customer-initiated feedback, whether communicated directly to the firm or to other customers, should be seen as a goldmine of brand experience insights. By applying these insights, the firm makes sure that service innovation is directed toward improving customers' brand experience.

5. Service innovation should focus on exploiting these opportunities by developing a customer feedback system.
6. Service innovation is founded on how customers behave and co-create value in their life and business contexts.
7. For service innovation to become sustainable, all engaged actors evaluate the value that is important to them. Most often, customers and firms capture different types of value from an innovation.
8. This chapter uses a narrative approach to explore the retail innovation journey of INGKA Group (as an IKEA franchisee).

Introduction

Getting feedback and learning from customers and other users is critical for success in progressive and more competitive markets. Feedback on products, services, and customer brand experiences is a cornerstone in market orientation. The importance of feedback implies that the firm is aware of its environment, takes in information from the market and customers, disseminates the information, and acts on it (Kohli and Jaworski, 1990; Narver and Slater, 1990). Thus, information from customers is widely used to improve service provision. Customer feedback is collected for many purposes such as quality improvement, advancing customer experiences, and evaluating complaint handling processes to enforce successful service recovery, as well as creating the basis for service innovation. Customer feedback is crucial throughout the stimulation, realization, and value capture of the service innovation process. Thus, customers are invited to provide their views and suggestions when innovations are created, and not only when an innovation is launched in the market. Customer feedback is an important guide for firm's service innovation efforts and for customer involvement in innovation processes (Alam, 2002, 2012).

Feedback from customers usually results from customers' unfavorable service experiences in connection with failures or malfunctions. Consequently, firms collect and analyze the information to improve service provision and the customer experience. This information may also be used when organizing and fostering service innovation. However, there is often a lack of systematic processes to use the feedback to develop novel offerings and solutions. Modesto *et al.* (1985) state that "the knowledge gained from failures is often instrumental in achieving subsequent successes ... in the simplest terms, failure is the ultimate teacher." Furthermore, Juran (1951) argues that failures are "gold in the mine," meaning that the cost of poor quality would be quickly reduced by investing in quality improvement programs and service innovation efforts.

Service innovation is driven by a need to develop more compelling value propositions (Lusch and Vargo, 2006). In particular, it is necessary to engage customers and other actors in the interrelated processes and interconnected relationships through which innovation occurs. An ecosystems approach is used for explaining "types" of innovation (that is, technological and market innovation) as they are driven by a common process (Vargo *et al.*, 2015). A service-ecosystems view centers on the collaborative creation of value, the integration of dynamic resources, and the institutions that influence, and are influenced by, interactions among multiple actors (Vargo and Lusch, 2011). In this view, technology is considered a dynamic resource, or potentially useful knowledge (Mokyr, 2004); markets are conceptualized as institutionalized solutions (Vargo *et al.*, 2015); and innovation is the collaborative recombination or combinatorial evolution of practices that provide novel solutions to new or existing problems (Vargo *et al.*, 2015). Feedback collected from customers seldom contributes to critical business and innovation processes, because of the small return of investments in these systems (Sampson, 2011). However, the problem lies in utilizing the feedback gathered in these systems (Goodman *et al.*, 1996) and the need to be persistent, combined with an increasing need to systematically build capabilities to capture and store feedback, and for the processes supporting the feedback to be channeled into the business. Consequently, firms should understand the value of connecting customer feedback to drive service innovation.

This chapter explores customer feedback that stimulates and realizes the service innovation process. We focus on the innovation process within INGKA Group (as an IKEA franchisee) and Inter IKEA (as the IKEA franchisor) using their Democratic Design as a starting point to show how they managed the overall innovation journey. This journey started with customer feedback and has resulted in an easy-assembly furniture system called the click system. The chapter is organized using a narrative approach. Consequently, this chapter intertwines the theory of customer feedback and service innovation with information about the two companies working under the IKEA brand (interviews, internal documents, and presentations). A service innovation framework is used and applied to explore this innovation journey.

Democratic Design as a Basis for Customer-Centric Innovation

The organizations working under the IKEA brand are values-driven companies built upon "a passion for life at home". Every IKEA product is based on the idea of creating a better home for many people. On a global scale, currently 402 IKEA stores are open across 49 countries; 2.3 million people visited an IKEA store in 2017. The IKEA vision starts with the idea of providing a range of home furnishing products that are affordable to many people, not just a few. A fundamental part of the approach, is to ask if there is a better way to create a living solution? The IKEA vision exists in every part of the company, from design, sourcing, packing, and distributing through to the business model. Thus, IKEA customers play an important role in the value-creation process. The IKEA vision implies, "We do our part, you do your part, together we save money." Consequently, customers get involved in many ways, from collecting the furniture in the store to assembling the flat-pack products.

The IKEA design and innovation is based on "Democratic Design". IKEA of Sweden head of design, Engman (2017), states that "Democratic Design is more than a catchphrase; it influences every step of the design process. Democratic Design is the backbone of IKEA, its heart and soul. It's our tool to fulfil our vision — to create a better everyday life for the many people." He continues, explaining that "A home isn't just a place. It's a feeling. Like being in the most comfortable space in the universe. So for us, understanding people's life at home is the most natural place to start. Every year, we visit homes all around the world to find out what people dream about. We then pair their needs with the abilities of our suppliers to create new solutions that, hopefully, will make everyday life a little better."

Customer feedback

A firm should always be encouraged to listen to the "voice of the customer". Collecting and analyzing customer feedback is important because it allows organizations to learn in a continuous manner, and to adapt their offerings to customer preferences (Sun and Li, 2011). The effective capturing of customer feedback can help firms act swiftly in improving the quality of their service and value-creating ecosystems. Accordingly, the assembly or resource integration of IKEA products becomes important for the overall customer experience. Appropriate utilization of customer feedback allows the firm to identify the areas of organization-level practices that can be improved to enhance the customers' everyday life. Developing a customer feedback process is a multilevel process that begins with defining the challenges facing the customer and thereafter gives priorities to the organization in its innovation efforts.

Customer feedback is defined as customer communication concerning a product or a service (Erickson and Eckrich, 2001) as well as the experience of the brand. Several scholars have contributed with knowledge about customer feedback management and have identified different outcomes, such as customer complaining behavior (Tronvoll, 2012), facilitation of organizational learning (Babbar and Koufteros, 2008), enhancement of overall service quality (Wirtz *et al.*, 2010), improved decision making (Bitner *et al.*, 1994), and the generation of competitive advantage (Lusch *et al.*, 2007). The customer feedback literature includes both solicited (the firm requested the information) and unsolicited (the firm did not request the information) feedback. However, this literature tends to focus on a restricted number of negative topics, such as customer complaining behavior, customer dysfunctional behavior, customer rage, and service recovery (Daunt and Harris, 2014). The topics are mostly directed at solving problems and providing guidelines for a firm to learn from unfavorable experiences and avoid them in the future. Only few studies have observed the positive side of customer feedback (for example, Erickson and Eckrich, 2001; Nasr *et al.*, 2014, 2015; Ordenes *et al.*, 2014) and the importance of relating this feedback to service innovation.

IKEA companies have collected both solicited and unsolicited feedback from customers through surveys, chatbot in the store, observing people in the store, and visiting customers at home. In internal IKEA documents, it is stated that "We prefer to ask, What can we do to make things better, so that everyday life will be better? ... Today, we've move[d] beyond the conventional way of looking at home furnishing. Instead of seeing rooms, we look at activities. What are people doing in the home? How do they do it, and when?" (Internal documents, Inter IKEA 2018). Most firms focus on creating customer experiences by listening and learning from the customer. Maria Möllerskov-Jonzon, (2018), IKEA customer experience knowledge and insight leader, states that "Across IKEA companies we are committed to create a new way of listening and taking actions based on what our customers are telling us. We are developing initiatives enabling us to better understand, and take meaningful actions to improve our customers' experience across the customer journey. Understanding our customers and their experiences is crucial for a customer centric future to keep a relevant IKEA in the heart and minds of the many people" (Jonzon, 2018).

The company is also recognizing changing market trends and that these trends create altered customer behavior. This recognition appears in IKEA internal documents (2018): "With technology and economic development bringing people closer together than ever before, the world is growing smaller and tighter by the minute. Living habits and standards are changing at a faster pace." Inter IKEA and INGKA Group are adapting their systems for customer feedback to suit customer habits; as Jonzon (2018) argues, "Today, customers are providing feedback however they want, whenever they and wherever they want ... we listen, process and act on all this feedback. By consolidating the feedback across multiple moments and touchpoints of the customer journey, we are for the first time able to, in a truly holistic way, understand the total experience of the company on a grand scale."

Internally, company initiated and customer initiated feedback is differentiated. The former is feedback asked for in specific moments of the customer's journey, from seeking inspiration about what to buy to evaluating the furniture assembled in their homes. The latter is feedback delivered by customers on their terms, in whatever form they want to give it. Solicited feedback is somewhat created from an inside-out perspective, securing validation or confirmation of current performance on dimensions internally perceived to be important for the customer, and known to be important to the business. The unsolicited feedback keep an internal focus on what is most relevant to customers and on detecting emerging pain points. All customer initiated feedback, whether it is communicated directly to the company or happening between customers — all the online reviews and communication customer-to-customer — is seen as a gold-mine of insight and perspectives to staying relevant. By feeding these insights into the business, the business will have the internal confidence that actions taken to improve or innovate are truly done with the customer in mind, aiming to create a better customer experience.

The feedback collected has made it clear that "We know that it can be difficult to assemble IKEA furniture. And to be honest, some of our current furniture is poorly adapted to the way people move today, which requires them to dissemble and assemble furniture more often" (Inter IKEA internal documents, 2018). Consequently, their main resulting challenge is summed up, "We have set out to revolutionize IKEA assembly, cutting down assembly time and creating products that better lasts being taken apart and put together again" (Inter IKEA internal document, 2018). Numerous customers' feedback has created the inspiration to meet these challenges and make the furniture even easier to assemble, as well as easier to disassemble to take when a customer moves.

Service innovation

Edvardsson and Tronvoll (2013, p. 27) define service innovation as "changes in structure that stem from either a new configuration of resources or a new set of schemas and that result in new practices that are valuable for the actors in a specific context." This definition emphasizes that service innovation is about institutionalized change in the engaged actors' resource integration efforts as well as structural changes. These changes are expressed in, for example, efforts to change norms, rules, and habits, shaping practices in a way that allows actors to extract value in novel and, for them, useful ways. This is consistent with Vargo *et al.*'s (2015, p. 33) conceptualization of service innovation as the co-creation or collaborative recombination of practices that provides novel solutions for new or existing problems. The role of structures or institutional arrangements (sets of interrelated institutions, including enduring multiple rules, norms, habits, values, and beliefs) is providing "the rules of the game" (North, 1990) that shape service innovation processes and outcomes. Innovation as a process of changing value co-creation practices entails reconfiguring these institutional arrangements in service ecosystems (Vargo and Lusch, 2016). Thus, Vargo *et al.* (2015, p. 1) argue that "maintenance, disruption and change of institutions — [is] a central process of innovation."

Service innovation is driven by engaged actors and expressed through a value proposition; that is, an invitation to other actors to join forces in co-creating value. The realization of a value proposition needs support from an aligned service ecosystem (Lusch and Vargo, 2014). Lusch and Nambisan (2015) define service innovation as the rebundling of diverse resources that creates novel resources that are beneficial to some actors in a given context. The authors argue for an ecosystem and dynamic view of service innovation, emphasizing the role of institutional arrangements, and describe this innovation as (1) a collaborative process involving a diverse network of actors with agency, (2) an application of specialized competences for the benefit of another actor or the self and as the basis of all exchange, (3) increasing resource liquefaction and resource density, and (4) resource integration as the fundamental way to innovate. Vargo *et al.* (2015) argue that institutionalization and the disruption and change of institutions is a central process of service innovation, since institutional arrangements influence actors' behaviors and actors' behaviors can also change institutionalized norms, rules, and habits.

The IKEA vision is based on the idea of providing a range of home furnishing products that are affordable for many people and not just a few. The products should be perceived as solutions to real life problems at home for many people. One important means to achieve this, according to Jonzon (2018), is as follows: "By tapping into feedback provided on the customers' terms, we strengthen the outside in perspective by not letting our internally defined focus areas and questions define what the customers are telling us. And combining multiple sources of data creates a common knowledge base and support the breakdown of knowledge and organisational siloes. ... [This] is the first step toward closing the feedback loop. Based on the business vision and the constant feedback provided, this constitutes the foundation for combining function, quality, design and value — always with sustainability in mind. These five principles are the core of Democratic Design (form, function, quality, sustainability and low price). We want the form to contribute to making everyday life a little bit more joyful and beautiful. Function means that the product meets all the needs of everyday life. Quality means that our products last over time. And the low price makes the product accessible to all the many people. Lastly, sustainability is about much more than just the choice of material or how something is manufactured. We want to take long-term responsibility all the way from how we source the material, to the people who are producing it, and all the way on to the customer. We want to help people make sustainable choices that influence our future in a good way. Our goal is to create maximum value at minimum cost" (Inter IKEA internal documents, 2018).

Democratic Design is embedded in everyday life across the IKEA business practice. "It's pretty much about having a dialogue all the way from the original idea to the reality on the factory floor, into the store and all the way to the customer. To turn an idea, a vision into reality, you need to be pretty dedicated, on the verge of being obsessed actually. It's a huge challenge to deliver on the five principles of Democratic Design, but it's also very rewarding when we get it right. You need to be both systematic and chaotic in the process. And you need to ask a lot of questions along the way. Does humanity really need yet another cozy sofa? How can we minimize the use of resources? How can we be even more efficient when using materials? Can we prolong the life of a product, maybe use it again by altering it? One of the most exciting ways to answer questions is to innovate, to think differently from the very start" (Inter IKEA internal documents, 2018).

The five principles of Democratic Design are intertwined and "the whole idea is to fulfill all five principles in one product. We can't separate them if we want to contribute to something meaningful in people's lives. You can't compromise on quality to lower the price. It's this impossible equation that inspires and challenges us. And it's also the reason why it sometimes takes up to three years to develop a product. If it doesn't fulfill all five principles, it won't go into production" (Inter IKEA internal documents, 2018). This is made possible by focusing on innovation, claiming, "It demands a great deal of innovation from our side. We need to turn every stone and find new ways of developing products. We need to try new methods, new materials. We need to think new. And we need to do it together with our suppliers, but also with our customers. We have to listen to our customers' needs and at the same time explore our suppliers' possibilities when it comes to inventing new techniques and solutions. And it's only when we work together that we succeed in making better products" (Inter IKEA internal documents, 2018).

Service innovation is understood as an institutionalized, novel, and useful way for multiple actors to co-create value. We view an innovation as being embedded in a service ecosystem emphasizing a multi-actor-centric approach, including actors with different value outcomes in mind. Innovative actors and entrepreneurs challenge and change existing institutionalized norms, rules, and habits in service ecosystems, and thereby co-create value with and for engaged actors (Lusch and Vargo, 2014). Entrepreneurs create constellations of actors with complementing resources and create the necessary coordinating mechanisms to make sure that resource integration works in practice. Based on multiple actors' social setting and the understanding of value-in-social-context, Edvardsson *et al.* (2011) highlight social interaction as part of the service ecosystem. Social interaction frames the innovation and exchange, enabling actors to integrate resources within the particular relation setting, guided by the present institutions and institutional arrangements. The actors participating in different systems have access to various potential resources that they may activate and operate upon, and that are enabled or constrained by institutions. Edvardsson and Tronvoll (2013, p. 20) suggest that "to understand and enhance service innovation, it is necessary to understand the social context in which the service innovation takes place; the service system; and social structures, such as schemas [institutions], resources, and actors' abilities to acquire, integrate, and use the available structures in the social context."

Service innovation framework from an ecosystem view

Service ecosystems exist and transform through the efforts of multiple actors joining forces to break, make, and maintain the institutionalized rules of resource integration to achieve their intentions, as well as value in their business or life context. Innovation as a process of reconfiguring the institutional structure in service ecosystems is not straightforward or without conflicts and tensions. As changes in service ecosystems include the efforts of multiple actors' practices drawing on different resources and intentions and guided by various institutional arrangements, the institutionalization of new rules of resource integration occurs through multiple adjustments and changes over time, until it becomes accepted and shared (Zietsma and McKnight, 2009).

Recently, Edvardsson *et al.* (2018) introduced an innovation framework that can be viewed as an integrative duality of structuration (Giddens, 1984) that conceptualizes the innovation process, from idea to market creation. Their "structuration of innovation" features three interdependent domains: agency, structure, and the states of the innovation process. The authors argue that the agency-driven concepts include value propositions, actors, and resources; the structure-driven concepts consist of institutions and institutional arrangements; and firms have a coordinating role in the different states of the innovation process (initiating, realizing, and outcoming). Service innovation relies on the actors' knowledge about the recombination of resources and the structure that exists in the market and society. To understand how innovative (novel and useful) ways of co-creating value emerge, the firm must address this duality and include interdependencies in the process of innovation. The structuration of the innovation framework is grounded in previous research, such as Orlikowski (2000, p. 405), who states that "a structurational perspective is inherently dynamic and grounded in ongoing human action." Not only business structures but also social structures affect actors and their service innovation efforts.

Service innovation is a manifestation in practice, and is founded in what actors do and how they act. For service innovation to become sustainable, all engaged actors need to understand the value of being engaged and benefit from the value being co-created. Engaging in such value co-creation asymmetry is crucial; that is, different actors contribute with complementary resources, but, even more important, are able to extract value in line with their (often very different) intentions and needs.

These *actor-driven concepts* capture the IKEA value proposition of making everyday life easy for many people; that is, the easy assembly of furniture and disassembly/reassembly when moving. The value proposition is denoted as an invitation from one actor, or a constellation of actors, to other actors to join in value co-creation efforts. IKEA retailers do invite customers to design their own home and get inspired from solutions provided in the catalog, on the IKEA website, in advertising, and not least in IKEA stores. Many actors are engaged to fulfill the IKEA value proposition, such as suppliers, partners, and external and internal experts with different roles and resources as part of the ecosystem all over the world. The actors represent packaging developers, material suppliers, logistic service providers, and distributors. Many of these firms are certified IKEA partners; for example, those that transport furniture to customers' homes and offer the customers help in assembling the furniture at the home. Others are suppliers, for example, of raw material such as textile, wood, and food. All actors and resources are orchestrated by IKEA employees, including designers, cost and quality controllers, auditors, and brand managers.

The *structure-driven concepts* focusing on norms, values, and beliefs can be linked to the IKEA Demographic Design through the five principles described previously. These principles (form, function, quality, sustainability, and low price) are expressions of key values that are institutionalized in the IKEA ecosystem (employees, customers, and suppliers), and they are rigorous rules of compliance in areas such as design, material, cost, and function. The structure-driven concepts are also shown in the document "People and Planet," describing how to create a positive impact on people and the planet: "That's why we're going all-in on things that really matter, from switching our entire lighting range to energy-efficient LED to sourcing all of the cotton we use in our products from more sustainable sources. We will also develop and promote solutions that inspire and enable customers to live a more sustainable life at home, whether it is saving or producing energy, reducing water use or sorting waste" (IKEA. com). People and Planet is only one of many guiding principles that specify Democratic Design, thus shaping and directing innovation in the IKEA system.

The innovation process is managed using an approach reflected in *state-driven concepts*. The initiating state in the IKEA value chain is enabled by a small number of passionate people doing "skunk works"; that is, doing innovation work outside the traditional organization, although supported by top management. This work is always grounded in a customer focus, applying the Democratic Design principles; that is, contributing to solving problems in the home for many. However, even more important is how to industrialize the innovation in the IKEA ecosystem, including the manufacturing processes, the use of machines and other equipment in production lines, and not least the logistics flow. "Since then we've continued to apply these methods and to work with suppliers right on the factory floor. What we today call democratic design influences and benefits every part of IKEA — from our development facilities in Älmhult, to our suppliers around the globe, including local artisans in places like India and South East Asia. Over the years we've learnt that by constantly asking ourselves, 'Is there a better way?', bright ideas can come from just about anywhere, from anyone" (Inter IKEA internal documents, 2018).

After the initiating state, the realizing state becomes a formalized project with a separate budget, and necessary competences are put together mainly from internal funding, but also from external expertise as well as suppliers and partners. A formalized innovation project always needs a sponsor higher up in the organization, to ensure that the project has the right focus and is provided with funding and other resources.

The outcoming state is most often expressed in how one supplier or a small group of suppliers diffuse or scale up as a result of the many new actors invited and becoming engaged in co-creating value. When many actors are engaged, including actors with very different knowledge and skills and access to other resources, the focus on easy to use, and easy to assemble, becomes a challenge. The many global sourcing systems of IKEA products, including tight control, and the coordination of production and distribution also become challenges. These challenges are met by an advanced logistics and ITC system, which also enables the scaling up of different innovations.

The state-driven concepts of initiating, realizing, and outcoming can be compared with IKEA innovation projects that are directed by a process of (1) concept design (the co-creation of customer experience performance), (2) proof of concept (showing the business value and testing underlying assumptions), and (3) embed and scale (incorporating new ways of working into the organization; Jonzon, 2018). The project to make it even easier for customers to assemble furniture and to make it possible to assemble IKEA furniture in a completely new way resulted, after some years of work by a small team "under the radar," in an innovation — the click system — that launched in June 2017. It is a unique and patented method that does not include any screws or the need for tools such as an adjustable wrench or screwdriver.

The innovative click system

By starting with customer feedback, the problem of easy assembly was identified and made a focus of the IKEA service innovation efforts. The traditional assembly technique using screws and wooden sticks will become outdated as IKEA products that snap together "like a jigsaw puzzle" are introduced.

By developing a new type of joint "system," called a wedge dowel, customers have been given a quicker and simpler way to assemble products, with no need for screws, bolts, screwdrivers, and hex keys. The small, ribbed protrusion comes ready-installed in flat-packed furniture panels, and fits into pre-drilled holes. The innovation was partly driven by customers' resistance to the often slow and frustrating experience of putting together IKEA products, and partly as a way to save resources, since assembly no longer requires dozens of metal fittings. IKEA range and supply manager at the time, Jesper Brodin, speaking at the Design Indaba conference in Cape Town, argued that "IKEA furniture typically contains quite a lot of fittings. We see some challenges in the time and interest in doing that. So we thought, what happens if we try to take them out totally? We are now into the implementation phase of making it possible for you to click your furniture together" (Brodin, 2017).

The wedge dowel was first introduced in 'Regissör' storage products and 'Stockholm' cabinets in 2014 to test the concept. Brodin (2017) said, "I actually put together a table which used to take me 24 minutes to assemble but took me three minutes to click together." He went on to explain that the company has developed a new type of joint called a wedge dowel, which gets rid of the need for screws and traditional fixings on wooden items. The furniture's panels come with small ribbed protrusions, which easily slot into pre-drilled holes in the panels they're meant to connect to. There's no need for glue or screws, and the bits can be taken apart and reassembled as many times as you fancy. The wedge dowel requires no glue, yet it can be taken apart and reassembled many times without loss of structural integrity. "This means the products will last longer and are better suited to modern lifestyles," stated Brodin. "People move a lot more now. There are more divorces. So if you get kicked out [of your house] in the morning you can reassemble your table in the afternoon.... It's actually better to be honest, because some of our [current] furniture if you dissemble it and assemble it again it might lose some of the strength of the fittings."

Discussion

This chapter explores how customer feedback can stimulate and realize service innovations. Customer feedback can facilitate and inform the service innovation process. Customers are invited to provide their views and suggestions when innovations are created, and not only when an innovation is launched in the market. Customer feedback is thus an important guide for a firm's service innovation efforts and for customer involvement in innovation processes. The chapter applies a theoretical framework of the "structuration of innovation" with its three concepts of agency, structuration, and states. The state concepts of the innovation process have three pillars: initiating (idea generation and selection), realizing (integration of the innovation in an existing service ecosystem), and outcoming (diffusion and scaling up); these pillars provide the structure for an empirical analysis of innovation challenges.

We studied and learned from the IKEA business, which is often referred to as one of the most innovative brands and businesses in the world. The IKEA companies have been able to renew their business over the years through a stream of innovations. "We began learning about the production of furniture 60 years ago. We had just begun to design our own furniture and needed to learn how best to match the possibilities of the supplier with the needs of the customer. Bringing the two closer together was how we would keep prices low" (Inter IKEA internal document, 2018). This chapter focused on the IKEA innovation process using their Democratic Design concept as a starting point, to show how they manage innovation processes and projects. One important basis for innovations is continuous customer feedback; this chapter focused on the innovation project of the easy assembly furniture system called the click system. The click system will have a major impact on the IKEA production and distribution systems, as well as on customers, making it easier for customers to assemble and disassemble furniture. The click system also resonates with the IKEA focus on environmental responsibility, a concept that is also important for more and more customers.

What can other companies and organizations learn from the IKEA approach and this chapter, to stimulate and realize innovations in their businesses, creating value for their customers and other stakeholders?

First, connecting customer feedback to innovation creates an important source of potential areas, challenges, or issues to focus on in innovation projects. Customer feedback should include both big data and the big picture as well as individual customer's journeys, experiences, and hurdles. This feedback can be used in all states of the innovation process, including initiation, realizing the innovation (checking with the customer), and the outcome (through diffusion or scaling up within a business ecosystem). The analysis of the click system shows how important it is to think about the industrialization and integration of an innovation into an existing service ecosystem (Edvardsson *et al.*, 2018).

Second, the outcome of innovation projects must be integrated into the existing service ecosystem. An effective integration of the outcomes of service innovation projects requires the control and coordination of innovation processes and projects from a business and operations perspective. A major challenge is to arrive at the institutionalization of all changes needed for the "outcoming" of the innovation in business practice. In this case, the IKEA vision together with the principles of Democratic Design serves as an innovation platform to guide and direct innovation activities and projects. Each organization must develop a platform and guidelines that fit its vision, mission, and business context.

Third, for an innovation to become sustainable and make a real difference, the solution must create favorable customer experiences and be preferred compared to other options. A wide range of actions, including innovation projects, are focused on improving customers' experiences across IKEA channels. Understanding how favorable customer experiences are formed and how to avoid unfavorable experiences provides important input into service innovation projects. Therefore, customer experience knowledge and insights become critical for sustainable innovation. The IKEA companies are creating a new way of listening to customers and taking actions based on what customers say. Each firm must develop a way of linking customer feedback to innovation, to foster service innovation.

References

Alam, I. (2002). An exploratory investigation of user involvement in new service development. *Journal of the Academy of Marketing Science*, **30**(3), 250–261.

Alam, I. (2012). New service development in India's business-to-business financial services sector. *Journal of Business & Industrial Marketing*, **27**(3), 228–241. doi: 10.1108/08858621211207243.

Babbar, S. and Koufteros, X. (2008). The human element in airline service quality: contact personnel and the customer. *International Journal of Operations & Production Management*, **28**(9), 804–830.

Bitner, M. J., Booms, B. H., and Mohr, L. A. (1994). Critical service encounters: The employee's viewpoint. *Journal of Marketing*, **58**(4), 95–106.

Brodin, J. (2017). IKEA range and supply manager. Design Indaba Conference, Cape Town, South Africa.

Daunt, K. L. and Harris, L. C. (2014). Linking employee and customer misbehaviour: The moderating role of past misdemeanours. *Journal of Marketing Management*, **30**(3–4), 221–244. doi: 10.1080/0267257X.2013.812977.

Edvardsson, B. and Tronvoll, B. (2013). A new conceptualization of service innovation grounded in S-D logic and service systems. *International Journal of Quality & Service Sciences*, **5**(1), 19–31.

Edvardsson, B., Tronvoll, B., and Gruber, T. (2011). Expanding understanding of service exchange and value co creation. *Journal of the Academy of Marketing Science*, **39**(2), 327–339.

Edvardsson, B., Tronvoll, B., and Witell, L. (2018). An ecosystem perspective on service innovation. In F. Gallouj (ed.), *A Research Agenda for Service Innovation*, Cheltenham, UK: Edward Elgar Publishing.

Engman, M. (2017). IKEAs Head of Design. *IKEA Democratic Design Day 2017*, Älmhult, Sweden: IKEA.

Erickson, G. S. and Eckrich, D. W. (2001). Consumer affairs responses to unsolicited customer compliments. *Journal of Marketing Management*, **17**(3–4), 321–340.

Giddens, A. (1984). *The Constitution of Society: Outline of the Theory of Structuration.* Cambridge, UK: Polity Press.

Goodman, J., DePalma, D., and Broetzmann, S. (1996). Maximizing the value of customer feedback. *Quality Progress*, **29**, 35–39.

Inter IKEA internal documents (2018). Internal documents and presentations within Inter IKEA.

Jonzon, M. M. (2018). IKEAs Customer experience knowledge and insight leader In: Tronvoll, B. & Edvardsson, B. (eds.) *Transcript from interview.*

Juran, J. M. (1951). *Quality-Control Handbook.* New York: McGraw-Hill.

Kohli, A. K. and Jaworski, B. J. (1990). Market orientation: The construct, research propositions, and managerial implications. *Journal of Marketing*, **54**(2), 1–18.

Lusch, R. F. and Nambisan, S. (2015). Service innovation: A service-dominant logic perspective. *MIS Quarterly*, **39**(1), 155–176.

Lusch, R. F. and Vargo, S. L. (2006). *The Service-Dominant Logic of Marketing: Dialog, Debate, and Directions.* Armonk, NY: M. E. Sharpe.

Lusch, R. F. and Vargo, S. L. (2014). *Service-Dominant Logic: Premises, Perspectives, Possibilities.* Cambridge, UK: Cambridge University Press.

Lusch, R. F., Vargo, S. L., and O'Brien, M. (2007). Competing through service: Insights from service-dominant logic. *Journal of Retailing*, **83**(1), 5–18.

Modesto, A., Maidique, M. A., and Zirger, B. J. (1985). The new product learning cycle. *Research Policy*, **14**(6), 299–313.

Mokyr, J. (2004). *The Gifts of Athena: Historical Origins of the Knowledge Economy.* Princeton: Princeton University Press.

Narver, J. C. and Slater, S. F. (1990). The effect of a market orientation on business profitability. *Journal of Marketing*, **54**(4), 20–35.

Nasr, L., Burton, J., and Gruber, T. (2015). When good news is bad news: The negative impact of positive customer feedback on front-line employee well-being. *Journal of Services Marketing*, **29**(6/7), 599–612. doi: 10.1108/JSM-01-2015-0052.

Nasr, L., Burton, J., Gruber, T., and Kitshoff, J. (2014). Exploring the impact of customer feedback on the well-being of service entities: A TSR perspective. *Journal of Service Management*, **25**(4), 531–555. doi: 10.1108/JOSM-01-2014-0022.

North, D. C. (1990). *Institutions, Institutional Change and Economic Performance.* Cambridge, UK: Cambridge University Press.

Ordenes, F. V., Theodoulidis, B., Burton, J., Gruber, T., and Zaki, M. (2014). Analyzing customer experience feedback using text mining: A linguistics-based approach. *Journal of Service Research*, **17**(3), 278–295. doi: 10.1177/1094670514524625.

Orlikowski, W. J. (2000). Using technology and constituting structures: A practice lens for studying technology in organizations. *Organization Science*, **11**(4), 404–428.

Sampson, S. E. (2011). An empirically defined framework for designing customer feedback systems. *Quality Management Journal*, **6**, 64–80.

Sun, B. and Shibo, Li. (2011). Learning and acting on customer information: A simulation-based demonstration on service allocations with offshore centers. *Journal of Marketing Research (JMR)*, **48**(1), 72–86. doi: 10.1509/jmkr.48.1.72.

Tronvoll, B. (2012). "A dynamic model of customer complaint behaviour from the perspective of service-dominant logic." *European Journal of Marketing*, **46**(1/2), 284–305.

Vargo, S. L. and Lusch, R. (2016). Institutions and axioms: An extension and update of service-dominant logic. *Journal of the Academy of Marketing Science*, **44**(1), 5–23. doi: 10.1007/s11747-015-0456-3.

Vargo, S. L. and Lusch, R. F. (2011). It's all B2B... and beyond: Toward a systems perspective of the market. *Industrial Marketing Management*, **40**(2), 181–187. doi: 10.1016/j.indmarman.2010.06.026.

Vargo, S. L., Wieland, H., and Akaka, M. A. (2015). Innovation through institutionalization: A service ecosystems perspective. *Industrial Marketing Management*, **44**(1), 63–72. doi: 10.1016/j.indmarman.2014.10.008.

Wirtz, J., Tambyah, S. K., and Mattila, A. S. (2010). Organizational learning from customer feedback received by service employees. *Journal of Service Management*, **21**(3), 363–387. doi: 10.1108/09564231011050814.

Zietsma, C. and McKnight, B. (Eds.), (2009). *Building the Iron Cage: Institutional Creation Work in the Context of Competing Proto-institutions*. New York: Cambridge University Press.

Chapter 6

Resource Integration Processes as a Microfoundation for Service Innovation

Rolf Findsrud and Sebastian Dehling

Högskolen i Innlandet, Karlstad University, Sweden

Key takeaways

1. Microfoundations look at the origin of phenomena and thus can explain what drives service innovation and how it emerges.
2. The purpose of this chapter is to integrate and relate the microfoundational characteristics and language with the lexicon and characteristics of resource integration and service innovation in a service-dominant logic (SDL) perspective to establish resource integration as a microfoundation of service innovation.
3. Resource integration creates learning opportunities for discovering better practices. Resource integration represents the raw material from which service innovation emerges. Service innovations occur when learning from resource integration creates a change in practice at a higher level of aggregation.

4. The chapter is independent of context and conceptual, based on theory.
5. Any reader who finds this chapter interesting should also see Chapters 4 and 5.

Introduction

Service innovation is a primary source of competitive advantage (Carlborg *et al.*, 2014; Kindström and Kowalkowski, 2014; Paswan *et al.*, 2009), as seen in contemporary digital services (for example, Netflix, Spotify, and Uber) that offer novel combinations of existing resources, allowing new methods of service exchange and customer experiences at scale. Ostrom *et al.* (2015) emphasize that identifying the drivers of sustained service innovation is an important direction for future research in service innovation. Early studies of service innovation considered new technology as the main driver of service innovation (Toivonen and Tuominen, 2009; Ordanini and Parasuraman, 2011), but technology plays a different role in service innovation. Even though technology is critical for service innovation (Carlborg *et al.*, 2014), it functions as an enabler of service innovation, leaving the question of what drives service innovation unanswered.

Service innovation often manifests as a change in the competences of the company, the competences of the customer, the prerequisites of the offering, or what the customer co-creates (Gustafsson *et al.*, 2012). Existing research (for example, Nonaka, 1994; Grigoriou and Rothaermel, 2014) argues that competences are the key driver for innovation, which emphasizes the role of individual competences as the microfoundations of firm-level capabilities (Felin and Foss, 2005). However, following a service-dominant logic (SDL) perspective, it is not an actor's individual competence as such that has value but rather its use (Findsrud *et al.*, 2018, see also Zimmermann, 1951). Further, use of knowledge and skills implies an agency effort, meaning it is the actor's ability to act purposefully that drives resource integration (Findsrud *et al.*, 2018, see also Kleinaltenkamp *et al.*, 2012; Edvardsson *et al.*, 2014). According to Peters (2014, p. 254), resource integration represents 'a continuous process consisting of "a series of activities performed by an actor" (Payne *et al.*, 2008, p. 86) for the benefit of another party, which is conceptually aligned with service. The driver of service innovation is based on customers' demand for new services (Barrett *et al.*, 2015; Storey *et al.*, 2016; Ratny *et al.*, 2017) and service providers' desire to create new services for existing markets or to find new markets for existing services (Barrett *et al.*, 2015; Ratny *et al.*, 2017). Hence, service innovation is actor driven (Edvardsson and Tronvoll, 2013) through the use of knowledge and skills to co-create value (Edvardsson *et al.*, 2011). To understand what drives actors involved in service innovation, focus is needed on how and why actors engage in activities and behaviors that lead to service innovation. Therefore, we propose resource integration as a microfoundation from which service innovation emerges.

Hollebeek *et al.* (2016) and Storbacka *et al.* (2016) argue that SDL is a promising candidate for a macrofoundational theory, and is suitable for studying service innovation (Ordanini and Parasuraman, 2011). Further, microfoundations are the theoretical building blocks of macrofoundational theory that have narrower conceptual applicability, rendering these building blocks closer to the realm of marketing practice (Hollebeek *et al.*, 2016). Accordingly, this chapter adapts an SDL perspective on service innovation and positions resource integration as a microfoundation of service innovation.

Theoretical microfoundations enable us to understand how these higher-level factors, such as service innovation, originate from individual-level factors. Resource integration represents the use of competences through individual actions and interactions, and through that lens we can better explain how resource integration and the interaction of actors lead to emergent and collective service innovations, and how relations between macrovariables are mediated by resource integration actions and interactions (see Hollebeek *et al.*, 2016; Felin *et al.*, 2015). By zooming in on resource integration as the key driver of service innovation at the micro-level, we seek insights into the mechanisms that shape the process of service innovation. Accordingly, resource integration enhances our understanding of what happens in practice when actors apply their knowledge and skills to improve their competitive advantage and engage in learning processes. The purpose of this chapter is to integrate and relate the micro-foundational characteristics and language with the lexicon and characteristics of resource integration and service innovation within the SDL to establish resource integration as a microfoundation of service innovation (MacInnis, 2011; Vargo and Lusch, 2016).

The remainder of the chapter is organized as follows: First a theoretical framing lays out the basis for reasoning in this chapter, providing a conceptualization of (1) service innovation and (2) the characteristics of microfoundations and principles of resource integration. Second, the chapter relates how resource integration as a microfoundation informs service innovation from a micro-level to a macro-level by focusing on (1) actors and their collaboration and (2) change in practices through the aggregation of interactions. Finally, the chapter concludes by delineating theoretical and managerial implications.

Theoretical Framing

A conceptualization of service innovation

Witell *et al.* (2016) argue that scholars have missed the chance to define service innovation clearly, leaving a gap for further conceptual development (Ostrom *et al.*, 2010) especially on the processes and actors (Carlborg *et al.*, 2014). Traditional perspectives on service innovation are mainly rooted in a goods-dominant logic (GDL) that privileges product and process innovation (Lusch and Nambisan, 2015) with a focus either on the service offering or on the service process (Ostrom *et al.*, 2015). Witell *et al.* (2016) found that defining service innovation as a "new service" is the most common interpretation of service innovation across the different perspectives (assimilation, demarcation, or synthesis), but how the newness emerges and aggregates still represents a knowledge gap in the literature.

In recent years, research on service innovation has been extended through a synthesis view of innovation (Gallouj and Savona, 2009) that proposes a value co-creation perspective beyond the GDL (Rubalcaba *et al.*, 2012; Lusch and Nambisan, 2015). Service innovation research using a synthesis view resonates well with the SDL that focuses on value co-creation through resource integration (Edvardsson and Tronvoll, 2013; Helkkula *et al.*, 2018). The SDL literature proposes that actors are generic resource integrators (not separating between the customer or provider roles) that co-create value in service ecosystems coordinated by institutional arrangements (Vargo and Lusch, 2016). Actors are embedded in these institutional arrangements that are the social and economic structures (Edvardsson *et al.*, 2011). These structures provide "the rules of the game" (North, 1990; Koskela-Huotari and Vargo, 2016) and influence actors' resource integration practices.

Vargo *et al.* (2015) argue that the key processes for service innovation are in changing practices, since service innovation emerges and aggregates through novel and improved ways of resource integration (Lusch and Nambisan, 2015; Vargo *et al.*, 2015). Service innovations occur when practices to integrate resources depart from previous practices through a learning and institutionalization process that leads to significant changes in organizational capabilities and the service ecosystem (Perks *et al.*, 2012; Koskela-Huotari *et al.*, 2016). As a result, the service innovation process can be characterized as event driven, dynamic, and highly dependent on correspondence and reciprocity (Ballantyne *et al.*, 2011; Edvardsson *et al.*, 2012). Chandler and Lusch (2015) suggest that actors alone cannot sustain value creation and therefore offer value propositions as invitations to other actors to co-create value. Lusch and Nambisan (2015) thus argue that the fundamental way to innovate is to engage multiple actors in collaborative processes. Even though actors engage in collaborative processes, service innovation is still based on the individual user's point of view, since actors experience value individually, and service innovation can be seen as changes in the service experience (Helkkula *et al.*, 2018).

Resource integration practices are driven by actors' needs (Toivonen and Tuominen, 2009) and motivation (Findsrud *et al.*, 2018), which allows traces of a Schumpeterian view of service innovation assuming that innovation provides benefits to the developer. This view also conceptualizes the idea that innovation must be carried into practice. This idea conforms with the aggregation or institutionalization of new practices, entailing that innovations are reproducible (Toivonen and Tuominen, 2009; Snyder *et al.*, 2016). To enhance service innovation, actors need to design conditions that allow resource integration mechanisms to change (Edvardsson and Tronvoll, 2013), which breaks, makes, or maintains the mechanisms' coordinating institutions in practice (Koskela-Huotari *et al.*, 2016). Such conditions might request more dynamic capabilities (Teece *et al.*, 1997) that can enable service innovation (den Hertog *et al.*, 2010). This chapter thus positions resource integration as a microfoundation for service innovation and uses an SDL perspective to conceptualize service innovation. Further, we explain how service innovation originates from resource integration and its aggregation.

Microfoundations and principles of resource integration

Earlier in this chapter, we stated that service innovation is a subjective macro-level construct that like any other macro-level construct is built of several conceptual elements. Foss (2011) suggests that there cannot be a direct causal relationship between a construct like service innovation and other macro-level constructs (for example, institutional arrangements) because macro-level constructs are always mediated by microfoundations rooted in individual action and interaction. Macro-level constructs might influence the conditions for microfoundations aggregating toward changes in other macro-level constructs, but theorizing micro-level causality still holds explanatory primacy (Abell *et al.*, 2008). Thus, Barney and Felin (2013) describe microfoundations in relation to individual action, interaction, and the additive or emergent aggregation shaping macro-level factors.

Microfoundations look at the origins and nature of the macro-level (Barney and Felin, 2013). However, simply referencing a micro-concept (for example, learning, competences) does not suffice as a microfoundation, as the concept itself needs to change or evolve given aggregation and interaction in the context of an organization or other social settings (Barney and Felin, 2013). The SDL narrative on value co-creation proposes that resources only have potential value (Zimmermann, 1951), and the actual value an actor can gain from a resource depends on how it is operated on in specific contexts with specific intentions (Edvardsson *et al.*, 2014). Resource integration is conceptualized as a process or an activity (Plé, 2016), where the activity in itself can be behavioral or cognitive (McColl-Kennedy *et al.*, 2012).

The microfoundation perspective sees individuals as independent actors with their own preferences and interests. Similarly, the SDL lens on resource integration sees actors as individuals or groups (Edvardsson *et al.*, 2014) with agency (Kleinaltenkamp *et al.*, 2012; Edvardsson *et al.*, 2014) driven by motivation (Findsrud *et al.*, 2018), using resources (for example, knowledge, skill) with the purpose of co-creating value (Vargo and Lusch, 2016). Skålén *et al.* (2015b) argue that resource integration may be conducted by one actor in isolation when creating value-in-use, and Löbler (2013) argues the pure process of resource integration might be carried out by a single person, several people, or many people. However, from an SDL perspective, value is always co-created, and thus resource integration cannot occur in isolation.

So the question becomes, if an individual has a particular preference, knowledge, or skill, where did these operant resources come from? In other words, when we look at the individual actor's resource integration activities as a microfoundation for service innovation, why not regress further? This question is referred to as the infinite regression problem, and microfoundations do not necessarily demand extreme reduction (Barney and Felin, 2013). The infinite regression problem can be "solved" in the sense that there are natural punctuations (Barney and Felin, 2013), and for microfoundations in social sciences, the individual provides a natural stopping point for reduction and the appropriate starting point for analysis (Barney and Felin, 2013). SDL is primarily intersubjective (Peters *et al.*, 2014; Löbler, 2011) and has mainly been conceptualized based on social aspects, for instance, institutions (for example, Vargo and Lusch, 2016; Koskela-Huotari and Vargo, 2016; Edvardsson *et al.*, 2014), structuration theory (for example, Edvardsson *et al.*, 2011), or practice theory (for example, Echeverri and Skålén, 2011). Thus, the individual actors become a natural starting point for analysis on service innovation in an SDL perspective. The lack of consensus on the number of actors needed for resource integration is related to a methodological perspective of the researchers. However, this is not an issue in regard to using resource integration as a microfoundation since microfoundational research does not necessarily need to regress to the level of the individual skills of an actor, although it does need to regress to a lower analytical level than the collective phenomenon that is to be explained.

One common misconception about microfoundations is that they only focus on the individual; however, micro-levels may focus on the individual or the collaboration (Barney and Felin, 2013). In the SDL, it is important that the act of resource integration unfold in the context of the service ecosystem (Laud *et al.*, 2015), and integrating resources emphasize collaborations among actors and the ways actors engage with others in their service network to integrate resources (McColl-Kennedy *et al.*, 2012). Resource integration often occurs while interacting with and operating on other resources (Laud *et al.*, 2015) or in collaboration with actors (Kleinaltenkamp *et al.*, 2012) through interactive practices in order to realize value-in-social-context (Edvardsson *et al.*, 2011). The microfoundation perspective sees individuals as performing within structures (Barney and Felin, 2013). Barney and Felin (2013) state that a microfoundation approach systematically looks at how choices and interactions create structure, the behavior of individuals within structures, and the role of individuals in shaping the evolution of structures over time. The same is true for resource integration, where shared institutional arrangements guide both how resources are integrated and value co-creation in service ecosystems (Vargo and Akaka, 2012; Edvardsson *et al.*, 2014; Lusch and Vargo, 2014; Koskela-Huotari and Vargo, 2016). Institutions represent frames of reference that condition and coordinate actors' choices to motivate action, and their sense of self and identity (Thornton *et al.*, 2012; Edvardsson *et al.*, 2014), and comprise regulative, normative, and cultural-cognitive elements that provide stability and meaning to social life (Koskela-Huotari and Vargo, 2016). Institutional arrangements are sets of interrelated institutions (Vargo and Lusch, 2016).

Peters (2016) conceptualized two different paths that resource integration can take to value creation leading to either summative (homopathic) or emergent (heteropathic) outcomes. In the article, Peters (2016) argues that in homopathic resource integration episodes, the resources combined have the same effect as when integrated separately, whereas in heteropathic instances of resource integration, the combination of resources lets new resources with new effects emerge, increasing the potential value beyond the sum of its constituents. An emergent effect might happen at the individual level, or summative effects at the individual level might transform into emergent effects on an aggregate level.

The different aggregation paths of actors integrating resources through collaboration hold a key role in how service innovation occurs, and might even trigger implications for service innovation in terms of incremental and radical outcomes. The microfoundational view on aggregation almost mirrors the resource integration perspective, suggesting that the resource characteristics an actor begins with, in the additive perspective (homopathic) of a collective phenomenon, are more important than the interaction practice and its coordinating institutional arrangements (Barney and Felin, 2013). From the additive perspective, actors seem more independent and do not seem to influence each other much. On the contrary, the heteropathic view in microfoundation research puts the focus on the reciprocal influence individuals have on each other, and their interactions may lead to emergent aggregate outcomes that cannot be reduced back to their originating constituents (for example, company culture).

In summary, resource integration is driven by actors with agency (Vargo and Lusch, 2011), and performed by a single actor or in collaboration (Löbler, 2013). Furthermore, the outcome of resource integration is value co-creation at multiple levels of aggregation (Laud *et al.*, 2015), and the process can be homopathic or heteropathic (Peters, 2016). This description can be directly linked to the characteristics of microfoundations that Barney and Felin (2013) delineated, as independent individuals interact within structures, such that additive or emergent effects aggregate into collective phenomena.

Informing service innovation with resource integration as a microfoundation

In the last decade, microfoundational research has increasingly been applied in the management literature (Devinney, 2013) to break down how macro-level constructs (for example, service innovation) emerge as a consequence of micro-level factors (Baer *et al.*, 2013; Foss and Pedersen, 2016). For instance, in service and marketing management research, Kindström *et al.* (2013) identified several "microfoundations" of dynamic capabilities (for example, sensing opportunities) as activities (for example, technology exploration) that enable service innovation. Since managers cannot directly change these dynamic capabilities, Kindström *et al.* (2013) identified activities that might create the conditions to enable service innovation.

Since service innovation continues to gain relevance, it is important to understand where it originates and how it forms from separate activities into a collective phenomenon. Therefore, individual actor's resource integration behavior within practices, the development of practices through resource integration, and the role of the actors in changing practices over time deserve careful consideration when theorizing about service innovation (Felin and Foss, 2005). As a result, we reconcile the principles of resource integration and microfoundations in relation to service innovation in the following sections: (1) actors and collaboration (micro-level) and (2) forms of aggregation (micro to macro). Table 1 summarizes the key points of the following section.

Actors and collaboration

Service innovation often gets linked to new, actor-driven ways to integrate resources, use resources, or capture value within service systems (Edvardsson and Tronvoll, 2013), and many ideas come from daily business activities (Toivonen and Tuominen, 2009). Accordingly, resource integration represents the raw material from which potentially better ways of realizing value can be found. Lusch and Nambisan (2015) argue that innovation occurs as actors seek better density and improved methods of value co-creation. Accordingly, service innovation is actor driven, and is about actors using resources (including their knowledge and skills) in specific contexts (Edvardsson and Tronvoll, 2013) to create value. Traditionally, the value of innovation is measured by the economic growth of the developing firm (Witell *et al.*, 2016), but from the SDL perspective, both in service innovation research and in resource integration research, the value created is from an actor perspective and determined by the beneficiary (Helkkula *et al.*, 2018).

Institutions are important within the SDL literature in general, and thus also play an important role in the service innovation literature. First, actors are guided by social values and institutional arrangements that determine how resources are to be understood, accessed, used, and integrated in achieving service innovation (Helkkula *et al.*, 2018), and innovation in service ecosystems entails reconfiguring the institutional structure by changing the institutionalized rules of resource integration

Table 1. Summary of characteristics relating microfoundations, resource integration, and service innovation.

Microfoundations	Resource integration Micro	Service innovation Macro
Individuals are independent of each other, with their own preferences and interests	Actors have agency (Kleinaltenkamp et al., 2012), have individual sets of knowledge and skills, and are driven by motivation	The prime mover of organizational competences is the individual actors (Nonaka, 1994)
The behavior of individuals is within structures	Actors have subjective experiences, as value is phenomenological determined by the beneficiary	Innovation is something which provides benefit to its developer
Microlevels may focus on the individual or the collaborative	Actors increase their knowledge and skill through resource integration	Service innovation cannot occur without learning
	Actors are guided by institutional arrangements	Innovation in service ecosystems entails reconfiguring the institutional structure by changing the institutionalized rules of resource integration (Koskela-Huotari et al., 2016)
	The pure act of resource integration may be carried out by a single actor, or in collaboration (Löbler, 2013)	Discovering better practices may come from individual use of resources or collaborative use of resources
		Innovations are the outcomes of behaviors and interactions between individuals and organizations (Perks et al., 2012)

Actor and collaboration

(*Continued*)

Table 1. (*Continued*)

	Microfoundations	Resource integration Micro	Service innovation Macro
Aggregation	Microfoundations cannot be without aggregation	The purpose of resource integration is to co-create value at various levels of aggregation (Vargo and Lusch, 2016)	Service innovation is change at a higher level of aggregation
	Choices and interactions create structure and shape the evolution of structures over time	Value outcomes from resource integration (may) lead to or change practices (Kleinaltenkamp et al., 2012)	Service innovation is a process of breaking, making, and maintaining institutionalized rules of resource integration (Koskela-Huotari et al., 2016)
			Innovation is something carried out in practice
			Innovation is something that is reproducible
	Aggregation from microfoundations may be additive or emergent	The resource integration may be homopathic or heteropathic (Peters et al., 2016)	Individuals influence each other, and their interaction may lead to aggregate outcomes that can be unforeseen, surprising, and emergent

(Koskela-Huotari *et al.*, 2016). Second, service innovation can be understood as a process of breaking, making, and maintaining institutionalized rules of resource integration (Koskela-Huotari *et al.*, 2016). Thus, not only do institutions shape the actors' behavior, but the behavior also shapes the institutions. In other words, institutions not only guide actors' resource integration, but resource integration creates new institutions and shapes existing institutions.

Collaboration is also recognized as a powerful tool for achieving successful service innovation (Agarwal and Selen, 2009; Kindström *et al.*, 2013), as innovations are the outcomes of behaviors and interactions between individuals and organizations (Perks *et al.*, 2012), and many ideas come from interactions with customers and partners (Toivonen and Tuominen, 2009). Human resources and collaboration are more important for service innovation then they are for product innovation (Edvardsson and Tronvoll, 2013), as many service organizations create new service offerings and service concepts through collaborative arrangements and partnerships (Agarwal and Selen, 2009). Thus, engaging in networks is a key dynamic capability for service innovation (den Hertog *et al.*, 2010).

Further, service innovation is also centered on dynamic and relational interactions between suppliers and customers (Randhawa and Scerri, 2015). Research by Ordanini and Parasuraman (2011) found that employee collaboration is likely to have a positive effect on the volume of service innovation but not the radicalness. Further, they found that customer collaboration contributes to innovation volume, serving as a source of new service ideas, and business-partner collaboration contributes to the radicalness of innovation, but not volume. Finally, only when partner collaboration was coupled with customer collaboration did a truly innovative and profitable set of services emerge (Ordanini and Parasuraman, 2011). Accordingly, collaboration may lead to interaction effects of service innovation, which may be of an additive or emergent nature. Additive and emergent aggregation will be further discussed later in the chapter.

Increasing knowledge and skills through learning is hypothesized to be an important asset for service innovators (den Hertog *et al.*, 2010). In the resource integration literature, knowledge and skills are considered a prerequisite that enables effective resource integration. Actors increase their knowledge and skills through resource integration, as resource integration processes and outcomes provide information to involved actors, influencing their motivation to continue to integrate resources (Findsrud *et al.*, 2018). Thus, resource integration processes and outcomes also provide insights into changed or new knowledge and skills needed for future resource integration efforts. Thus, an actor has learning opportunities every time the actor integrates resources. Learning is important in the accumulation and development of competences and plays an important role in service innovation processes, since service innovation cannot occur without learning (Drejer, 2004).

Since the prime mover of organizational competences is the individual actors (Nonaka, 1994), a focus on individuals and their interactions may provide crucial insight to service innovation. Even though learning strengthens the potential for further innovation, learning does not equal innovation. For learning to be considered an innovation, it must be carried into practice (Toivonen and Tuominen, 2009). Accordingly, service innovation occurs when learning from resource integration creates a change in practice, and should be understood as a process of ongoing negotiations, experimentation, competition, and learning (Koskela-Huotari *et al.*, 2016).

To summarize, resource integration as a microfoundation focuses on the individual actors using operant resources individually or in collaboration, guided by institutional arrangements; this creates learning opportunities for discovering better practices and opportunities for reshaping or creating new practices and institutions. In the next section, we discuss how these micro-level activities of resource integration lead to additive or emergent innovations that change at the macro-level (for example, practices, institutions).

Changes in practice through the aggregation of interactions

The name "microfoundations" implies that microfoundations are the constituents of collective phenomena and that therefore their key condition is to aggregate to a higher level than that at which they are located. Individual actors and their interactions are such microfoundations and are fundamental to understanding the collective phenomena of the organizational or service ecosystem level and how these collective phenomena change.

Microfoundational analysis should therefore be mainly concerned with how actors and their mutual resource integration efforts aggregate toward macro-level constructs such as service innovation. We conceptualize service innovation as new or changed resource integration practices based on reconfiguring resources and institutional arrangements leading to changes in the service ecosystem that are of value to actors (Koskela-Huotari *et al.*, 2016; Vargo *et al.*, 2015). The key mechanism for service innovation to emerge and change ecosystems is the social processes of aggregation and the interaction of individual variables. Resource integration processes are sequences of interdependent episodes that require individual action and interaction through practice. Thus, looking at interactions among individuals may provide insights into how practices emerge.

Basically, practices are the routine activities and sensemaking frameworks that people carry out and apply in specific contexts (Skålén *et al.*, 2015a). When actors perform new or changed activities to co-create value, they might create new or break given practice and institutions (Koskela-Huotari *et al.*, 2016). If this scenario makes sense or creates value also for other actors, those actors might adopt this new or changed way of integrating resources. Thus, via actors, this practice and its sensemaking frameworks are further diffused into wider practice, becoming a service innovation (Koskela-Huotari *et al.*, 2016). However, temporal and nonreproducible changes are not sufficient to aggregate sustainably to a collective level and become service innovations (Schumpeter, 1934; Snyder *et al.*, 2016).

The aggregation of new or changed activities, transforming them into routines and practices that make, break, or maintain institutions and lead to service innovation, is the result of two different types of resource integration process. Peters (2016) argues that one should differentiate between (1) homopathic resource integration processes and (2) heteropathic resource integration processes. Similarly, Barney and Felin (2013) argue that actors and their interactions aggregate either in a simple additive or in a complex way. The homopathic or additive process assumes that single effects of each resource integration episode aggregate to the sum of their single effects (Peters, 2016; Barney and Felin, 2013). On the contrary, the heteropathic or complex resource integration process assumes that effects aggregate to emergent effects that are original and not reducible to their former constituent parts (Peters, 2016). These totally new resources with new properties and potential effects might hold more potential value than the sum of the parts they originated from.

Emergent resource integration processes are characterized by the reciprocal influence of interacting actors on each other, and less on the independence of resources in summative aggregation processes (Barney and Felin, 2013). Therefore, the heteropathic resource integration pattern seems to organize actors and interaction in a certain way instead of just simply aggregating them. According to von Koskull and Strandvik (2014), the innovation process has interestingly been modeled in the service innovation literature either as a strongly structured and sequential process or as an unstructured and circular process. The latter supports an emergence perspective that emphasizes the interactions between participating actors, their sensemaking, and the emergence of innovations within the process (von Koskull and Strandvik, 2014). The more structured process tends to be an additive resource integration process since there is little room for interactions to unfold, and it puts more emphasis on the single resources as an input to the process.

However, actors are not equal in their ability to obtain value from their resource integration activities (Hibbert *et al.*, 2012), which brings some uncertainty as to which resource integration pattern is most valuable for which kind of actor and desired outcome. It is the managers' task to create the conditions for emergent or summative resource integration patterns to occur so that aggregation toward the desired change is more feasible.

Conclusion

With the increased relevance of service innovation as an important source of competitive advantage, it becomes imperative for researchers, students, and practitioners to understand where service innovation originates and how it comes about. Therefore, this chapter used a microfoundational perspective to position and relate the principles of resource integration as the source and driver of service innovation — its microfoundation. The focus in this chapter has been on the individual, interactions, and the process of aggregation rather than on the type of service innovation. Service innovation research should focus more on microfoundations rooted in individual action and interaction that mediates service innovation, and in other macro-level constructs (for example, institutional arrangements; Foss, 2011). Furthermore, this chapter theoretically contributes to the service innovation literature by using resource integration as a theoretical framework for understanding an individual actor's resource integration behavior within practices, the development of practices through resource integration, and the role of actors in changing practices over time.

The additive and emergent paths of resource integration as sources for service innovation might suggest different outcomes. Conditions that are designed to facilitate emergent resource integration might lead to more radical service innovation, whereas additive resource integration might evolve into more incremental service innovation. These varying outcomes have some clear managerial implications for organizations that seek service innovation. As argued previously in this chapter, practices emerge from the activities and interactions of actors, and service innovation occurs when changes in practices spread through learning processes in the organization. Accordingly, the focus of managers should not be on creating practices, but rather on creating learning environments where practices can emerge; a bottom–up approach might facilitate service innovation better than a top–down approach.

Managers can also try to create different innovation environments aiming to explicitly facilitate additive or emergent resource integration paths for different desired outcomes. One challenge for managers with emergent service innovation is that it may be hard to replicate or reproduce, and in those instances, it can arguably be considered as not being an innovation. Thus, focusing on resource integration helps researchers and managers to understand where service innovation originates and how it spreads, and therefore must receive careful consideration when theorizing about service innovation.

References

Abell, P., Felin, T., and Foss, N. (2008). Building micro-foundations for the routines, capabilities, and performance links. *Managerial and Decision Economics*, **29**, 489–502.

Agarwal, R. and Selen, W. (2009). Dynamic capability building in service value networks for achieving service innovation. *Decision Sciences*, **40**, 431–475.

Baer, M., Dirks, K. T., and Nickerson, J. A. (2013). Microfoundations of strategic problem formulation. *Strategic Management Journal*, **34**, 197–214.

Ballantyne, D., Frow, P., Varey, R. J., and Payne, A. (2011). Value propositions as communication practice: Taking a wider view. *Industrial Marketing Management*, **40**, 202–210.

Barney, J. and Felin, T. (2013). What are microfoundations? *The Academy of Management Perspectives*, **27**, 138–155.

Barrett, M., Davidson, E., Prabhu, J., and Vargo, S. L. (2015). Service innovation in the digital age: Key contributions and future directions. *MIS Quarterly*, **39**, 135–154.

Carlborg, P., Kindström, D., and Kowalkowski, C. (2014). The evolution of service innovation research: A critical review and synthesis. *The Service Industries Journal*, **34**, 373–398.

Chandler, J. D. and Lusch, R. F. (2015). Service systems: A broadened framework and research agenda on value propositions, engagement, and service experience. *Journal of Service Research*, **18**, 6–22.

Den Hertog, P., Van der AA, W., and De Jong, M. W. (2010). Capabilities for managing service innovation: Towards a conceptual framework. *Journal of Service Management*, **21**, 490–514.

Devinney, T. M. (2013). Is microfoundational thinking critical to management thought and practice? *The Academy of Management Perspectives*, **27**, 81–84.

Drejer, I. (2004). Identifying innovation in surveys of services: A Schumpeterian perspective. *Research Policy*, **33**, 551–562.

Echeverri, P. and Skålén, P. (2011). Co-creation and co-destruction: A practice-theory based study of interactive value formation. *Marketing Theory*, **11**, 351–373.

Edvardsson, B., Kleinaltenkamp, M., Tronvoll, B., Mchugh, P., and Windahl, C. (2014). Institutional logics matter when coordinating resource integration. *Marketing Theory*, **14**, 291–309.

Edvardsson, B., Skålén, P., and Tronvoll, B. (2012). Service systems as a foundation for resource integration and value co-creation. *Review of Marketing Research*, **9**, 79–126.

Edvardsson, B. and Tronvoll, B. (2013). A new conceptualization of service innovation grounded in SD logic and service systems. *International Journal of Quality and Service Sciences*, **5**, 19–31.

Edvardsson, B., Tronvoll, B., and Gruber, T. (2011). Expanding understanding of service exchange and value co-creation: a social construction approach. *Journal of the Academy of Marketing Science*, **39**, 327–339.

Felin, T. and Foss, N. J. (2005). *Strategic Organization: A Field in Search of Micro-foundations.* London, Thousand Oaks, CA, and New Delhi: SAGE Publications.

Felin, T., Foss, N. J., and Ployhart, R. E. (2015). The microfoundations movement in strategy and organization theory. *The Academy of Management Annals*, **9**, 575–632.

Findsrud, R., Tronvoll, B., and Edvardsson, B. (2018). Motivation: The missing driver for theorizing about resource integration. *Marketing Theory*, https://doi.org/10.1177/1470593118764590.

Foss, N. J. (2011). Invited editorial: Why micro-foundations for resource-based theory are needed and what they may look like. *Journal of Management*, **37**, 1413–1428.

Foss, N. J. and Pedersen, T. (2016). Microfoundations in strategy research. *Strategic Management Journal*, **37**, E22–E24.

Gallouj, F. and Savona, M. (2009). Innovation in services: A review of the debate and a research agenda. *Journal of Evolutionary Economics*, **19**, 149.

Grigoriou, K. and Rothaermel, F. T. (2014). Structural microfoundations of innovation: The role of relational stars. *Journal of Management*, **40**, 586–615.

Gustafsson, A., Kristensson, P., and Witell, L. (2012). Customer co-creation in service innovation: A matter of communication? *Journal of Service Management*, **23**, 311–327.

Helkkula, A., Kowalkowski, C., and Tronvoll, B. (2018). Archetypes of service innovation: Implications for value cocreation. *Journal of Service Research*, **21**(3), 284–301. https://doi.org/10.1177/1094670517746776.

Hibbert, S., Winklhofer, H., and Temerak, M. S. (2012). Customers as resource integrators: Toward a model of customer learning. *Journal of Service Research*, **15**, 247–261.

Hollebeek, L. D., Srivastava, R. K., and Chen, T. (2016). SD logic-informed customer engagement: Integrative framework, revised fundamental propositions, and application to CRM. *Journal of the Academy of Marketing Science*, 1–25. https://doi.org/10.1007/s11747-016-0494-5.

Kindström, D. and Kowalkowski, C. (2014). Service innovation in product-centric firms: A multidimensional business model perspective. *Journal of Business & Industrial Marketing*, **29**, 96–111.

Kindström, D., Kowalkowski, C., and Sandberg, E. (2013). Enabling service innovation: A dynamic capabilities approach. *Journal of Business Research*, **66**, 1063–1073.

Kleinaltenkamp, M., Brodie, R. J., Frow, P., Hughes, T., Peters, L. D., and Woratschek, H. (2012). Resource integration. *Marketing Theory*, **12**, 201–205.

Koskela-Huotari, K., Edvardsson, B., Jonas, J. M., Sörhammar, D., and Witell, L. (2016). Innovation in service ecosystems — Breaking, making, and maintaining institutionalized rules of resource integration. *Journal of Business Research*, **69**, 2964–2971.

Koskela-Huotari, K. and Vargo, S. L. (2016). Institutions as resource context. *Journal of Service Theory and Practice*, **26**, 163–178.

Laud, G., Karpen, I. O., Mulye, R., and Rahman, K. (2015). The role of embeddedness for resource integration: Complementing SD logic research through a social capital perspective. *Marketing Theory*, **15**, 509–543.

Löbler, H. (2011). Position and potential of service-dominant logic — Evaluated in an 'ISM' frame for further development. *Marketing Theory*, **11**, 51–73.

Löbler, H. (2013). Service-dominant networks: An evolution from the service-dominant logic perspective. *Journal of Service Management*, **24**, 420–434.

Lusch, R. F. and Nambisan, S. (2015). Service innovation: A service-dominant logic perspective. *MIS Quarterly*, **39**, 155–175.

Lusch, R. F. and Vargo, S. L. (2014). *Service-Dominant Logic: Premises, Perspectives, Possibilities*. Cambridge, UK: Cambridge University Press.

Macinnis, D. J. (2011). A framework for conceptual contributions in marketing. *Journal of Marketing*, **75**, 136–154.

Mccoll-Kennedy, J. R., Vargo, S. L., Dagger, T. S., Sweeney, J. C., and Van Kasteren, Y. (2012). Health care customer value co-creation practice styles. *Journal of Service Research*, **15**, 370–389.

Nonaka, I. (1994). A dynamic theory of organizational knowledge creation. *Organization Science*, **5**, 14–37.

North, D. C. (1990). *Institutions, Institutional Change and Economic Performance*. Cambridge, UK: Cambridge University Press.

Ordanini, A. and Parasuraman, A. (2011). Service innovation viewed through a service-dominant logic lens: A conceptual framework and empirical analysis. *Journal of Service Research*, **14**, 3–23.

Ostrom, A. L., Bitner, M. J., Brown, S. W., Burkhard, K. A., Goul, M., Smith-Daniels, V., Demirkan, H., and Rabinovich, E. (2010). Moving forward and making a difference: Research priorities for the science of service. *Journal of Service Research*, **13**, 4–36.

Ostrom, A. L., Parasuraman, A., Bowen, D. E., Patricio, L., and Voss, C. A. (2015). Service research priorities in a rapidly changing context. *Journal of Service Research*, **18**, 127–159.

Paswan, A., D'Souza, D., and Zolfagharian, M. A. (2009). Toward a contextually anchored service innovation typology. *Decision Sciences*, **40**, 513–540.

Payne, A., Storbacka, K., and Frow, P. (2008). Managing the co-creation of value. *Journal of the Academy of Marketing Sciences*, **36**, 83–96.

Perks, H., Gruber, T., and Edvardsson, B. (2012). Co-creation in radical service innovation: A systematic analysis of microlevel processes. *Journal of Product Innovation Management*, **29**, 935–951.

Peters, L. D. (2016). Heteropathic versus homopathic resource integration and value co-creation in service ecosystems. *Journal of Business Research*, **69**, 2999–3007.

Peters, L. D., Löbler, H., Brodie, R. J., Breidbach, C. F., Hollebeek, L. D., Smith, S. D., Sörhammar, D., and Varey, R. J. (2014). Theorizing about resource integration through service-dominant logic. *Marketing Theory*, **14**, 249–268.

Plé, L. (2016). Studying customers' resource integration by service employees in interactional value co-creation. *Journal of Services Marketing*, **30**, 152–164.

Randhawa, K. and Scerri, M. (2015). Service innovation: A review of the literature. *The Handbook of Service Innovation*. Berlin: Springer, Chapter 2, pp. 27–51.

Ratny, S., Arshad, A. M., and Gaoliang, T. (2017). The effect of service-driven market orientation on service innovation: Literature review and new research framework. *Journal of Applied Business Research*, **33**, 999–1012.

Rubalcaba, L., Michel, S., Sundbo, J., Brown, S. W., and Reynoso, J. (2012). Shaping, organizing, and rethinking service innovation: A multidimensional framework. *Journal of Service Management*, **23**, 696–715.

Schumpeter, J. A. (1934). *The Theory of Economic Development: An Inquiry into Profits, Capital, Credit, Interest, and the Business Cycle*. Cambridge, MA: Harvard University Press.

Skålén, P., Gummerus, J., Koskull, C., and Magnusson, P. (2015a). Exploring value propositions and service innovation: A service-dominant logic study. *Journal of the Academy of Marketing Science*, **43**, 137–158.

Skålén, P., Aal, K. A., and Edvardsson, B. (2015b). Co-creating the Arab Spring: Understanding transformation of service systems in contention. *Journal of Service Research*, **18**, 250–264.

Snyder, H., Witell, L., Gustafsson, A., Fombelle, P., and Kristensson, P. (2016). Identifying categories of service innovation: A review and synthesis of the literature. *Journal of Business Research*, **69**, 2401–2408.

Storbacka, K., Brodie, R. J., Böhmann, T., Maglio, P. P., and Nenonen, S. (2016). Actor engagement as a microfoundation for value co-creation. *Journal of Business Research*, **69**, 3008–3017.

Storey, C., Cankurtaran, P., Papastathopoulou, P., and Hultink, E. J. (2016). Success factors for service innovation: A meta-analysis. *Journal of Product Innovation Management*, **33**, 527–548.

Teece, D. J., Pisano, G., and Shuen, A. (1997). Dynamic capabilities and strategic management. *Strategic Management Journal*, **18**(7), 509–533.

Thornton, P. H., Ocasio, W., and Lounsbury, M. (2012). *The Institutional Logics Perspective: A New Approach to Culture, Structure, and Process.* Oxford: Oxford University Press.

Toivonen, M. and Tuominen, T. (2009). Emergence of innovations in services. *The Service Industries Journal*, **29**, 887–902.

Vargo, S. L. and Akaka, M. A. (2012). Value cocreation and service systems (re) formation: A service ecosystems view. *Service Science*, **4**, 207–217.

Vargo, S. L. and Lusch, R. F. (2011). It's all B2B... and beyond: Toward a systems perspective of the market. *Industrial Marketing Management*, **40**, 181–187.

Vargo, S. L. and Lusch, R. F. (2016). Institutions and axioms: An extension and update of service-dominant logic. *Journal of the Academy of Marketing Science*, **44**, 5–23.

Vargo, S. L., Wieland, H., and Akaka, M. A. (2015). Innovation through institutionalization: A service ecosystems perspective. *Industrial Marketing Management*, **44**, 63–72.

Von Koskull, C. and Strandvik, T. (2014). Discovering the unfolding of service innovations. *Journal of Business & Industrial Marketing*, **29**, 143–150.

Witell, L., Snyder, H., Gustafsson, A., Fombelle, P., and Kristensson, P. (2016). Defining service innovation: A review and synthesis. *Journal of Business Research*, **69**, 2863–2872.

Zimmermann, E. W. (1951). *World Resources and Industries: A Functional Appraisal of the Availability of Agricultural and Industrial Materials.* Dordrecht, Netherlands: Harper & Brothers.

Chapter 7

Service Teams and Understanding of Customer Value Creation

Besma Glaa[*,†], **Per Kristensson**[*] **and Lars Witell**[*,†]

*Karlstad University, Sweden
†Linköping University, Sweden*

Key takeaways

1. The research concerns what type of teams exist in service firms and what the literature has identified as their key characteristics.
2. This chapter reports on how the configuration of teams used for new service development (in this chapter referred to as "service teams") affects the understanding of the customer value creation process.
3. The shift from products to services can be described as a change from value creation through the product's efficiency alone to value co-creation through the product's efficiency and effectiveness within the customer's production process. A value driver that has a certain effect will over time lose this effect; to continue to co-create value, resources have to be committed to activate new value drivers in the business relationship.
4. The chapter concerns service teams and is relevant for most types of firms.
5. Those interested in this chapter may also find Chapters 8 and 12 interesting.

Introduction

Technological advancement and changing markets make service businesses work in highly competitive environments. Moreover, the development and launch of new services is becoming more important to sustain the competitiveness and growth of the service business (Froehle *et al.*, 2000). In this context, new service development (NSD) strives to add value for customers and respond to customers' needs (Alam, 2006). These goals influence customer loyalty and create an urgent need for service firms to understand customer value creation (Gebauer *et al.*, 2011). However, the service research has shown that organizing NSD is complex and given it little consideration (Jaakkola and Hallin, 2017). Recent research specifies that to improve firm performance, firms need to consider several NSD structures in parallel (Blindenbach-Driessen and Ende, 2014). Research and business practice have shown the increasing popularity of the team-based organizational structure, which "reflects the widely shared belief that teamwork offers the potential to achieve outcomes that could not be achieved by individuals working in isolation" (West, 1996, p. 53). Thus, an understanding of the diversity and the characteristics of service teams (that is, teams used for NSD) is needed.

Previous research has mostly focused on different types of service teams, such as project teams (for example, Alvesson, 1995; Leiponen, 2006; Lievens and Moenaert, 2000a; de Brentani, 2001; Jaakkola and Hallin, 2017), multidisciplinary teams (West, 1996; Meyer and DeTore, 1999), cross-functional teams (Davenport, 1993; Froehle *et al.*, 2000; de Brentani, 1991; Zomerdijk and Voss, 2011; Gallouj and Weinstein, 1997), integrated development teams (Edvardsson *et al.*, 2013; Hull and Tidd, 2002), or co-design teams (Trischler *et al.*, 2018). In most of these studies, the main focus was not the service teams themselves but rather NSD. Moreover, these studies have provided increasing evidence that team-based organizational structures are needed to develop innovative services and respond to customers' needs (West, 1996). Few prior studies have clearly focused on exploring the variety and characteristics of service teams in the context of NSD, and far less attention has been given to how the different configurations of service teams affect the understanding of the customer value creation process.

To address this lack of comprehensive understanding of existing service teams' configurations in the context of NSD and how these configurations affect the customer value creation process, we explore this subject with an extensive literature review. This chapter identifies similarities and differences between the different team configurations and provides guidance for researchers and managers interested in understanding service teams and their role in service firms.

Service Innovation as a Change in the Customer Value Creation Process

Service innovation can be viewed as a change in the value creation process for customers (Witell *et al.*, 2016). In this view, a service provides the prerequisites for value creation in use. The customer contributes the knowledge, skills, and activities that facilitate the realization of value using the prerequisites provided through the service. The notion that value arises in use requires firms to adjust their way of thinking and their actions to create business models that facilitate value creation. Witell *et al.* (2016) use the example of ice cream: "The value of ice cream is not realized until it is eaten. Resources required for value creation are, aside from the ice cream itself, a wafer and perhaps a park bench to sit on and a newspaper to read … If it starts to rain while sitting on the park bench, the experienced value of the ice cream will be affected." This means that the provider of ice cream can only influence parts of the customer experience; if the park bench is occupied, if it is raining, or if the newspaper is boring has a huge influence on the customer experience, but these factors are outside the control of the service provider.

What is a Service Team?

The production and delivery of the service doesn't happen without customer involvement. Due to the presence of the customer as part of the process, service organization cannot separate production and marketing activities. Therefore, the operations function producing the service and the marketing function dealing with the customer should be interdependent

(Lievens and Moenaert, 2000a). There is increasing evidence that the interaction between these functions is crucial for the success of the service offering (Lovelock *et al.*, 1988; Chase, 1981; Chase and Tansik, 1983; Mahajan *et al.*, 1994). In this context, service teams are defined according to Langeard *et al.* (1981) "as a task force that offers a way to integrate functional viewpoints during new service development" (as cited in Lievens and Moenaert, 2000a, p. 47). Such a team is characterized by team members with a range of specialization areas and with a variety of experiences and expertise who collaborate to complete NSD projects. To do so, service teams should communicate internally (within the team) and externally with customers or suppliers (Lievens and Moenaert, 2000a).

In an empirical investigation of about 500 firms working with NSD, Edvardsson *et al.* (2013) conclude that about 65% of firms use service teams to develop new services. In a follow-up study in 2017 covering several countries such as Sweden, Finland, Italy, Austria, Germany, Switzerland, and Mexico and including about 1000 NSD projects, the average NSD project took about 7 months and was performed by a service team consisting of six employees with different competences and cooperating with external partners, either suppliers or customers.

Different Configurations of Service Teams

Many scholars have investigated the role of teams and their importance for NSD (Meyer and DeTore, 1999; Sundbo, 1998; Froehle *et al.*, 2000; Edvardsson *et al.*, 2013; Hull and Tidd, 2002). Different types of teams have been identified in previous research, such as cross-functional teams, multidisciplinary teams, integrated development teams, project teams, agile teams, and co-design teams. For instance, Davenport (1993) and Terrill (1992) highlighted the relevance of teamwork and integration for process innovation. In particular, the authors argued that effective process innovation teams have special knowledge and capabilities and can overcome traditional organizational boundaries. Likewise, Pisano (1997) emphasized the importance of integration and cross-functional work. In his paper, he argued that the speed of completion of development projects is higher when the organization is integrated and cross-functional compared to when the organization is separated functionally. The author also suggested that integrated and cross-functional firms accomplish development projects with less effort. Moreover, Froehle *et al.* (2000) showed that although cross-functional teams normally do not accelerate a NSD process, they have a strategic effect on increasing the effectiveness of the development process. Their empirical study of 175 US service firms revealed that the use of diverse and cross-functional team structures can directly influence the overall success of NSD and the effectiveness of the NSD process. The authors explain that the diversity and the fruitfulness of ideas created by the cross-functional teams benefit the NSD process. In a similar manner, Gallouj and Weinstein (1997) underlined the importance of flexible cross-functional teams for the success of development work. The authors attributed this success to the novelty in knowledge and skills that characterize cross-functional teams. Other scholars have also stressed the importance of cross-functional NSD teams with a range of multiple specialization areas in the NSD process (de Brentani, 1991; Froehle *et al.*, 2000). These teams can increase the availability of various information and expertise in the NSD process (Zomerdijk and Voss, 2011). Edvardsson *et al.* (2013) also showed the relevance of an assortment of knowledge and competencies in integrated development teams in NSD. In their study, cross-functional teams are created using functional areas that are considered as resource pools. The authors argue that improved communication and dual perspectives can strongly affect the success of NSD and performance development (Hull and Tidd, 2002).

In the same way, communication by project team members within financial service organizations has been considered vital because it helps to have market information about customers and competitors (Lievens and Moenaert, 2000a). Lievens and Moenaert named project teams "new service teams" and considered them "information processing systems" (p. 46). In addition, Lievens and Moenaert distinguished between intra-project and extra-project communication. Intra-project communication is communication among the members of a project team, whereas extra-project communication is the communication of project team members with external factors such as customers. Project teams are able to deal with the uncertainty caused by the specific services' characteristics and the nature of financial service innovation

(Lievens *et al.*, 1999). Extra-project communication is similar to the concept of "team boundary spanning" that is defined as teams' efforts to create and manage external relationships both within the organization or across organizational boundaries (Marrone, 2010; Marrone *et al.*, 2007).

Galbraith (1973) defined project teams as "a form of horizontal contact which is designed for problems of multiple departments" (p. 319). These teams can integrate different functional perspectives during NSD (Langeard *et al.*, 1981) and are able to decrease innovative uncertainty (that is, customer, resource, and technological uncertainty) during NSD by acting as "information processing organisms operating in a complex and dynamic environment" (Lievens and Moenaert, 2000a, p. 47). Lievens and Moenaert (2000a) showed the relevance of cross-functional cooperation for ensuring effective communication and subsequently a reduction in innovative uncertainty. For instance, the reduction of customer and resource uncertainty has an important effect on both financial and technological success (Lievens and Moenaert, 2000a). Similarly, a recent study by Jaakkola and Hallin (2017) discussed diverse NSD structures. One of these structures was NSD in temporary project teams. The composition of these teams was variable according to the task they were supposed to execute. The studied teams were characterized by a flexible mix of professionals that included a wide variety of specialization areas in terms of professional fields and expertise in NSD.

In the same context, Meyer and DeTore (1999) emphasized the relevance of multidisciplinary teams for NSD. This type of team, according to West (1996), brings together experts that have diverse knowledge backgrounds and has the potential to create innovative ideas for new services. Similarly, Mintzberg (1979) defined multidisciplinary teams as a group of specialists deployed in "small market-based project teams" (p. 433). Zomerdijk and Voss (2011) considered multidisciplinary teams particularly relevant for experiential services due to the diversity of functions that collaborate to deliver a good customer experience. The main strength of these teams is the availability of a quantity and diversity of information in the NSD project (Zomerdijk and Voss, 2011). However, it is time consuming to create multidisciplinary teams due to the time needed for the team to start working in a group and creating a shared vision for the new service requirements (Froehle *et al.*, 2000).

Another configuration of teams that has been adopted by an increasing number of organizations is agile teams. With agile teams, the development work is done in teams with fixed membership. These teams are small, cross-functional, self-organized, and able to contribute both to efficiency and to small-scale innovation (Lindkvist *et al.*, 2017). According to Lankhorst *et al.* (2012, p. 13), "the iterative character of agile processes, with a focus on people and interactions, close contact with customers, and cross-functional teams that tackle different aspects of development at the same time, is a much better fit with the complex and multidimensional nature of service development." Each iteration is a closed loop with an adaptive character that helps to evaluate and adapt the work of the agile team. These closed loops and the adaptive character are the most relevant success factors of agile processes compared to the traditional open-loop processes used in development work (Lankhorst *et al.*, 2012).

Service Teams and Their Understanding of Customer Value Creation

"Customers are fundamentally changing the dynamics of the market-place. The market has become a forum in which consumers play an active role in creating and competing for value" (Prahalad and Ramaswamy, 2000, p. 80). Consequently, customers are increasingly considered critical for NSD and an indispensable element in service design. Chan *et al.* (2010) highlighted customer participation in service design as contributing both to improving the economic value to the customer and to reinforcing the relationship between customers and services employees. Customer engagement during a service development project via an active dialogue enables a firm to understand customer needs (Prahalad and Ramaswamy, 2000; Kristensson *et al.*, 2004; Matthing *et al.*, 2004). Moreover, the involvement of multiple functions simultaneously during the early stages of the development process can strongly affect the NSD performance (Hull and Tidd, 2002).

In particular, previous research has investigated the role of the customer and his participation with service teams. For instance, the use of multidisciplinary teams can improve consumer satisfaction with a new service more than the use of a single function can (Froehle *et al.*, 2000). Moreover, research has shown that a positive relationship exists between the quality of project communication within the innovation project teams and the decrease of customer uncertainty (Lievens and Moenaert, 2000a, 2000b; Lievens *et al.*, 1999). Zomerdijk and Voss (2011) underlined the importance of collaboration within multidisciplinary teams in order to deliver a good customer experience. The concept of customer experience is considered by service designers ever more important and essential to any service design project (Teixeira *et al.*, 2012). However, the intangible nature of services stresses the need to create tangible evidence in order to simplify the communication between the development team and the customers (for example, de Brentani, 1991; Zomerdijk and Voss, 2011).

Similarly, Edvardsson *et al.* (2013) underlined the relationship between service teams and the customer. The authors argue that the diversity of knowledge and resources that characterize an integrated development team offers a different understanding of customer information. The research further identified an interaction effect between the use of integrated development teams and customer co-creation such that "the greater the use of integrated development teams, the stronger the positive effect of customer co-creation on NSD performance" (p. 19). Lee and Chen (2009) suggest a positive correlation between project performance and integrated development teams. Furthermore, Jaakkola and Hallin (2017) have shown that temporary project teams in NSD offer a flexible service development that uses the best possible combination of resources, and that these teams are considered a crucial factor in finding the solution to the customer's problem.

In particular, learning from and with customers has been shown relevant to NSD. This learning can be achieved through intensive and early customer involvement in NSD and the use of cross-functional teams that are able to respond to customers' needs (Matthing *et al.*, 2004). In order to explore customer involvement, Matthing's research highlights the use of several sources of knowledge and skills (Mendes *et al.*, 2017). Kristensson *et al.* (2004) emphasized the ability of ordinary customers to create innovative and valuable ideas and to be engaged in the innovation process. Previous research recognized these customers as a critical external source of knowledge (for example, Edvardsson *et al.*, 2013). Thereby, the incorporation of service users together with in-house professionals into a co-design team can contribute to understanding customers' needs. These insights about the customers are needed for service teams to convert pertinent knowledge into original outcomes (Trischler *et al.*, 2018).

Meyer and DeTore (1999, p. 70) suggested that "understanding the knowledge and/or convenience drivers among customers will prove to be one of the more powerful techniques for focusing service development and marketing." Accordingly, the integration of representatives of the end-users into service teams can increase customer satisfaction with new services. The design of multidisciplinary teams should ensure that the potential needs of all customers can be satisfied by a single team. In this way, the interface between the customer and the organization is simplified by the service teams, and the quality of the service received can be improved (West, 1996). Moreover, from this interface originates vital information that is needed to reduce the uncertainty generated by the innovation project (Lievens and Moenaert, 2000b).

Davenport (1993) has even proposed considering the customer's perspective not only in the final process design but also in the early stages and post-implementation activities. Davenport suggests including customers on the process design teams and allowing them to participate in prototyping and refining the design. This is similar to the concept of agile teams presented by Lindkvist *et al.* (2017). Agile teams are in close contact with the customers and are assigned short tasks of 2–4 weeks in order to guarantee flexibility and that new customer needs are frequently added. "A team should plan for regular contacts with (internal or external) customers, e.g., in connection with the presentation of a demo, to check whether requirements have been interpreted correctly, if something is missing, etc." (Lindkvist *et al.*, 2017, p. 580). This close relation with the customer has been also highlighted by Lankhorst *et al.* (2012) as a necessary element in agile team work.

The following table (Table 1) summarizes the four main team configurations investigated in the literature.

Table 1. Configurations of service teams in relation to customer value creation.

Team	Characteristics of the service team	Sources
Multidisciplinary teams	— Are diverse — Foster the collaboration of diverse functions — Deliver a good customer experience — Bring together experts with different backgrounds — Generate innovative ideas for new services — May include representatives from marketing or end users — Are designed to ensure that all of a customer's potential needs can be met — Simplify the customer-organization interface and may improve the service received	Meyer and DeTore (1999); West (1996); Teixeira *et al.* (2012); Mintzberg (1979)
Cross-functional teams	— Contain a diversity of experience, expertise, and knowledge — Are able to innovate processes that traverse organizational boundaries and areas of management responsibilities — Contain a broad perspective — Foster synergy based on team interaction — Improve creativity — Improve problem solving — Span traditional organizational boundaries — Have members with unique abilities and knowledge	de Brentani (1991); Froehle *et al.* (2000); Gallouj and Weinstein (1997); Zomerdijk and Voss (2011); Terrill (1992)

Project teams	— Are diverse	Alvesson (1995); Leiponen (2006); Lievens *et al.* (1999); Jaakkola and Hallin (2017)
	— Are seen primarily as information processing systems	
	— Have specific communication patterns	
	— Have communication flows among team members	
	— Must be able to deal with work-related uncertainty introduced by the specific service characteristics (intangibility, simultaneity of production and consumption, heterogeneity, and perishability)	
Agile teams	— Are diverse	Silva da Silva *et al.* (2011); Lindkvist *et al.* (2017)
	— Are small teams where everybody is visible	
	— Focus on efficiency improvements	
	— Have a stable team principle, "locked-in" into a team	
	— Involve a local representative of the client	
	— Have a short feedback loop between the team and the customer	

The literature review shows that all service teams' concepts or configurations are highly linked to customer value creation. Consequently, all the service teams' configurations reviewed have an impact on the success of NSD when the customer is integrated in the NSD process. In addition, the literature review provides evidence that all service teams' configurations are characterized by diversity. This criterion has been expressed differently by many scholars. For instance, scholars have used a variety of knowledge backgrounds; diversity of experience, expertise, and knowledge; fruitfulness of ideas; and a broad perspective to express the diversity of service teams. Diversity is needed when designing the service team to ensure that the team has all the skills and knowledge required to respond to all customers' potential needs.

Furthermore, the concept of the integration of the customer in the service design process is also relevant for NSD. The integration of customer knowledge with the different skills of service teams' members has been highlighted as a key factor in the NSD process (Edvardsson *et al.*, 2013). The success of NSD has been associated with the presence of both employees and customers in development projects (Melton and Hartline, 2010). Many researchers have emphasized communication with the customer to achieve this integration. For instance, learning from and with customers has been shown relevant to NSD (Matthing *et al.*, 2004). However, securing and enabling external and internal learning should be accomplished in the right stage of the NSD process. Facilitating knowledge sharing and transfer between service teams' members and customers has the potential to improve NSD performance (Edvardsson *et al.*, 2013). Many scholars have suggested interaction between the service team and the customers. This interaction has the potential to improve the effect of customer co-creation on NSD (Matthing *et al.*, 2004).

The literature review also showed that NSD researchers tend to use the different designations of service teams interchangeably. For instance, Edvardsson *et al.* (2013) use the designations integrated development teams, cross-functional teams, and project teams to describe teams that are used for NSD. Edvardsson *et al.* (2012) use terms such as development teams, service development teams, and design teams. The terms project teams, new service teams, and cross-functional teams have been used by Lievens and Moenaert (2000a). The lack of a common understanding of what should constitute a service team might explain this use of multiple terms.

Conclusion

In this chapter, we presented a literature review of the different configurations of service teams used for NSD and particularly how these configurations affect customer value creation. We identified diversity as a common characteristic of all service teams' configurations; this diversity is needed to make sure that customers' needs are met. We explored the interaction between service teams' members and the customer, and the necessity of the integration of customer knowledge with the different skills of service teams' members. That service teams in many ways represent the integration of customer knowledge into organizations is becoming more and more evident. Recently, new concepts, such as DevOp-teams (Brunnert *et al.*, 2015), have been introduced that represent a type of service team where operational knowledge regarding customer value creation is coupled with technological knowledge of the offering from the organization. All these elements have been shown to be key factors to the success of NSD.

Additionally, in this chapter we shed light on the lack of a common understanding of what constitutes a unique service team. The interchangeable use of many designations of service teams indicates this lack of common understanding, as does the blurred and inexistent common definition of a service team in the context of NSD.

For managers, this chapter shows that much of the existing research on service teams provides guidance on team work in general, but less guidance on the specifics of different types of service teams. In general, the research suggests that managers should support diversity in service teams and enable and support interactions between team members. Since most service firms use service teams in different forms (development teams, project teams, quality improvement teams), understanding how to get the most out of these teams is important. Much of the research on the efficiency and effectiveness of teams is in management research, but less is in service research.

References

Alam, I. (2006). Removing the fuzziness from the fuzzy front-end of service innovation through customer interactions. *Industrial Marketing Management*, **35**(4), 468–480.

Alvesson, M. (1995). *Management of Knowledge-Intensive Companies*. Berlin: Walter de Gruyter.

Blindenbach-Driessen, F. and Ende, J. (2014). The locus of innovation: The effect of a separate innovation unit on exploration, exploitation, and ambidexterity in manufacturing and service firms. *Journal of Product Innovation Management*, **31**(5), 1089–1105.

Brunnert, A., van Hoorn, A., Willnecker, F., Danciu, A., Hasselbring, W., Heger, C., and Koziolek, A. (2015). Performance-oriented DevOps: A research agenda. arXiv preprint arXiv:1508.04752.

Chan, K. W., Yim, C. K. B., and Lam, S. S. K. (2010). Is customer participation in value creation a double-edged sword? Evidence from professional financial services across cultures. *Journal of Marketing*, **74**(3), 48–64.

Chase, R. B. (1981). The customer contact approach to services: Theoretical bases and practical extensions. *Operations Research*, **29**, 698–706.

Chase, R. B. and Tansik, D. A. (1983). The customer contact model for organization design. *Management Science*, **29**(9), 1037–1050.

Davenport, T. H. (1993). *Process Innovation: Reengineering Work through Information Technology*. Boston: Harvard Business School Press.

De Brentani, U. (1991). Success factors in developing new business services. *European Journal of Marketing*, **25**(2), 33–59.

De Brentani, U. (2001). Innovative versus incremental new business services: Different keys for achieving success. *Journal of Product Innovation Management*, **18**(3), 169–187.

Edvardsson, B., Kristensson, K., Magnusson, P., and Sundstrom, E. (2012). Customer integration in service development and innovation — methods and a new framework. *Technovation*, **32**(7/8), 419–429.

Edvardsson, B., Meiren, T., Schäfer, A., and Witell, L. (2013). Having a strategy for new service development: Does it really matter? *Journal of Service Management*, **24**(1), 25–44.

Froehle, C. M., Roth, A. V., Chase, R. B., and Voss, C. A. (2000). Antecedents of new service development effectiveness: An exploratory examination of strategic operations choices. *Journal of Service Research*, **3**(1), 3–17.

Galbraith, J. R. (1973). *Designing Complex Organizations*. Reading, MA: Addison-Wesley.

Gallouj, F. and Weinstein, O. (1997). Innovation in services. *Research Policy*, **26**, 537–556.

Gebauer, H. Gustafsson, A. and Witell, L. (2011). Competitive advantage through service differentiation by manufacturing companies. *Journal of Business Research*, **64**(12), 1270–1280.

Hull, F. and Tidd, J. (2002). *Service Innovation: Organizational Responses to Technological Opportunities and Market Imperatives.* London: Imperial College Press.

Jaakkola, E. and Hallin, A. (2018). Organizational structures for new service development. *Journal of Product Innovation Management*, **35**(2), 280–297.

Kristensson, P., Gustafsson, A., and Archer, T. (2004). Harnessing the creative potential among users. *Journal of Product Innovation Management*, **21**(1), 4–14.

Langeard, E., Bateson, J. E. G., Lovelock, C. H., and Eiglier, P. (1981). Integrating different functional perspectives in service businesses. In Langeard, E., Bateson, J. E. G., Lovelock, C. H., and Eiglier, P. (eds.), *Services Marketing: New Insights from Consumers and Managers*, Cambridge, MA: Marketing Science Institute, pp. 81–95.

Lankhorst, M. M., Janssen, W. P. M., Proper, H. A., and Steen, M. W. A. (2012). Introducing agile service development. In M. Lankhorst (Ed.), *Agile Service Development: Combining Adaptive methods and Flexible Solutions* (pp. 1–15). The Netherlands: Springer.

Lee, Y.-C. and Chen, J.-K. (2009). A new service development integrated model. *The Service Industries Journal*, **29**(12), 1669–1686.

Leiponen, A. (2006). Managing knowledge for innovation: The case of business-to-business services. *Journal of Product Innovation Management*, **23**(3), 238–258.

Lievens, A., Moenaert, R. K., and S'Jegers, R. (1999). Linking communication to innovation success in the financial services industry: A case study analysis. *International Journal of Service Industry Management*, **10**(1), 23–47.

Lievens, A. and Moenaert, R. K. (2000a). New service teams as information-processing systems reducing innovative uncertainty. *Journal of Service Research*, **3**(1), 46–65.

Lievens, A. and Moenaert, R. K. (2000b). Project team communication in financial service innovation. *Journal of Management Studies*, **37**(5), 732–766.

Lindkvist, L., Bengtsson, M., Svensson, D. M., and Wahlstedt, L. (2017). Replacing old routines: How Ericsson software developers and managers learned to become agile. *Industrial and Corporate Change*, **26**(4), 571–591.

Lovelock, C. H., Langeard, E., Bateson, J. E. G., and Eiglier, P. (1988). Some organizational problems facing marketing in the service sector. In Lovelock, C. H. (ed.), *Managing Services: Marketing, Operations and Human Resources*, London: Prentice-Hall, pp. 359–366.

Mahajan, J., Vakharia, A. J., Paul, P., and Chase, R. B. (1994), An exploratory investigation of the interdependence between marketing and operations functions in service firms. *International Journal of Research in Marketing*, **11**, 1–15.

Marrone, J. A. (2010). Team boundary spanning: A multilevel review of past research and proposals or the future. *Journal of Management*, **36**(4), 911–940.

Marrone, J. A., Tesluk, P. E., and Carson, J. B. (2007). A multi-level investigation of antecedents and consequences of team member boundary spanning behavior. *Academy of Management Journal*, **50**, 1423–1439.

Matthing, J., Sanden, B., and Edvardsson, B. (2004). New service development: Learning from and with customers. *International Journal of Service Industry Management*, **15**(5), 479–498.

Melton, H. L. and Hartline, M. D. (2010). Customer and frontline employee influence on new NSD performance. *Journal of Service Research*, **13**(4), 411–425.

Mendes, G. H. S., Oliveira, M. G., Gomide, E. H., and Nantes, J. F. D. (2017). Uncovering the structures and maturity of the new service development research field through a bibliometric study (1984–2014). *Journal of Service Management*, **28**(1), 182–223.

Meyer, M. H. and DeTore, A. (1999). Product development for services. *Academy of Management Executive*, **13**(3), 64–76.

Mintzberg, H. (1979). *The Structuring of Organizations*. Englewood Cliffs, NJ: Prentice Hall.

Pisano, G. P. (1997). *The Development Factory*. Boston: Harvard Business School Press.

Prahalad, C. K. and Ramaswamy, V. (2000). Co-opting customer competence. *Harvard Business Review*, **78** (January–February), 79–87.

Silva da Silva, T., Martin, A., Maurer, F., and Silveira, M. (2011). User-centered design and agile methods: A systematic review, Agile Conference, Agile 2011, 77–86.

Sundbo, J. (1998). *The Organization of Innovation in Services*. Frederiksberg, Denmark: Roskilde University Press.

Teixeira, J., Patrício, L., Nunes, N. J., Nóbrega, L., Fisk, R. P., and Constantine, L. (2012). Customer experience modeling: From customer experience to service design. *Journal of Service Management*, **23**(3), 362–376.

Terrill, C. A. (1992). The ten commandments of new service development. *Management Review*, **81**, 24–27.

Trischler, J., Kristensson, P., and Scott, D. (2018). Team diversity and its management in a codesign team. *Journal of Service Management*, **29**(1), 120–145.

West, M. (1996). The consequences of diversity in multidisciplinary work teams. In West, M. A. (ed.), *The Handbook of Work Group Psychology*, Chichester: John Wiley & Sons, Ltd., pp. 53–75.

Witell, L., Snyder, H., Gustafsson, A., Fombelle, P., and Kristensson, P. (2016). Defining service innovation: A review and synthesis. *Journal of Business Research*, **69**, 2863–2872.

Zomerdijk, L. G. and Voss, C. A. (2011). NSD processes and practices in experiential services. *Journal of Product Innovation Management*, **28**(1), 63–80.

Chapter 8

Creating the Perfect Match: Roles and Archetypes of Open Service Innovation

Per Myhrén*, Lars Witell[†,‡] and Maria Åkesson[†]

*Paper Province, Sweden
†Karlstad University, Sweden
‡Linköping University, Sweden

Key takeaways

1. Open service innovation has been suggested as a solution by which firms can become more innovative and better cooperate with other actors to develop and introduce new services on the market. However, there is scarce research on how open service innovation happens in practice and how it should be organized.
2. This chapter identifies the roles of actors in role constellations and illustrates how the roles influence knowledge provision in the innovation process, from idea generation to commercialization, in open service innovation.
3. We find that different role constellations are needed for different archetypes of open service innovation, and that a new role, the

Constitutional Monarch, is key to success in bringing new services to the market.

4. The chapter presents multiple case studies involving a B2B company organizing an innovation network with nine open service innovation groups in the pulp and paper industry.

5. Those interested in this chapter may also find Chapters 7, 13, 14, and 15 interesting.

Introduction

Many firms turn to open innovation, based on cooperation with customers, partners, and other actors, to improve their innovativeness and gain a competitive advantage (van de Vrande *et al.*, 2009; Syson and Perks, 2004; Möller and Svahn, 2003). Open innovation views the innovation process as an open system engaging multiple actors (West *et al.*, 2014), where the exchange of technologies, ideas, and information allows firms to improve efficiency and effectiveness and reduce uncertainty in the development of new products and services (Wallin and Von Krogh, 2010; Elmquist *et al.*, 2009). Previous research has failed to investigate open innovation grounded in constellations of different actors, often referred to as strategic alliances or innovation networks (Vanhaverbeke, 2006; Vanhaverbekke and Cloodt, 2014).

Collaboration with different business actors is beneficial for firms (Hsueh *et al.*, 2010; Faems *et al.*, 2005; Koschatzky, 1999; Freytag and Young, 2014). Membership in an innovation network entails shared research and development (R&D) risks (Pittaway *et al.*, 2004), costs, and access to specialized skills, complementary assets, and valuable competences, and creates competitive advantages that are difficult to imitate (Landsperger and Spieth, 2011; Rampersad *et al.*, 2010). Open service innovation networks consist of different actors, or more commonly constellations of actors, including individuals, organizations, firms, customers, consultants, and universities. These intentionally created constellations of actors deliberately work together to perform complex, customized work to develop businesses (Jones *et al.*, 1998). Myhren *et al.* (2018) identify three archetypes of open service innovation, suggesting that open service innovation needs to be organized in different ways depending on the aim of the open service innovation project.

The efficiency and innovativeness of an archetype of open service innovation depend on the actors taking on different roles and contributing with their creativity and knowledge (Schon, 1963; Allen, 1970; Nambisan and Sawhney, 2008). These roles include different intended contributions, tasks, and responsibilities. The assigned role does not necessarily result in a corresponding enacted role with the assumed agency, where agency refers to the capability to act purposefully (see e.g., Giddens, 1984). The assigned role might thus be far from the enacted role in practice, making the open service innovation network less efficient or not in line with the aim and strategy of the innovation. This possibility will influence the management of the constellations of actors (Heikkinen *et al.*, 2007).

The flow of knowledge and skills provided by the actors shapes the creation of new ideas or novel solutions to existing problems (Mu *et al.*, 2008). The innovativeness of the outcome depends on the design of the actor constellations (Vanhaverbekke and Cloodt, 2006) and on how well the different actor roles complement one another (Åkesson, 2011). Thus, competitive advantage no longer is determined by the performance of the actors within a firm, but by the cooperation of resourceful constellations of actors (Gomes-Casseres, 1996, 2003) often carried out in open service innovation groups.

This chapter builds on the case of an innovator firm and its network partners. It identifies the roles of actors in role constellations and illustrates how the roles influence knowledge provision in the innovation process, from idea generation to commercialization, in open service innovation. In particular, the chapter intends to (1) increase understanding of how to manage open service innovation groups; (2) highlight the conditions of long-lasting open service innovation groups; (3) explore the situation when the innovator firm works as a facilitator, coordinating activities; and (4) show how results from open service innovation groups are developed into solutions in an industrial B2B context.

Open Innovation, Service Innovation, and Networks

Innovation as a result of internal R&D activities has been challenged by the success of open innovation (Chesbrough, 2003). The increased importance of open innovation and the interest among both researchers and practitioners is explained by shorter innovation cycles, industrial R&D's escalating costs, and scarce resources (Gassmann and Enkel, 2004). Firms need to open up the innovation processes to exchanges of technologies, ideas, and knowledge in order to improve efficiency, effectiveness, and management of risk in innovation processes and to co-create value (Wallin and Von Krogh, 2010; Elmquist *et al.*, 2009). Internal R&D is no longer the strategic asset it once was, since organizations use new ways to come up with ideas and bring them to the market (Chesbrough, 2003). Chesbrough and Bogers (2014, p. 17) view open innovation as "a distributed innovation process based on purposively managed knowledge flows across organizational boundaries, using pecuniary and non-pecuniary mechanisms in line with the organization's business model." The inbound flows of externally created knowledge speed up development processes in a firm. The outbound flows of internally created knowledge concern technology spillovers not aligned with the firm's business model. The vast majority of research is on R&D projects and technology transfer, with less emphasis on market introduction and commercialization (Vanhaverbeke and Cloodt, 2006).

The service sector's importance for the growth of the global economy has increased and expanded service innovation as an emerging research field (Ostrom *et al.*, 2010). This field has grown from a narrow focus on the service sector (demarcation) to service innovation as a perspective on innovation in all sectors (synthesis; Coombs and Miles, 2000). This growth has changed the view of service innovation from being evaluated by characteristics such as offer and firm toward emphasizing characteristics such as product, process, exist, more, and value (Witell *et al.*, 2016). This suggests that the view of service innovation is developing and that the definitions are becoming more inclusive to cover new types of offerings. Innovations often result as new combinations of existing resources (Arthurs *et al.*, 2009), suggesting that partners can contribute with complementary resources. A traditional Schumpeterian view on innovation is that (a) it should be produced in practice, (b) be beneficial for the developing firm, and (c) be reproducible (Toivonen and Tuominen, 2009). To extend the Schumpeterian view of service innovation, it should be beneficial and create value for customers, employees, business owners, alliance partners, and communities (Ostrom *et al.*, 2010).

As previously discussed, service innovation as an outcome of firms' or organizations' development processes rarely results from strictly internal activities but rather from collaboration in constellations with different partners, in open service innovation networks. The reasons for firms to engage in such networks are access to complementary information, markets, and technologies (Corsaro *et al.*, 2012). Open service innovation networks consist of actors from independent organizations, rather loosely and informally composed and with different timeframes, who collaborate on one or more steps of the innovation process for the development of new products or services (DeBresson and Amesse, 1991; Landsperger and Spieth, 2011). Networks in general can be viewed as borderless self-organizing systems (Möller and Rajala, 2007), in the broadest sense not manageable for one single actor (Möller and Rajala, 2007; Heikkinen *et al.*, 2007). In contrast, intentional business networks have a deliberate structure with negotiated roles of actors and agreed upon goals, also called value nets or strategical nets (Möller and Rajala, 2007).

Three Archetypes for Open Service Innovation

To be effective, open service innovation networks thus require varied resources, actors with knowledge and skills that depend on the scope and objectives of the project. The ability to establish diverse relationships is crucial to using these resources and also to developing a firm's innovation capacity (Calia *et al.*, 2007). The innovation processes can be seen as the flows of ideas and activities directed by actors that combine and recombine these resources (Freytag and Young, 2014). The access to such knowledge and how it is used in the innovation process determines the output from open service innovation. Myhren *et al.* (2018) identified three archetypes on how to organize open service innovation, built on three different dimensions: competences of the participants, ties between the participants, and how the development work is performed.

The first archetype is called "Internal Group Development" and is primarily used to improve existing services; that is, incremental service innovation. It is designed for a situation in which the objective is narrow and has scarce human capital. A key ingredient is to gather senior participants within the area of interest, obtain agreement on how to perform the work, and run all development work within the group. The development work in this archetype is performed within the open service innovation group.

The second archetype, "Satellite Team Development," concerns incremental service innovation but involves larger development tasks. The development work follows a standardized method for improving services. The work starts with the open service innovation groups, which suggest an improvement, design a project, and form a development team. The actual development work is not performed within the open service innovation group, but by a development team that performs service improvements using recruited specialists; consequently, greater coordination between the open service innovation group and the development team is required. The development team presents the results for approval by the open service innovation group. Due to the need for more people to be involved and the larger number of tasks to undertake, this archetype involves less formal ties.

The third archetype, "Rocket Team Development," concerns radical service innovation projects involving participants with rather heterogeneous competences. A cross-functional team of senior participants with different competences and perspectives is selected to initiate a new development project. The results of such initiation projects determine whether to start a full-scale development project or not. This type of open service innovation group should have informal and wide ties among the participants. The development work can then take place within the group or it can be outsourced to a development team of specialists. This decision is based on the complexity of the task and the competences of the participants in the open service innovation group.

These archetypes of open service innovation are role constellations with a set of actors who perform roles and provide complementing knowledge. Gomes-Casseres (2003) argues that competitive advantages no longer are determined at the firm level but at a constellation level dependent on the actors involved, the size of the constellation, its technological capabilities, the market reach, a unifying vision, leadership, and no internal competition among the participants. In accordance with Ford *et al.*

(2003), we agree on the complexity of management on open service innovation networks but would rather focus on a level suitable for managers. The point of departure for this chapter is therefore an innovator firm that is responsible for an open service innovation network involving nine open service innovation groups.

Role Constellations in Open Service Innovation

Each archetype is designed to include a constellation of actors with various assigned roles. These can be seen as role constellations enabling knowledge flows and directing innovation. A role constellation is a relatively stable combination of different roles that emerges as an effect of mutual adaptability (Åkesson, 2011). This means that through the interaction within the open service innovation group, the actors adapt to the needs, strengths, weaknesses, etc. of each other. Thus, a role constellation concerns the adaptable tasks and knowledge and skills that bring actors together in relationships, as well as the social constraints and opportunities associated within these. When roles adapt to each other, the actors' roles should ideally complement each other in a specific situation, due to complementing knowledge, skills, and motivation as well as complementing expectations of each other's roles.

Actor roles — the role concept

A role guides and directs an actor in a given setting (Solomon *et al.*, 1985). The understanding of different roles can be used to explain how actors perform tasks, interact, collaborate, and work together to acquire and exchange knowledge (Herrmann *et al.*, 2004). The research on roles in the social sciences has a long tradition, among the first being Mead's (1934) work. Mead was a devotee of the notion of symbolic interactions that assumes that society is composed of interactions and these interactions develop a role structure (Herrmann *et al.*, 2004). Another view on roles is the functionalistic perspective in which society determines roles defined by a set of normative expectations and sanctions. Both these perspectives on roles wish to explain the relationship between the individual and society or between a person and the system (Herrmann *et al.*, 2004).

The functionalistic view argues there is an existence of objective structures that determine the individual's behavior, while the symbolic interaction argues that roles are formed on the subjective will of the actors (Herrmann *et al.*, 2004). In agreement with Mead, we share the view that a role structure results from interactions (symbolic interactions).

According to Herrmann *et al.* (2004, p. 168), "a role is the sum of all behavior expectations of a social system towards a concrete role actor." They argue that a role can be divided into four characteristics: (1) Position: A role always includes a position that has relations to other positions in a social system. (2) Function/Task: These occur in the form of explicit and documented expectations, rights, and obligations (for example, job descriptions and task assignment). (3) Behavior/Expectations: A role includes implicit expectations such as informal notions and agreement on how to behave. (4) Social interaction: An actor learns how to behave, what to do, and what not to do in order to be accepted in a group. The institutionalized norms, rules, and habits direct and shape the actors and form their roles. This change can also be described as a result of negotiations with other actors in a social system where the role expectations transform into actual behaviors.

Roles and knowledge provision

In open service innovation groups, internal and external actors perform several tasks. To manage these processes requires clarity on the objectives and who performs the different tasks to meet the objectives. Different innovation actors provide different knowledge in the development process. A review of the previous research resulted in seven innovator roles (see Table 1) with regard to the knowledge provision of different actors.

The actors who typically enact the role of *Gatekeeper* possess technology and resource knowledge, and they have the ability to collect and translate external knowledge and diffuse the information to the network to enthuse the participants. Actors enacting the role of *Orchestrator* are task masters. They have the skills and knowledge to identify and articulate problems of interest for further development. They possess knowledge on leadership and have the power to overcome obstacles and barriers and to make decisions; they also have knowledge on how to

Table 1.   Innovator actors in innovation networks and their knowledge provision.

Innovator role	Knowledge provision	Reference	Related roles
Gatekeeper	Technology and resource knowledge and translation of external knowledge	Allen (1970) and Heikkinen et al. (2007)	Expert promotor (Witte, 1977)
Orchestrator	Leadership knowledge to orchestrate the whole network	Nyström et al. (2014)	Power promotor (Witte, 1977)
Producer	Specialized knowledge necessary for the development process	Heikkinen et al. (2007)	Planner (Heikkinen et al., 2007), Adapter (Nambisan and Sawhney, 2008)
Integrator	Coordination knowledge; how to integrate heterogeneous knowledge, ideas, and technologies	Nyström et al. (2014)	Project manager (Gemünden et al., 2007)
Messenger	Communication knowledge; forward and disseminates information in the network; does not join the innovation development	Heikkinen et al. (2007)	Advocate (Heikkinen et al., 2007), Agent (Nambisan and Sawhney, 2008)
Compromiser	Relationships knowledge to avoid contradictions or conflicts	Heikkinen et al. (2007)	Webber (Heikkinen et al., 2007)
Bridger	Relationships knowledge, acting as a coordinator	Bessant and Rush (1995)	Champion (Schon, 1963), Process promotor (Witte, 1977), Technology-related relationship promotor (Gemünden et al., 2007), Coordinator (Nyström et al., 2014)

design the innovation network and process knowledge to build structure and coherence into the activities and to envision and direct the innovations; and finally, they have resource knowledge, determining what actors to engage for the development process.

Actors that provide different kinds of specific technical or specialized knowledge in the different stages of the development process often enact the role of *Producers*. *Bridgers* has internal relationship knowledge to establish relationships among participants, and external relationship knowledge to promote the innovation project to external partners either from a technical or market know-how perspective.

Enacting the role of a *Messenger* implies having communication knowledge to forward and disseminate information in the network. However, this role does not join the innovation development phase. *Compromisers* possess relationship knowledge and are useful in avoiding contradictions or conflicts. *Integrators* are those with coordination knowledge, the ability to provide heterogeneous competences and technologies and to bring different ideas together.

The Gatekeeper interprets external information, assimilates and translates it before diffusion to the network. The Orchestrator uses knowledge and experience to evaluate and decide how to problematize and use the received information. The Orchestrator knows what network design is the best and also has the power to carry through the preparation of an innovation project. With the information from the Gatekeeper and the Orchestrator, the Integrator knows what competences to look for and which suitable personal resources, developers, and performers, to engage.

Five of the seven roles are present in the development stage. This stage starts with the forming of a development team of Producers. The Producers are recruited because of their specific or specialized knowledge necessary for the development process. They use the prerequisites from the Orchestrator as input values for their work. During the progress, there is an ongoing flow of knowledge from the Gatekeeper, the Integrator, and the Orchestrator to fertilize the development process. In this stage, an additional innovator actor is included, the Bridger. The Bridger is responsible for the coherence of the innovation project. The Bridger coordinates the knowledge flows among the involved actors to foster the development of a new innovation but also provides knowledge about the project to external partners outside the innovation project.

Now that we have identified the seven roles and how they interact, we will explore case studies, and then match the seven roles with the participants we encountered in the case studies.

A Multiple Case Study of Open Service Innovation

To obtain new knowledge on the actors involved, their roles, and their knowledge provision in an open service innovation network, we employed a multiple case study approach (Eisenhardt, 1989; Yin, 2014). Meredith (1998) suggested that case study research is beneficial when theory can be generated by observing and analyzing actual practice. Voss *et al.* (2002) emphasized that studying a single case (that is, a firm) may actually involve a number of different cases that enable comparisons that clarify whether an emergent result can be consistently replicated (Eisenhardt and Graebner, 2007; Siggelkow, 2007). We identified nine open service innovation groups in the case firm (the innovator firm) and used them as cases in our study.

Data collection and analysis

Data collection can be divided into three different stages. First, we performed seven in-depth interviews with project managers at the innovator firm responsible for the open service innovation groups. Second, during 20 site visits, we performed 38 in-depth interviews with participants of the open service innovation network. Altogether, we performed 45 in-depth interviews with participants in nine different open service innovation groups where the interviewees reflected on different open service innovations.

The transcribed interviews from the multiple case studies were inductively coded and categorized. Each interviewee was asked to describe his or her involvement in the open service innovation group. To better understand and describe the open service innovation groups and their actors, we used role theory. The different categories from the coding were analyzed using the characteristics of the role concept (Herrmann *et al.*, 2004). The four characteristics were built on the following open coded categories:

- Position: *The project manager, Assignment*
- Function/Task: *The project manager, Assignment*
- Behavior/Expectations: *Idea generation, Idea management, Development process*
- Social Interaction: *Discussion climate, Commitment, Customer involvement, Engagement, Knowledge transfer across boundaries, Power.*

We performed a within-case analysis of each of the nine open service innovation groups. The firms studied had open service innovation groups for Delivery Contracts, Inventory Database, Structural Engineering, Mechanical Engineering, Electrical Engineering, Instrumental Engineering, Pipe Engineering, Surface Protection, and Safety. We followed this analysis with a cross-case synthesis using the three archetypes of organizing for open service innovation (Myhrén *et al.*, 2018). This synthesis resulted in a set of tables and templates for deepening the understanding (Yin, 2014; Miles *et al.*, 2014) of the different innovator actors and their roles and knowledge provision in open service innovation. We revisited and interviewed the innovator firm's project managers several times during the research process to confirm our findings.

The innovator firm: Open service innovation

The innovator firm is owned by six multinational pulp and paper companies and facilitates an open service innovation network. Altogether nine open service innovation groups have been formed, each consisting of seven to ten participants and a project manager. The purpose of the groups is to maintain and improve existing services and, in some cases, also to identify new services based on the needs of the pulp and paper industry. The participants have all signed a competition guideline that hinders them from discussing business models, pricing, and customers to prevent cartels. The ideas and solutions are further developed by the innovator firm and introduced to the market as industrial services.

In the following, we present the actors involved, their roles, and the knowledge they provide in the different stages in the innovation process. For each open service innovation group, the majority of the actors take part in more than one stage of the innovation processes, implying that the actors assume multiple roles. We have investigated the role constellations across the three different archetypes:

- Internal Group Development,
- Satellite Team Development, and
- Rocket Team Development.

Roles in internal group development

This archetype is used by the Delivery Contract, Inventory Database, and Structural Engineering groups. The outcome is the maintenance and improvement of existing services. Five different actors can be identified: the chairman, senior participants, specialists, the innovator firm representative, and an external expert. The external expert is only involved in idea generation. The competence profile of the chairman is the same as that of the senior participants but with a longer experience working in the open service innovation network. Together with the innovator firm representative, the chairman prepares and organizes the meetings, runs the agenda, activates the different actors, and makes sure everyone is listened to.

> *It's of course an important role as a chairman to make sure that the reticent participants also will be heard. [Chairman]*

The chairman and the innovator firm representative allocate different tasks in the development stage and finally make sure a decision is made on a refined or updated service solution. The innovator firm representative coordinates all practical matters before, during, and after the meetings. The senior participants are experts within their field. Together with the chairman, they play a vital role in idea generation. They jointly identify problems that need to be solved and also configure the setup of competences for the development stage. The innovator firm representative is also involved in idea generation, keeps track of earlier versions of the services, and suggests updates, but also provides information that can be used in idea generation.

Finally, one open service innovation group had a fourth actor involved in idea generation and development, the specialists. Specialists are technical consultants invited to the network to provide user knowledge into the innovation process.

We have invited consultants, experts who have explained different questions related to the delivery contract. [Innovator firm representative]

These specialists are not regular participants and not actively involved in the innovation process.

In summary, the development work is done by the actors, either all together or in development teams. The chairman or a senior participant is responsible for the development, whereas the other actors contribute with their knowledge.

The innovator firm representative coordinates the work and updates the service innovation group on the progress. Once the development work is finished, the actors (except the innovator firm representative) make a decision on the new service solution. The improved service is given to the the innovator firm representative, who brings it back to the innovator firm (which has market knowledge) for final design and pricing before it is released on the market (see Table 2).

Roles in satellite team development

The archetype called Satellite Team Development is used by the Mechanical Engineering, Instrument Engineering, Electrical Engineering, and Pipe Engineering groups. The identified actors are the chairman, senior participants, a specialist, the innovator firm representative, and developers. The objectives of this archetype are similar to those of Internal Group Development with one exception. Where Internal Group Development has only one or very few services to refine, Satellite Team Development has multiple services to work with. Due to the simultaneous improvement of several services, the chairman, senior participants, and specialist at the end

Table 2. Actors in internal group development.

Internal group development	Position	Function/Task	Behavior/Expectations	Social interaction
Senior OSI participant (Chairman)	Major impact	Meeting facilitator, taskmaster, developer, decision-maker	Conducting, executing, being committed, being responsive, idea generating, decision making	Open atmosphere, Balance active/passive
Innovator firm representative	No decision power, but influential	Organizer, facilitator, executor	Bringing coherence, being efficient, driving	Balance active/passive, humble participation
Senior OSI participant	Major impact	Taskmaster, developer, decision-maker	Investigating, idea generating, being committed, decision making	Open atmosphere, transparency, acceptance, knowledge, experience
OSI specialist	Certain impact	Controlled performer	Providing user knowledge	Open atmosphere, knowledge, experience
External expert	No impact	Special knowledge deliverer	Providing informative delivery on the spot	Knowledge, Experience

of the idea generation stage need to identify external competences outside the open service innovation group to recruit as developers. These developers are normally colleagues of the chairman, senior participants, or the specialist. For the development stage, a development team is formed that consists of the chairman or one of the senior participants, the developers, and in many cases also the specialist and the innovator firm representative. Development takes place in this team. The chairman or one of the senior participants is responsible for development, but the innovator firm representative has an active role. He/She coordinates the meetings, collects information from the involved actors, and shares the information with the development team. He/She also informs the open service innovation group about the progress of the development work. When the work is done, the development team delivers a suggestion for a new service (see Table 3).

Roles in rocket team development

The Surface Protection and Safety groups use the archetype called Rocket Team Development. The result of the development process with this archetype is a radical new service. Because of the broader objectives for these groups, they require a wider range of experience and knowledge, which affects which actors to involve. For the Surface Protection group, the following actors are identified: chairman, senior participants, specialists, innovator firm representative, developer, and external experts.

The actors in the groups in this archetype are equipped to illuminate different perspectives and the needs for new services. The actions of the chairman, the senior participants, and the specialists in the idea generation stage are similar to those in the Internal Development Group; the difference is that the actors can handle a wider range of problems because of their heterogeneous backgrounds and experiences. The role of the innovator firm representative in idea generation is to inform on the latest versions of the services and to help prioritize.

In development, the chairman or one senior participant and one or two specialists perform the development work. While the chairman is in charge, the innovator firm representative organizes and administrates, and the specialists provide the necessary knowledge. Development takes place either within the open service innovation group, or outside the open

Table 3. Actors in satellite team development.

Satellite team development	Position	Function/Task	Behavior/Expectations	Social interaction
Senior OSI participant (Chairman)	Major impact	Organizer, meeting executor, taskmaster, resource allocator, remitter, decision maker	Driving, committed, idea generating, idea screening, governing	Open atmosphere, strive for consensus
Innovator firm representative	Little impact but participating	Organizer, facilitator, coordinator, executor	Bringing coherence, committed, engaged, driving	Humble/active participation
Senior OSI participant	Major impact	Idea generator, taskmaster, resource allocator, remitter, decision maker	Committed, idea generating, idea screening, resource identifying	Open atmosphere, reflection, negotiation, verbal skills, knowledge/ experience
OSI specialist	Certain impact	Idea generator, idea screener, remitter, developer, decision maker	Committed, idea generating	Advising
Developer	Little impact	Competence, knowledge provider, controlled performer	Informative, autonomous	Persuasive behavior

service innovation group in a development team. The suggested solution for a new service is presented to the open service innovation group for consideration and a decision (with no participation of the innovator firm representative; see Table 4).

Discussion

In this chapter, we describe how a service firm works with open service innovation to achieve incremental or radical service innovation. The innovator firm uses a deliberate strategy to match the archetypes, types of innovations, and actors in the right roles to reach the specific goal of the open service innovation group.

What roles do we need?

Internal Group Development and Satellite Team Development function in a similar way, with a primary objective of incremental service innovation. The main difference between the two archetypes is the number of services to improve, with Internal Group Development focusing on one service while Satellite Team Development works with several services. The Rocket Team Development archetype is used when the objectives are more complex or the scope is broader; that is, when the focus is on radical service innovation.

Role constellations within all the archetypes have similar setups of actors, but their innovation roles differ. There should be a senior actor with the mandate to foster the constellation, a chairman. In addition, there should be senior actors in supporting roles. Together these actors constitute the foundation for knowledge creation and provision in the open service innovation group. Normally, a specialist provides a user perspective. External experts are also included. Developers are part of the development for constellations within the third archetype and occasionally in constellations in the second archetype. Finally, the innovator firm is represented in all archetypes. Table 5 describes the actors of open service innovation and their identified innovation roles in the three archetypes, which are described below.

Table 4. Actors in rocket team development.

Rocket team development	Position	Function/Task	Behavior/Expectations	Social interaction
Senior OSI participant (Chairman)	Major impact	Meeting facilitator, taskmaster, resource allocator, remitter, developer, decision-maker	Controlling, executing, engaged, decision making	Open atmosphere, transparency, responsive, knowledge, experience
Innovator firm representative	No decision power, but influential	Planner, organizer, facilitator, executor	Supportive, engaged, responsive, driving	Balance active/passive participation
Senior OSI participant	Major impact	Idea generator, competence recruiter, taskmaster, resource allocator, remitter, developer, decision-maker	Engaged, knowledge sharing, reflecting, idea managing, decision making	Open atmosphere, active participation, transparency, knowledge, experience gives negotiation power
OSI specialist	Certain impact, authority	Problem solver, developer, controller, decision maker	Observing, arguing	Transparency, knowledge, experience, open atmosphere, power demonstrations
Developer	Little or no decision power, but influential	Developer, controlled performer	Developing, reporting	Verbal skills, persuasive behavior
External expert	Limited impact	Special knowledge (perspective) deliverer	Informing	Knowledge, Experience

Table 5.   Actors and innovator roles in open service innovation.

Archetype	Actor	Innovator role
Internal Group Development	Chairman	Orchestrator/Bridger
	OSI senior participant	Integrator
	OSI specialist	Producer
	IFR	Gatekeeper/Constitutional Monarch
	External expert	Gatekeeper/Messenger
Satellite Team Development	Chairman	Gatekeeper
	OSI senior participant	Integrator
	OSI specialist	Producer
	IFR	Constitutional Monarch
	Developer	Producer
Rocket Team Development	Chairman	Orchestrator/Integrator
	OSI senior participant	Gatekeeper/Integrator
	OSI specialist	Gatekeeper/Producer
	IFR	Compriser/Constitutional Monarch
	Developer	Producer
	External expert	Messenger/Integrator

Matching roles in internal group development

The chairman has the knowledge, experience, and support from the other participants to be the *Orchestrator* of the open service innovation group. The chairman contributes with ideas that need solutions and also has the power to make decisions. In this archetype, the chairman is actively involved in development, often as a *Bridger* with relationship knowledge. Each senior participant mostly has the same background as the chairman with long experience and broad knowledge, making it possible for them to enact the role of *Integrators*. In idea generation, they identify current problems and actively participate in discussions. The specialist functions as a *Producer* when contributing with specialized knowledge necessary for development. In this archetype, the external expert only appears occasionally in idea generation, in the role of a *Messenger* providing external knowledge, but not allowed to participate in the development process. This is because the objective within this archetype is quite narrow, so therefore the archetype has scarce human capital. As a consequence, there is no room for external experts when development work is performed.

Matching roles for satellite team development

In this archetype, the chairman has a major impact and mainly enacts the role of a *Gatekeeper* with technology and resource knowledge. The senior participants play a vital role as *Integrators* with knowledge on how to find and integrate heterogeneous perspectives in idea generation. They are also actively involved in development by knowledge provision. Just as in Internal Group Development, the specialist functions as a *Producer*, but in contrast with that archetype, developers may be involved in development. As with the specialist, these developers enact the role of *Producers* due to their user knowledge. Developers are involved in development due to the large number of tasks to undertake.

Matching roles for rocket team development

In Rocket Team Development, the chairman enacts the role of *Orchestrator* in idea generation but is less actively involved in the development phase, where he acts as an *Integrator*, identifying what actors to involve and how to support them. In the consideration/decision phase, the chairman leads the open service innovation group toward a decision. In this archetype, the senior participants enact the role of *Integrator* to identify, involve, and support suitable actors in the development work. In the consideration/decision phase, the senior participants act as *Gatekeepers* with the knowledge and power to make decisions. The specialist is brought in as a *Gatekeeper* and *Producer* to contribute with user knowledge in idea generation and development. In the consideration/decision phase, the specialist provides technical expert knowledge on the service concepts. Just as in Satellite Team Development, developers have no role in the idea generation phase; the outcomes of this phase are used to identify developers, who are invited due to their specific knowledge and skills to perform during the development phase. They act as *Producers* to provide deep, specialized user knowledge.

In addition to appearing as a *Messenger,* who in idea generation provides external knowledge and information to enhance the performance, the external expert is also involved in development and in consideration/ decision as an *Integrator* providing information and incremental knowledge to support the decision being made. External experts are essential due to the fact that the radical service innovation projects undertaken call for more heterogeneous competences.

New role: The constitutional monarch

Note that the descriptions matching the roles have not yet mentioned the innovator firm representative, who has a central role in all archetypes. The role seems different from the roles identified in previous research; therefore we describe a new innovator role in open service innovation: the *Constitutional Monarch.* The Constitutional Monarch has a central position in the open service innovation group and is involved throughout the innovation process. It is a role enacted by an actor that other actors go to for advice and for getting help.

> *If I have something I want to inform the network I just ask the innovator firm representative and he'll fix it. [OSI senior participant]*

The Constitutional Monarch is a performer with relational skills to promote and market the open service innovation group externally, responsible for information, actively participating in the organization and administration of activities, and largely involved in the coordination and facilitation of the actors in the network.

> *I think it's the project manager who spends the most time, preparing the agenda and in some way is the cohesive link ... I don't think these groups, this kind of collaborations would work without them. [Member of open service innovation group]*

But when it comes to decision making, the Constitutional Monarch has no power due to the constitution of the network:

According to the constitutions we actually have no voting rights; we rather function as catalysts or coordinators. [Innovation firm representative]

Long-lasting open service innovation groups

In contrast to previous research, this study focuses on an innovator firm that has been involved in a long-lasting open service innovation network. The nine open service innovation groups have operated since the 1970s because they create value: value for the pulp and paper industry, the group participants, and the innovator firm.

The actors in the role constellations use their accumulated knowledge to solve common problems and develop them into new services.

You don't have to do the engineering work, calculations on every site. You just use standards ... you save a lot of engineering hours in both smaller and bigger investment projects. [OSI senior participant]

These standards are used by a large proportion of the process industry. As such, they create value in terms of reduced costs in calculation and engineering work, increased efficiency since the services can be used as a negotiating tool during procurement with contractors and suppliers, and decreased uncertainties in big and small construction projects.

The open service innovation groups also create value for the participants. Knowledge provision from the different actors enhances each actor's activities, which is beneficial for the actors in their ordinary work. For some participants, this is in fact the primary incentive for joining the open service innovation groups.

I'm basically just there for the network, to be able to discuss certain issues ... it is a great network when you run into problems and need someone to ask for advice ... Whenever we have made any major construction, I have called the guys in the network and we have together sorted things out. [Member of open service innovation group]

Finally, the outcomes from the open service innovation groups also create value for the innovator firm, not just in terms of the user-driven development of new services such as business agreements, education, technical standards, and guidelines, but also through building the brand and reputation, showing an innovator firm as a trusted third part, a neutral actor in respect to the other actors, that brings trust to the activities in the open service innovation groups.

Conclusions

In the study, we use the role concept (Herrmann *et al.*, 2004) to highlight actors' positions, tasks, behaviors, and social interactions to describe their innovator roles in the innovation process, from idea generation to commercialization. We show how actors take on multiple innovator roles in the innovation process of open service innovation. The more radical changes, the more roles each actor takes on, a finding that aligns with Rese *et al.* (2013), who argue that role accumulation, not role specialization, is beneficial in interorganizational contexts.

In contrast to previous research (Vanhaverbeke and Cloodt, 2006), this study describes a central innovator firm, an organizer of an open service innovation network that neither is in charge of the design of the innovation process nor has any impact on the resource allocation decisions of the actors in the network. The firm has to act on the outcomes from the different open service innovation groups and from there adjust the business model to create value for the customers and the firm. We argue that the firm's representative enacts the role of the Constitutional Monarch. By identifying this new role, we add to previous research of innovator roles. The Constitutional Monarch has a central position in all archetypes, but as the name implies, has no decision power. The research also sheds light on how the hub firm deploys not one but a portfolio of network orchestration processes (Nambisan and Sawhney, 2011) dependent on the archetype used for open service innovation.

References

Åkesson, M. (2011). *Role Constellations in Value Co-creation: A Study of Resource Integration in an E-government Context*. Diss. Karlstad University: Faculty of Economic Sciences, Communication and IT, Business Administration.

Allen, T.-J. (1970). Communication networks in R&D labs. *R&D Management*, **1**, 14–21.

Arthurs, D., Cassidy, E., Davis, C. H., and Wolfe, D. (2009). Indicators to support innovation cluster policy. *International Journal of Technology Management*, **46**(3–4), 263–279.

Bessant, J. and Rush, H. (1995). Building bridges for innovation: The role of consultants in technology transfer. *Research Policy*, **24**(1), 97–114.

Calia, R. C., Guerrini, F. M., and Moura, G. L. (2007). Innovation networks: From technological development to business model reconfiguration. *Technovation*, **27**(8), 426–432.

Corsaro, D., Ramos, C., Henneberg, S. C., and Naudé, P. (2012). The impact of network configurations on value constellations in business markets — The case of an innovation network. *Industrial Marketing Management*, **41**(1), 54–67.

Chesbrough, H. W. (2003). *Open Innovation: The New Imperative for Creating and Profiting from Technology.* (1st edn.), Boston, MA: Harvard Business School Press.

Chesbrough, H. W. and Bogers, M. (2014). Explication open innovation: Clarifying an emerging paradigm for understanding innovation. In Chesbrough, H., Vanheverbeke, W., and West, J. (eds.), *New Frontiers in Open Innovation* (1st edn.), Oxford: Oxford University Press, Chapter 1, pp. 3–28.

Coombs, R. and Miles, I. (2000). Innovation, measurement and services: The new problematique. In Metcalfe, S. J. and Miles, I. (eds.), *Innovation Systems in the Service Economy, Measurement and Case Study Analysis.* (Volume 18 edn.), Springer Link, Chapter 5, pp. 85–103.

DeBresson, C. and Amesse, F. (1991). Networks of innovators: A review and introduction to the issue. *Research Policy*, **20**(5), 363–379.

Eisenhardt, K. M. (1989). Building theories from case study research. *Academy of Management Review*, **14**(4), 532–550.

Eisenhardt, K. M. and Graebner, M. E. (2007). Theory building from cases: Opportunities and challenges. *Academy of Management Journal*, **50**(1), 25–32.

Elmquist, M., Fredberg, T., and Ollila, S. (2009). Exploring the field of open innovation. *European Journal of International Management*, **12**(3), 326–345.

Faems, D., Van Looy, B., and Debackere, K. (2005). Interorganizational collaboration and innovation: Toward a portfolio approach. *Journal of Product Innovation Management*, **22**(3), 238–250.

Ford, D., Gadde, L. E., Hakansson, H., and Snehota I. (2003). Managing business relationships. Chichester, UK: John Wiley & Sons Ltd.

Freytag, P. and Young, L. C. (2014). Introduction to special issue on innovations and networks: Innovation of, within, throughand by networks. *Industrial Marketing Management*, **43**(3), 361–364.

Gassmann, O. and Enkel, E. (2004). Towards a theory of open innovation: Three core process archetypes. In *The R&D Management Conference*, Lisbon, Portugal July 6–9.

Gemünden, H. G., Salomo, S., and Hölzle, K. (2007). Role models for radical innovations in times of open innovation. *Creativity and Innovation Management*, **16**(4), 408–421.

Giddens, A. (1984). *The Constitution of Society: Outline of the Theory of Structuration*. Berkley: University of California Press.

Gomes-Casseres, B. (1996). *The Alliance Revolution: The New Shape of Business Rivalry*. Harvard University Press.

Gomes-Casseres, B. (2003). Competitive advantage in alliance constellations. *Strategic Organization*, **1**(3), 327–335.

Heikkinen, M. T., Mainela, T., Still, J., and Tähtinen, J. (2007). Roles for managing in mobile service development nets. *Industrial Marketing Management*, **36**(7), 909–925.

Herrmann, T., Jahnke, I., and Loser, K.. (2004). The role concept as a basis for designing community systems. In Darses, F., Dieng, R.,Simone, C., and Zackland, M. (eds.), *Cooperative System Design: Scenario-Based Design of Collaborative Systems*. IOS Press, Amsterdam, pp. 163–178.

Hsueh, J.-., Lin, N., and Li, H. (2010). The effects of network embeddedness on service innovation performance. *Service Industries Journal*, **30**(10), 1723–1736.

Jones, C., Hesterly, W. S., Fladmoe-Lindquist, K., and Borgatti, S. P. (1998). Professional service constellations: How strategies and capabilities influence collaborative stability and change. *Organization Science*, **9**(3), 396–410.

Koschatzky, K. (1999). Innovation networks of industry and business-related services — Relations between innovation intensity of firms and regional inter-firm cooperation. *European Planning Studies*, **7**(6), 737–757.

Landsperger, J. and Spieth, P. (2011). Managing innovation networks in the industrial goods sector. *International Journal of Innovation Management*, **15**(6), 1209–1241.

Mead, G. H. (1934). *Mind, Self and Society*. Chicago: University of Chicago Press.

Meredith, J. (1998). Building operations management theory through case and field research. *Journal of Operations Management*, **16**(4), 441–454.

Miles, M. B., Huberman, M. A., and Saldana, J. (2014). *Qualitative Data Handbook: A Methods Sourcebook.* (3rd edn.). Thousand Oaks, California: Sage Publications, Inc.

Möller, K. and Rajala, A. (2007). Rise of strategic nets — New modes of value creation. *Industrial Marketing Management,* **36**(7), 895–908.

Möller, K. and Svahn, S. (2003). Managing strategic nets: A capability perspective. *Marketing Theory,* **3**(2), 209–234.

Mu, J., Peng, G., and Love, E. (2008). Interfirm networks, social capital, and knowledge flow. *Journal of Knowledge Management,* **12**(4), 86–100.

Myhren, P., Witell, L., Gustafsson, A., and Gebauer, H. (2018). Incremental and radical open service innovation. *Journal of Services Marketing,* **32**(2), 101–112.

Nambisan, S. and Sawhney, M. (2008). *The Global Brain — Your Roadmap for Innovating Faster and Smarter in a Networked World.* (1st Edn.). Upper Saddle River, New Jersey: Prentice Hall.

Nambisan, S. and Sawhney, M. (2011). Orchestration processes in network-centric innovation: Evidence from the field. *The Academy of Management Perspectives,* **25**(3), 40–57.

Nyström, A. G., Leminen, S., Westerlund, M., and Kortelainen, M. (2014). Actor roles and role patterns influencing innovation in living labs. *Industrial Marketing Management,* **43**(3), 483–495.

Ostrom, A. L., Bitner, M. J., Brown, S. W., Burkhard, K. A., Goul, M., Smith-Daniels, V., Demirkan, H., and Rabinovich, E. (2010). Moving forward and making a difference: Research priorities for the science of service. *Journal of Service Research,* **13**(1), 4–36.

Pittaway, L., Robertson, M., Munir, K., Denyer, D., and Neely, A. (2004). Networking and innovation: A systematic review of the evidence. *International Journal of Management Reviews,* **5**(3–4), 137–168.

Rampersad, G., Quester, P., and Troshani, I. (2010). Managing innovation networks: Exploratory evidence from ICT, biotechnology and nanotechnology networks. *Industrial Marketing Management,* **39**(5), 793–805.

Rese, A., Gemünden, H. G., and Baier, D. (2013). 'Too many cooks spoil the broth': Key persons and their roles in inter-organizational innovations. *Creativity and Innovation Management,* **22**(4), 390–407.

Solomon, M. R., Surprenant, C., Czepiel, J. A., and Gutman, E. G. (1985). A role theory perspective on dyadic interactions: The service encounter. *The Journal of Marketing,* **49**(1), 99–111.

Schon, D. A. (1963). Champions for radical new inventions. *Harvard Business Review*, **41**(2), 77–86.

Siggelkow, N. (2007). Persuasion with case studies. *The Academy of Management Journal*, **50**(1), 20–24.

Syson, F. and Perks, H. (2004). New service development: A network perspective. *Journal of Services Marketing*, **18**(4), 255–266.

Toivonen, M. and Tuominen, T. (2009). Emergence of innovations in services. *The Service Industries Journal*, **29**(7), 887–902.

van de Vrande, V., de Jong, J. P. J., Vanhaverbeke, W., and de Rochemont, M. (2009). Open innovation in SMEs: Trends, motives and management challenges. *Technovation*, **29**(6–7), 423–437.

Vanhaverbeke, W. (2006). The interorganizational context of open innovation. In Chesbrough, H. W., Vanheverbeke, W., and West, J. (eds.), *Open Innovation: Researching a New Paradigm*. (1st edn.). Oxford: Oxford University Press, Chapter 10, pp. 205–219.

Vanhaverbeke, W., and Cloodt, M. (2006). Open innovation in value networks. *Open Innovation: Researching a New Paradigm*, Chapter 13, pp. 258–281.

Vanhaverbekke, W. and Cloodt, M. (2014). Theories of the Firms and Open Innovation. In Chesbrough, H. W., Vanheverbeke, W., and West, J. (Eds.). *New Frontiers in Open Innovation*. (1st Edn.). Oxford: Oxford University Press, Chapter 14, pp. 256–278.

Voss, C., Tsikriktsis, N., and Frohlich, M. (2002). Case research in operations management. *International Journal of Operations and Production Management*, **22**(2), 195–219.

Wallin, M. W. and von Krogh, G. (2010). Organizing for open innovation: Focus on the integration of knowledge. *Organizational Dynamics*, **39**(2), 145–154.

West, J., Salter, A., Vanhaverbeke, W., and Chesbrough, H. W. (2014). Open innovation: The next decade. *Research Policy*, **43**(5), 805–811.

Witell, L., Snyder, H., Gustafsson, A., Fombelle, P., and Kristensson, P. (2016). Defining service innovation: A review and synthesis. *Journal of Business Research*, **69**(8), 2863–2872.

Witte, E. (1977). Power and innovation: A two-center theory. *International Studies of Management Organization*, **7**, 47–70.

Yin, R. K. (2014). *Case Study Research, Design and Methods*. (5th edn.). Thousand Oaks, California: SAGE Publications, Inc.

Chapter 9

Servitization Goes to the Psychologist

Per Kristensson and Peter R. Magnusson

Karlstad University, Sweden

Key takeaways

1. The idea of servitization has been around since 1989, but many industrial companies still struggle to servitize their businesses.
2. This chapter presents several useful theories of psychology that explain how companies can support servitization implementation processes.
3. Instead of attempting to depict phases or identify challenges in regard to servitization, managers should turn their attention toward five specific ways to accelerate servitization processes.
4. The chapter contains various illustrations of how B2B organizations are servitizing.
5. Those interested in this chapter may also find Chapters 7 and 12–14 interesting.

Introduction

A contemporary phenomenon among product-oriented firms is to expand their businesses by adding services (Neu and Brown, 2005).

Research shows that adding services increases competitiveness via flexibility and differentiation (Ulaga and Reinartz, 2011). This transition toward infusing more services into a business is labeled servitization and was introduced in the late 80s by Vandermerwe and Rada (1989). It is often divided into different phases where a company moves from providing services supporting the product to services supporting the customer (Mathieu, 2001). Examples of the former are maintenance and repair, while examples of the latter are services that help the customer better use the product or that optimize the process of installing the product. In the last instance, the firm thus takes a service perspective and focuses on offering solutions to customers' problems. This perspective has a kinship with the marketing trend of service logic (Vargo and Lusch, 2004) that emphasizes that value is created when customers use products and services. The object is thus not to sell products *per se*, but to see what the products can do for the customer, and to understand the value that the customer experiences.

Unfortunately, the servitization process has been troublesome for companies (Hertenstein *et al.*, 2005; Oliva and Kallenberg, 2003, Ostrom *et al.*, 2015), especially in the latter phases where servitization implies a thorough understanding of the customer. The seminal work of Vandermerwe and Rada (1989) has been cited more than 800 times, and the research has since then focused on producing models that outline the servitization process in distinct phases and pinpoint strategic steps. Despite this research, it is still difficult for manufacturing companies to implement servitization.

The change is slow for several reasons. In our research, we have seen that product-oriented companies often fall in love with their products and forget why customers buy them; that is, to use them for value creation. A major challenge to learn and understand more regarding the customer's processes and context confronts companies who seek to understand the value in use. Another challenge is that businesses worry that they'll lose core values such as R&D and technical excellence when adopting a service logic. Poor attempts at servitization occur when service functions as a sales support for products and when incentive programs are tied to meeting targets for product sales. In addition, services are often discounted or even free to support product sales, which implies that services are regarded merely as an add-on to a product.

To summarize, there is business potential in servitization, but many companies fail to implement it. Research has illustrated the problems with implementing servitization but has failed to help businesses implement it. As a consequence, we contend that instead of developing yet another servitization strategy, or identifying another barrier to servitization, it is time to take a new approach. Essentially what is missing for implementation is a process in which problems are overcome using contemporary psychology theories.

In this chapter, we thus address how to facilitate and implement servitization using several psychological principles that appear ready-made for facilitating change. Adopting the ideas of Nobel laureate Daniel Kahneman, we argue that servitization processes can be better managed by taking two cognitive systems into consideration, referred to as System I and System II (Kahneman, 2011). System II thinking is rational and slow, and depends on deliberate processes that require control and effort. It represents the conscious self that makes choices and decides what to do. System I thinking, on the other hand, is fast, automatic, and emotional, controls much of everyday behavior, and operates as an autopilot.

Present servitization research, outlining the steps of servitization, taps into the rational and slow System II thinking. Employees typically think of themselves as in control of their minds and behavior. More often than not, they characterize their behavior and organizational functioning as rational and intelligent. Nevertheless, System I often controls our thinking. Many organizations know they need to change, but it does not happen; change comes slowly or sometimes not at all. We argue that it is System I thinking, based on experiences, knowledge, and skills acquired over a long time period, that keeps preserving old habits. Therefore, to change behavior within an industrial organizational context, organizations need to take System I thinking into account. Through several case studies from our research, we illustrate how companies aiming to servitize can take new actions, hitherto neglected in previous research.

About the research

The overall research procedure was to follow leading Swedish industrial manufacturing companies in their attempts to servitize. The Swedish funding agency, the KK-foundation, explicitly informed Swedish companies that they had an opportunity to receive free research expertise on challenging management issues if they would allow researchers full access to employees, meetings, and documents. The agreement enabled co-production between researchers and industrial companies, with the overarching goal to contribute to both academically interesting research and managerially relevant actions.

To understand the challenges of servitization and how to overcome them, researchers participated in several projects by attending meetings and did cooperative work with leading managers within each of the firms. All projects were approved by top management and funded by the KK-foundation. The research was conducted between October 2011 and January 2017. Respondents included R&D managers, sales and marketing managers, and business segment managers with decision-making authority.

The Platform to Servitization

Taking the customer perspective — it is about value, not products

In essence, servitization implies taking a customer perspective on your industrial business offerings. Instead of selling a top-rated, quality-guaranteed super product, the company offers the customer help toward reaching an important customer goal. The product is probably one important part of reaching that goal, but focusing on the customer's goal instead of the product gives the company more things to accomplish (than merely the product) to help fulfill that goal. That is what servitization is all about.

Therefore, psychological tools to aid servitization will help organizations come closer to the customer and adopt a customer perspective. Too often, servitization is hindered by an internal focus on the business and a lack of understanding of the customer. In industrial settings, organizations often talk about the customer rationally and analytically, as expected by System II thinking, but viewing the customer instead as a subject, with intentions, needs, and wants (aligned with System I thinking) will facilitate servitization. Such a subjective understanding of the customer goes hand-in-hand with helping the customer realize his or her goals, and not only selling products. Therefore, actions on how to turn the customer into a subject are needed.

In one of our larger research projects, we asked customers of TeliaSonera, the leading telecom provider in Northern Europe, to share ideas for new cell phone services built on people's experiences. The ideas were later assessed for service innovation purposes. At the TeliaSonera, personnel typically talked about the customer as just "the customer". The customer was an object that the R&D personnel seldom came in contact with. Personnel did not particularly know much about the customer despite millions spent on large market surveys.

However, during the project, the experiences that the customers shared (that is, contextual information given by the ideas they generated) provided the personnel with illuminating and vivid information on the customers' activities and interests. There were, for example, stories on how the customers used the cell phone while grocery shopping, or when watching an interesting TV show. The R&D staff began to talk about these experiences and slowly, but steadily, the view of customers changed from them being distant objects to becoming subjects, just like you and me, with real emotions, motivations, and needs. Identifying the real-life experiences of customers can move employees from seeing only a product on the shelf to understanding the value-creating moments that the customer really values.

Another illuminating example comes from Experio Lab, a patient care services organization in the healthcare industry, which visited the organization they were working with (a hospital), pretending to be a patient. The fake patient videotaped the experience from the patient's point-of-view, from the ambulance picking him/her up to the hospital visit to the subsequent convalescence care at home. The video highlighted the dusty roof-lamps, incomprehensible statements from the doctor (which may have been normal phrases but in the ears of a patient sounded worrying), and absence of information about what was going on and what would happen next (and how long the patient would wait). The information gathered by Experio Lab were subsequently shared with health-care personnel, doctors, nurses, and administrative staff where they were shown the collected information, videos, and etcetera, and thereby were able to see the experiences from the customer perspective.

In terms of servitization, visits to customer plants (where a physical good are used into a factory) in order to see how the company's employees (e.g., a machine operator) and the customer's customers (downstream in the value-chain) are experiencing the use of the "product", and more importantly, what these customers are trying to achieve, is well-invested time and money. At Volvo Trucks, similar visits occur when Volvo engineers follow truck drivers on their long-distance drives to the southern parts of Europe and back. By ethnographic, *in situ* experiences, Volvo employees get a rich understanding of how the truck and truck-driver co-create value during use.

Finally, one striking and entertaining real-life example of how to not forget the customer comes from Jeff Bezos and Amazon, who reshaped a whole business sector. When all prominent executives have seated themselves in the boardroom, there is still one chair empty (Pink, 2013). The empty chair is there to remind everyone about the most important person: the customer. Whenever the debate goes back and forth about a new launch, strategy, or campaign, everyone can refer to the customer, who is less likely to be forgotten.

Five Techniques to Start and Perpetuate Change

We illustrate five techniques to start and perpetuate servitization. These are not rooted in traditional rational models of how an industrial firm should change, that is, System II thinking, as there are already several models relying on this type of thinking. Instead, the techniques aim to guide the irrational and emotional System I thinking. Two techniques help start the process: *head start* and *crisis awareness*. The remaining techniques help perpetuate the process: *labeling, social proof,* and *small wins*. For all techniques to work, the customer perspective, described above, needs to be present as a platform for servitization.

Head start

Imagine a typical transformation process where the C-level team introduces their vision to embrace servitization: big goals, strategies containing several steps, and a distant vision, all in line with System II thinking.

In contrast, head start makes employees feel that they have already started the transformation process. Head start reframes the process such that the first steps have already been accomplished rather than not yet begun. Instead of a long tiresome process ahead of them, employees have de facto already moved closer to the goal. According to psychological theory, and as found at our research at various companies, this view increases the likelihood of successful servitization and decreases completion time.

In an illuminating study on promotion campaigns, every customer who bought a car wash got a stamp on a loyalty card. In one set of customers, when the card filled with eight stamps, the customers got a free wash. In another set of customers, everything was the same except that the customers needed ten stamps (rather than eight), but they were given a *head start* as two stamps had already been added to the card. Which promotion campaign was the most successful? As Nunes and Dreze (2006; Heath and Heath, 2010) found out in their study, the customers who had a head start were both faster and more loyal, developing new car washing behaviors (34% versus 19%).

In terms of servitization at the Volvo Group, head start implies identifying steps that the manufacturing firm already has taken toward becoming a service-operating organization. Employees will then acknowledge that their company is already in the process of servitization, although they hadn't realized it.

At the Volvo Group, an important first step toward servitization is offering aftersales services to the customer (Gebauer *et al.*, 2010). Most manufacturing companies that provide physical goods offerings also need to, for their installed base, offer aftersales services. Aftersales services typically include activities such as supplying and installing spare parts, repair, and basic training of customers to ensure proper product functioning. The Volvo Group has offered aftersales services for a long time, but only recently have they been offered to increase customer accessibility. As a result, additional aftersales services are now offered, such as inspections and maintenance, to further help customers increase their time using their Volvos.

As the principle of head start shows, it is easier for employees to take the next step in servitization when they know they are already on their way. At the Volvo Group, employees were asked to identify and realize how they already were on the path to being servitized; for example, by participating in a workshop during which they explained why they offer spare parts. This process involves taking the customer perspective, as illustrated above. In a company where there is resistance to applying a service logic, recognizing to what extent they actually are already on their way toward becoming a servitized business will facilitate the process.

In addition, the Volvo Group renamed their spare parts to "soft products" to make it clear that the transformation to a service provider was not only ahead of them but already ongoing. Furthermore, the CEO of the company at the time, Leif Johansson, stated that at least 50% of all offerings of the Volvo Group should be soft products within eight years and that they were already on the path of realizing this goal.

Crisis awareness

In the absence of real threat, employees may keep on doing what they have always done and are comfortable with. Therefore, to make change happen, especially when change is hard, crisis awareness is needed.

Crisis awareness, or a strong sense of urgency as Kotter (2008) describes it, has always been an important factor in changing the behavior of organizations as well as of individuals. Consider, for example, how IBM used a crisis — at the time, the biggest financial loss ($8 billion) in the history of corporate America — to make the leap from selling products to offering services. Before the crisis, it had been impossible to change the organization. Creating strong urgency by pointing toward a potential, or real, crisis also works for individuals; consider how cigarette packages use warnings such as "smoking kills" to help people avoid the risky behavior of smoking. In terms of servitization, creating urgency implies letting employees analyze what staying with a product-oriented logic means for the company's future.

In today's globalized economy, low price entrants, typically from East Asia, represent a potential crisis. The most direct solution to such a threat, supported by rational System II, is for a company to lower its own prices. However, this is seldom a financially sustainable approach; even if the company runs the competitor out of business, it might not have much of its own business left when the fight is over. In such a case, servitization appears as a more sustainable alternative to price competition. Price competition can be used to create a sense of urgency. With crisis around the corner, the focus needs to shift toward how the company can better help its customers.

Crisis awareness is not only about displaying hard facts, for example, that low price entrants may compete for business, but also about creating emotional conviction. Thus, crisis awareness speaks directly to System I thinking. Emotionally engaging stories speak directly to the heart and thereby motivate employees to take action.

As an example, a Swedish industrial company that manufactures machines changed its employees' perception of the business by having R&D staff engage in dialogues, listening carefully to what their customers really cared for or experienced. From these dialogues, it became evident that there were only small differences between their offerings and lower-price competitors from Asia. The staff then understood that their offering could easily be replaced by such cheaper competitive offerings if they did not create value for their customers in a better way than before. They created this value by expanding their previous offerings to full-service offerings in which they took responsibility for parts of their customers' businesses, instead of simply selling the traditional product. The dialogues with customers had created emotionally strong stories that made the R&D staff realize the urgency to embrace servitization.

Perpetuating the Change

Once change starts, techniques to perpetuate the transformation process are needed. Labeling, social proof, and small wins are three such techniques.

Labeling

Labeling entails giving someone a describing characteristic with the intention that the individual in question will later act and think in a manner consistent with the label. More precisely, labeling implies a heightened self-perception of a certain behavior, which will result in an enhanced likelihood of displaying a label-consistent behavior later in time. In an experiment regarding labeling, Tybout and Yalch (1980) found that citizens who randomly were labeled "above-average probability of voting" were more likely to actually vote in an election a week later than those citizens labeled "average probability of voting". In essence, labeling relies on the underlying psychological fact that people wish and strive to behave in a consistent manner; having been ascribed a certain behavior, an individual is much more likely to continue displaying that behavior in the future. In terms of servitization, this implies changing the perception of what service really is. By helping employees internalize new actions as their own, labeling speaks directly to System II thinking.

A problem with introducing service operations in a product-oriented company is the low status and attention they receive. When we interviewed a business developer at Volvo Aero engines and asked about the revenue that services generated for the company, the answer was unexpected but revealing: "Revenue from services? Services are cost units." The view that services are expenses rather than potential profit makers is deeply rooted in many companies, largely due to services being offered "for free," included when the customer buys the product. It is no surprise that service operations have a very low status in many companies.

We have discovered that such companies should avoid the "S word" when labeling service. The word "service" can trigger people's minds in the wrong direction as they tend to equate service with non-knowledge-intensive operations such as cleaning; it can be dangerous to label the company as a service company. On the contrary, many services that product companies engage in are rather knowledge intensive, with knowledge about the products combined with a deep knowledge of the customers' applications. Therefore, using the label "knowledge" is often preferable. The Swedish manufacturer SKF had this experience. They see knowledge as the most powerful resource to developing new offerings and use the slogan, "The knowledge engineering company". Labeling servitization as capitalizing on knowledge has proven a successful route.

Another example of labeling comes from the Volvo Group. As mentioned in the head start example, then-CEO Leif Johansson declared in 2007 that by 2015, 50% of the company's revenue should come from "soft products" (which was the important label used for services), and that growth from service was a top priority for Volvo (Volvo Technology Corporation, 2010; Brown *et al.*, 2009). This declaration functioned as a label and emphasized the importance of services for Volvo; no longer was services the poor cousin to be despised.

Labeling can also come from the bottom–up. At Sandvik, a frustrated middle manager responsible for the unit's service operation got an idea. A product board made stage-gate decisions in the product development process. He set up a "service board". The mere label showing that services also had a board increased the status of services; the rest of the organization seemed to conclude that something worthy of a board must be important.

Social proof

In uncertain situations, when a new behavior is not given, the behavior that others are performing is often used as a heuristic shortcut to a new behavior. This principle, other people's behavior as guidance to your own, is referred to in the psychological literature as social proof (Cialdini, 2007). Social proof implies a type of conformity where individuals assume that the actions of others are the correct behavior and then, often unconsciously, use that information to influence their own behavior. Social proof works between companies or, as in the case of servitization illustrated below, between departments within a company.

At the Volvo Group, one business unit wanted to change the mindset from only delivering high quality products to enabling value creation for its customers. The latter required other changes, such as a new business model and integration with other offerings to create a seamless experience for the customer. The business unit only provided a rational business argument as to why the change was needed, which hampered the process. This is System II thinking, that an analysis based on financial estimates will lead to change. System I thinking requires seeing and experiencing what actions need to be taken before change is likely to occur.

The business unit started to identify and monitor several key performance indicators in order to benchmark best practices, by comparing themselves with another business unit in the company. The business unit could then show social proof of how the other unit had not only changed their actions and mindset but also improved their business, in comparison to the business of their own unit. With this information at hand, they invited several employees from the other business unit to show how they implemented and succeeded with servitization. These behaviors from the employee perspective served as social proof of actions leading to servitization that the employees of the first unit needed to take. Thus, by evaluating various servitization processes in relation to processes at other units within the company, the business unit could more easily sustain improvements and specific best practices that had previously been implemented elsewhere.

As best practice, benchmarking involves the evaluation of specifically defined aspects of a firm's processes and comparing these with competing companies' processes, it is a good example of how social proof can be used to transform a business. By best practice benchmarking, firms can monitor how important servitization is and understand how competing businesses move forward. As illustrated above, best practice works as a social proof that cuts through the clutter and, as hinted above, is stronger than quantitative, good-sounding but not engaging arguments, as it provides both evidence of the results and, importantly, examples of the actions to engage in.

Leif Johansson of Volvo looked at Ericsson, a multinational telecom company from Sweden, and saw how much Ericsson benefitted financially from offering service solutions to its customers. This ought to be the case for Volvo as well, he concluded to his employees at Volvo, in another example of the use of social proof.

To sum up, social proof helps people engage in less known and uncertain behaviors. Organizations can, as the business unit at the Volvo Group did, show how units within an organization are working with servitization processes, and by doing so encourage other units to follow suit. They can also look for examples at other organizations. Someone else engaged in servitization is social proof that servitization is acceptable or important.

Small wins

What is the best way to motivate employees to do new, innovative behaviors? According to Weick (1984) and Amabile and Kramer (2011), help them take a step forward, albeit a small step, every day. In an analysis of knowledge workers' diaries, Amabile and Kramer found that nothing contributed more to success in adopting new behaviors as making steps of progress, however small they might be. Small steps of progress are associated with experiences of fulfillment, enjoyment, and stimulation and build intrinsic motivation. Therefore, facilitating employees making small wins in transformation projects will perpetuate the change.

Compare this with the typical way of transforming an organization to become servitized: it usually focuses on a big and distant future vision where lucrative financial gains await. Such visions fit well with System II, but the opposite is required for System I. To get employees committed requires small steps that can be accomplished within a short time.

Weick (1984) defined small wins as fulfilling activities and goals that appear within reach, and are perceived as meaningful and will create motivation and thereby pave the way for further engagement in such activities. Imagine eating an elephant; you'd need to take it in small pieces over a long period of time. Servitization is an elephant. System II thinking leads to trying to eat the elephant too fast, in too big pieces. Instead, it takes time and persistence to move a firm from a product mindset to a mindset where the mission of the company is to solve the customers' problems.

Companies that succeed in implementing servitization do it step by step. A recipe for failure is to set up a grand servitization project coupled with a distant vision and to hope for the best. Successful companies like the gas manufacturing company AGA, within the Linde Group, instead take on servitization in smaller pieces. New service innovations emerge from specific customer problems that are solved one by one. A successful solution (a small win) is then analyzed by the so-called application engineers to generalize the solution into a generic service offered to many other customers. The advantages of this method are many: one small project is easier to survey, and is much less costly for the company.

Any success that follows can subsequently be spread to the rest of the organization (via labeling and social proof). By doing this, AGA continuously learns more and more about the customer use side of the business, in small steps, and then capitalizes on the knowledge by turning it into new service offerings. Servitization at AGA is thus in progress every day by solving customer's problems; that is, servitization via small wins.

Using the Five Techniques in Change Projects

This chapter focused on the organizational change of servitization; however, these five psychological techniques are worth applying in any situation where an organization is moving from A to B (such as by employing a new business model or making a switch from a hierarchic to a flat organization), not only in situations related to servitization. Whenever change is needed, and change is hard to accomplish, employees need more than a map that informs rationally about how the change may look; they need techniques that can aid in starting and perpetuating new employee behaviors toward the goal. We have illustrated five such techniques, observed in cases collected from the Swedish manufacturing industry: two techniques that help start the change process, and three techniques that aid in perpetuating the change.

What is unique and interesting about the techniques applied here is that they are not mentioned in rational models of how industrial organizations should servitize. Change is often difficult, and merely pointing out a goal that sounds fantastic is usually not enough. Well-informed planning, strategy documents, and spreadsheets with financial estimates will create knowledge about the change but won't necessarily lead to the change. Psychological techniques that guide the irrational and emotional System I thinking of Kahneman are also needed. Many research articles on servitization presuppose that change processes are all about pointing out the ideal end state. Unfortunately, history tells us that change is more troublesome than that, and that both System II and System I thinking need to be considered for true change to happen.

References

Amabile, T. and Kramer, S. (2011). *The Progress Principle: Using Small Wins to Ignite Joy, Engagement, and Creativity at Work*. Harvard Business Press.

Brown, S. W., Gustafsson, A., and Witell, L. (2009). Beyond products. *Wall Street Journal*, **253**(144), R7.

Cialdini, R. B. (2007). *Influence: The Psychology of Persuasion*. New York: Collins.

Gebauer, H., Gustafsson, A., and Witell, L. (2011). Competitive advantage through service differentiation by manufacturing companies. *Journal of Business Research*, **64**(12), 1270–1280.

Heath, C. and Heath, D. (2010). *Switch: How to Change When Change is Hard.* New York: Broadway Books.

Hertenstein, J. H., Platt, M. B., and Veryzer, R. W. (2005). The impact of industrial design effectiveness on corporate financial performance. *Journal of Product Innovation Management,* **22**, 3–21.

Kahneman, D. (2011). *Thinking, Fast and Slow* (1st ed.). New York: Farrar, Straus and Giroux.

Kotter, J. P. (2008). A sense of urgency. Boston: Harvard Business Press.

Mathieu, V. (2001). Service strategies within the manufacturing sector: Benefits, costs and partnership. *International Journal of Service Industry Management,* **12**(5), 451.

Nunes, J. C. and Drèze, X. (2006). Your loyalty program is betraying you. *Harvard Business Review,* **84**(4), 124.

Neu, W. A. and Brown, S. W. (2005). Forming successful business-to-business services in goods-dominant firms. *Journal of Service Research,* **8**(1), 3–17.

Oliva, R. and Kallenberg, R. (2003). Managing the transition from products to services. *International Journal of Service Industry Management,* **14**(2), 160–172.

Ostrom, A. L., Parasuraman, A., Bowen, D. E., Patricio, L., and Voss, C. A. (2015). Service research priorities in a rapidly changing context. *Journal of Service Research,* **18**(2), 127–159.

Pink, D. H. (2013). *To Sell is Human: The Surprising Truth About Moving Others.* New York: Penguin.

Tybout, A. M. and Yalch, R. F. (1980). The effect of experience: A matter of salience? *Journal of Consumer Research,* **6**(4), 406–413.

Ulaga, W. and Reinartz, W. J. (2011). Hybrid offerings: How manufacturing firms combine goods and services successfully. *Journal of Marketing,* **75**(6), 5–23.

Vandermerwe, S. and Rada, J. (1989). Servitization of business: Adding value by adding services. *European Management Journal,* **6**(4), 314–324.

Vargo, L. S. and Lusch, F. R. (2004). Evolving to a new dominant logic for marketing. *Journal of Marketing,* **68**(January), 1–17.

Volvo Technology Corporation (2010). *Process Description Service — Global Development Process S-GDP.* Göteborg: AB Volvo.

Weick, K. E. (1984). Small wins: Redefining the scale of social problems. *American Psychologist,* **39**(1), 40.

Chapter 10

Unveiling the Hidden Aspects of Service Innovation: Using Eye Tracking to Understand and Enhance Customer Experience

Wästlund Erik, Shams Poja, Otterbring Tobias*
and Matos Ricardo[†]

Service Research Center, Karlstad University, Sweden
[†]*Head of Training Programs, Tobii Pro, Sweden*

Key takeaways

1. This chapter furthers the understanding of how novel technology can be used in service innovation.
2. The chapter provides a new model — the 3S model — for studying the retail servicescape.
3. Customers' value creation process can be understood by means of novel technology such as eye tracking. In order to understand and enhance the customer experience of the retail servicescape, the servicescape should be looked at through the lens of the three levels of the 3S model: Store, Shelf, and Stock.

4. This is a retrospective chapter building on the results of seven experimental studies.
5. Those interested in this chapter may also find Chapters 7 and 9 interesting.

Introduction

Service innovation is a broad term used to explain many facets of the innovation process within a service firm. One dimension of service innovation is service experience, which represents the customer's interaction between the senses, mind, and environment, including other customers and employees, that together form the holistic impression of the service offering (Martin *et al.*, 2016; Verhoef *et al.*, 2009). Managing the service experience involves creating a sensory impression (Schmitt, 2003) and enhancing its holistic evaluation (Lam, 2001). Service experience is a process rather than an outcome (Grönroos, 1998; Yang *et al.*, 2012); consequently, scholars have argued that the focus should lie on the service process rather than the outcome of the service performance (Bolton *et al.*, 2014).

Thus, to fully understand the service experience, researchers have advocated to adopting tools that explore the service process. Novel technology such as eye tracking is one way to capture users' experiences in service innovation research. By capturing user experiences, it is possible to better understand users' value creation processes. The aim of this chapter, then, is to show how such technology can shed light on customers' experiences and decision making, and how it enhances the understanding of customers' value creation processes by unveiling the hidden aspects of service innovation.

To achieve this goal, we first delineate the importance of studying the process underlying customers' service experiences in the retail servicescape (cf. Bitner, 1992) and the necessity of including new technological tools in order to understand the decision-making processes underlying customers' service experiences. Next, we introduce a new conceptual model comprising three units of analysis for studying the retail servicescape, hereinafter referred to as the 3S model, with its components of

Store, Shelf, and Stock. This is followed by a retrospective approach on several published eye-tracking studies, which are looked at through the lens of the 3S model. We conclude the chapter by elucidating how eye tracking can be used in service research generally and in service innovation specifically.

Studying the Retail Servicescape from a Process Perspective

The process perspective of consumer decision making stems from behavioral decision theory, wherein consumers are thought of as satisficers rather than maximizers. Hence, consumers do not necessarily search for all available alternatives, but choose the alternative that exceeds a certain level of payoff (Simon, 1955). The payoff is dynamically influenced by processed information, such as stimuli in the surrounding environment. It is important to emphasize that the process perspective applies to complex decision making (Svenson, 1996), which can result from consumers' bounded cognitive capacity and be amplified by factors such as time pressure, level of experience, and the number of available alternatives (Payne *et al.*, 1992). When there are many alternatives, the decision process is divided into stages that screen for acceptable alternatives that can be evaluated in more detail. The initial stage is described as fast, crude, holistic, and parallel, while the subsequent stage is deliberate, attentive, detailed, and sequential (cf. Evans, 2008).

Process tracing has been advocated by researchers in the past as the decision outcome is not sufficient for understanding consumer decision making (Lohse and Johnson, 1996; Payne, 1976). Specifically, the use of eye movements in decision making has been advocated (Bettman *et al.*, 1998; Russo, 2011). When looking at the customer journey, we can position it in a process perspective, since the experience is constructed in the decision-making process (Verhoef *et al.*, 2009). In fact, the process perspective has been highlighted as an important perspective in customer experience research and as fundamental in understanding the customer journey (Lemon and Verhoef, 2016). It is within the process perspective that process tracing tools such as eye-tracking methodology are applicable, to get insights into the underlying experience during interactions with touchpoints, as visual attention is central to most forms of decision making (Russo, 2011). Hence, visual attention gives insight into the processed information and its influence on customers' service experience throughout the customer journey, and captures the customer's sequence of eye movements, and the factors that are influential in this process, from the first interaction to actual purchase or choice behavior (Russo, 2011; Wedel and Pieters, 2008).

In the past few years, there have been many advances in eye-tracking technology. There are several techniques for measuring eye movements, but the most common procedure is through video-based, combined-pupil/corneal reflection systems (Holmqvist *et al.*, 2011). Corneal reflection is created by infrared light and is measured relative to the location of the pupil center. Two types of equipment are used in the eye-tracking studies included in this chapter: the Tobii remote and Tobii mobile systems, produced by Tobii Technology. The remote system is used in lab-based studies, and the mobile system is used in field studies.

Many different eye-tracking measures can be extracted and analyzed. Eye movements can generally be divided between (1) eye movements toward and (2) eye position at a specific area of interest (AOI). Eye position measures are defined when the eyes rest for a short moment and visual information is gathered; this is known as a fixation (Holmqvist *et al.*, 2011; Rayner, 2008). The measures used in the studies in this chapter all originate from fixations that are aggregated in different ways. Time-to-first-fixation is the time it takes from stimulus onset until a specific AOI receives its first fixation. This measure shows the order of visual impact between different AOIs, expressed in time. Fixation count is the number of dwells within a specific AOI. Fixation count is either positively correlated with semantic importance (Henderson *et al.*, 1999) or negatively correlated with search efficiency (Goldberg and Kotval, 1999). Observation duration is one of the most important measures used in eye-tracking studies. The measure is defined as the aggregation of fixation duration within an AOI. Observation duration is a good indicator of consideration and choice in the context of point-of-purchase decision making as the chosen options have traveled furthest in the decision-making process, and hence aggregated the most attention.

The 3S Model

Lemon and Verhoef (2016) suggest that service experience includes the search, purchase, consumption, and after-sale phases. Hence, the perception of the product is influenced throughout the whole consumption process. The present research focuses on what customers perceive during the in-store shopping phase. One way to look at the in-store experience is through the servicescape lens (Bitner, 1992). The servicescape is a conceptualization of the impact that the physical surroundings of the service setting have on customers and employees. In the retail environment, this means that the store is filled with environmental cues that influence the cognitive and emotional dimensions of the customer, and that these cues influence perceived quality, satisfaction, and loyalty toward the retailer (Baker *et al.*, 2002).

A regular store visit can be viewed as a customer journey through the servicescape and its various touchpoints. According to Sorensen (2009), this journey can be divided into navigation and purchase consideration. In general, customers spend approximately 80% of their time navigating through the store and 20% considering purchases. However, Sorensen's dichotomization of the in-store journey fails to capture the different layers of the servicescape and their impact on the customer decision-making process. Therefore, there is a need for an elaborated and more nuanced view of the various segments constituting the in-store customer journey in order to fully understand the experience of the retail servicescape.

The 3S Levels Summarized: Stock, Shelf, and Store

The vast majority of all buying decisions are made at the point of purchase (POPAI, 1996). At the most fine-grained level, customers perceive visual elements such as brand logos, pictures, and verbal content on product packaging (Pilditch, 1961). Consistent with the terminology of inventory management in which a stock keeping unit (SKU) denotes a specific product for sale, we refer to this as the Stock level of the 3S model.

Taking a step back and looking up from the specific products reveals that stock units are not isolated entities but are rather part of a larger and more complex environment. Point-of-purchase material, brand displays, number of facings, and shelf placement all influence customers' attention and purchase decisions. Hence, in order to fully comprehend the customer decision-making process, it is necessary to also view a given stock unit in its natural habitat (that is, the context of the retail servicescape). We therefore treat the Shelf as the second level of analysis in the 3S model.

Zooming out even further, shelves are part of a larger servicescape consisting of everything in the entire retail environment. Although shelves and SKUs are parts of the entire retail environment, the focus of this level of analysis, the Store level, is to illuminate the customer's experiences of the servicescape while moving around in the store. The store level thus resembles the navigational phase described by Sorensen (2009); however, in addition to navigation, this level also includes aspects such as information acquisition, in-store search behavior, and resource depletion.

In what follows, we show how retailers can increase attention toward important areas of the servicescape with practices that involve changes at the Store, Shelf, and Stock levels of the 3S model. The overarching goal of this approach is to create decision support for customers and help them reach their goals during their multi-sensory journeys through the retail servicescape.

Stock

Product packaging is an influential tool in capturing customer attention (Berkowitz, 1987; Bloch, 1995) and communicating value (Page and Hen, 2002). Packaging that captures attention also facilitates quick in-store decision making (Silayoi and Speece, 2004). Customers choose with their eyes, which means that unseen products are unsold products (Clement, 2007). Textual and pictorial cues have been recognized as important in influencing perception. Pictorial elements are central for capturing and retaining customer attention (Childers and Houston, 1984; Pieters and Wedel, 2004; Underwood *et al.*, 2001), and textual elements have a large impact on customers' choices (Pieters and Wedel, 2004).

In the following studies, we describe how packaging cues can affect customers' visual attention and how the use of eye tracking has added deeper insights in how cue information influences customers' decision-making processes.

Even though the vast majority of purchase decisions are made at the point of purchase, customers enter the store with the goal of fulfilling a need. Goal specificity might range from very broad goals, such as satisfying a general desire, like thirst, to very specific goals, such as acquiring a particular product of a certain brand. In the former case, goal completion includes searching for possible options and evaluating them to find the best one. In the latter case, goal completion is solely the result of a successful search activity leading up to identification of the desired product. The ease with which a specific product can be found has been described as its findability. Thus, from a customer's point of view, findability is all about goal achievement. From a brand-owner's perspective, findability is about mitigating the apparent risk that a customer who is in search of a specific product or a product with a specific quality will find and choose a competing brand before finding the brand-owner's product, or will pick up the wrong product within the brand-owner's product line.

In our study, "Consumer perception at point of purchase: Evaluating proposed package designs in an eye-tracking lab" (Wästlund *et al.*, 2010), we compared four products (three new plus the current design) with a product from the same brand that the compared products where often confused with. The objective of the study was to investigate which, if any, of the four designs best conveyed a specific quality sought after by the customers. The 22 participants were ordinary customers visiting a shopping mall. 45% of the participants said that they occasionally picked up the wrong package when they were shopping. The study was a eye-traking based reaction-time experiment where the participants were shown four packages on a screen. One of the packages featured a new design and the remaining three packages featured the original design, and participants were instructed to click on the new one as fast as they could. This was repeated 16 times so that each of the four products appeared in each of the four possible positions. The packages were then compared in regards to the average response time and attention pattern, hence enabling a deeper understanding of both the process and the performance-based aspects of the designs.

From a performance-based perspective, it was clear that one of the three new designs was much easier to find than the others. Looking at the process, it was clear that most of the attention was focused on the design element conveying the desired quality. The other two new designs performed worse than the original design. From an attentional point of view, it was clear that these two new designs performed poorly, either because attention was focused on a design element not conveying the desired quality or because attention was scattered all over the packaging.

The results of this study clearly show that small changes to the packaging design can increase or decrease the findability of a product. From a customer's perspective, this can be the difference between easily finding the desired product or spending considerable time searching for it.

The question of how the design of packaging influences findability, customer judgment, and decision making is also the central theme of our study, "Left isn't always right: Placement of pictorial and textual package elements" (Otterbring *et al.*, 2013). However, unlike the previously described study, where the focus was the discrimination between a sought-after target product and several similar non-target products, the aim of this study was to investigate how the placement of design elements on packaging affects detection time.

The importance of packaging design for customer decision making has been highlighted by many (for example, Rettie and Brewer, 2000; Silayoi and Speece, 2007; Underwood and Klein, 2002), and packaging has been described as a silent salesman (Pilditch, 1973). Despite the importance of packaging design for facilitating both attention and information distribution at the point of purchase, there is a surprising lack of research examining how the placement of various packaging elements influences customers' visual attention toward the specific package and its respective elements. Previous research has rather focused on recall of design elements (Rettie and Brewer, 2000), overall packaging evaluation (Silayoi and Speece, 2007), and aesthetic appeal (Deng and Kahn, 2009; Levy, 1976), but none has, to our knowledge, focused on how the placement of design elements influences customers' visual attention toward such elements.

To measure the attentive effects of placement of pictorial and textual design elements, we conducted a between-subjects eye-tracking experiment, where the stimulus product was a snack package of potato chips that we had modified in six different ways. Two versions of the package contained a pictorial element (a clover symbol) placed in the top corner of the package, on the left- or right-hand side depending on the specific experimental condition. The remaining four versions contained textual elements (the text "New" or the text "Win 100 000"), again located in the top corner on either the left- or right-hand side of the package. The 199 participants were randomly shown one package and were instructed to look freely at the image while being informed that they would receive questions afterward.

Analyzing the time it took for participants to detect the packaging element in question revealed that both textual elements were detected faster when they were placed on the left-hand side of the package, whereas the pictorial element was detected faster when it was placed on the right-hand side. Furthermore, apart from influencing detection time, a larger number of participants were able to notice the packaging element in question within the time limit of 7.0 seconds when exposed to this element organization (text left, or picture right) rather than the complementary layout (text right, or picture left). This suggests that a suboptimal element organization may make important design elements on packaging virtually invisible, with customers taking a longer time to detect them and being less likely to look at them at all.

These results pinpoint the importance of a proper placement of design elements on packaging, as placement clearly affects the time it takes for customers to actually view the elements. Taken together with the study on findability, the joint takeaway message is that packaging design plays a crucial role in creating the opportunity for customers to make fast decisions, which is typically how decisions are made in various retail settings. Additionally, given that the element organization that facilitated detection time is congruent with a layout that has been found to increase evaluations of aesthetical appeal (Levy, 1976; Deng and Kahn, 2009; Silayoi and Speece, 2007), it is possible that a proper packaging design, with elements organized to maximize detection, may both enhance information acquisition and lead to more favorable packaging evaluations. Indeed, theories of processing fluency indicate that stimuli that are more fluently processed tend to be evaluated more positively, with downstream effects on customers' purchase decisions and choice behavior (for example, Novemsky *et al.*, 2007; Winkielman *et al.*, 2003).

The focus of both the aforementioned studies is the parts and design elements of packaging and their effect on customers' overt attentive process. Unlike this approach, our study "Unsold is unseen ... or is it? Examining the role of peripheral vision in the consumer choice process using eye-tracking methodology" (Wästlund *et al.*, 2018) emphasizes the whole product/packaging in order to investigate the customer's reliance of peripheral vision — or covert attention — during the decision-making process. Previous research has shown that approximately half of all products in a product category are observed at least once (Sorensen, 2009). Put differently, this means that the other half is not observed at all. However, it is unclear if not being directly observed is the same as not being processed in any way by the customer. Therefore, in a series of experiments conducted both in an eye-tracking lab and in a retail store, we investigated to what extent products can be excluded from consideration without being directly looked at.

The lab-based experiments were all designed to investigate whether or not participants could discriminate between target and non-target visual objects without looking directly at them. All stimuli consisted of an equal amount of target and non-target geometric objects, such as circles and triangles. Participants were asked to count one of the two types of objects while their eye movements were recorded. The question was if participants would be able to correctly count target objects without looking at the non-targets. A total of 101 students participated in the experiments. The results showed that irrespective of target type (circles or triangles), participants were able to count the targets without having to look at the non-targets. Although counting circles and triangles might seem like a long way from the shopping aisle, these results show that it is possible to exclude objects from consideration without directly observing them.

In order to validate the findings from the lab, we conducted a field experiment at a grocery store. Fifty-six ordinary customers where equipped with Tobii Glasses (a head-mounted eye-tracking system similar to a regular pair of glasses) and were given a short shopping list of products that they were instructed to select as if they were buying the products for themselves. One of the sought-for products was sandwich meat, which participants were able to pick up from two different shelves: one containing two brands of sandwich meats (in equal proportions), and the other containing sandwich meat on one side and assorted pickles on the other side (70% sandwich meat). In order to investigate the reliance on peripheral vision during the choice process, the gaze pattern of the participants was analyzed in a similar way as in the preceding lab-based study. At the shelf with the assorted pickles, sandwich meat was treated as the target. At the shelf containing two brands of sandwich meat, the brand that a customer ultimately chose was viewed as the target. The results of the analysis showed that irrespective of which shelf the participants chose from, the vast majority of observations of individual products fell on the target, thus mirroring the findings on circles and triangles. These results suggest that, rather than being overlooked, products that are not directly looked at might be selectively ignored based on the lack of interesting features they convey.

Taken together, the three papers presented above demonstrate the importance of investigating the impact of variations in the Stock level on the retail service experience. The results illustrate how packaging design influences the findability of a specific product as well as how easily a product conveys specific qualities. The reliance on peripheral vision shown in the research further accentuates the importance of product design, as uninteresting products are rarely viewed. Thus, to facilitate the decision-making process and create a positive service experience, the Stock level of analysis should be taken into account.

Shelf

As mentioned in the previous section, product packaging influences customer decision making. Nevertheless, the product is rarely unaccompanied by competitors in the shelf display; thus, factors such as category structure (Nedungadi *et al.*, 2001) also influence customers' attention and choice. Category structure influences customers because products at certain placements on the shelf can have a perceptual advantage (for example, an eye-level position grabs attention). Chandon *et al.* (2008) showed that almost all customers saw brands in the center of the shelf and that the likelihood of noticing a brand at shelf extremities was low. This result can be explained by the natural resting position of the eyes (Dréze *et al.*, 1994). In fact, previous research has identified a central fixation or center bias (Foulsham and Underwood, 2008; Parkhurst *et al.*, 2002) that can explain this effect.

Furthermore, customers make many product evaluation inferences during the decision-making process, and these inferential beliefs also influence the decision outcome (Huber and McCann, 1982). Product placement can influence customers if the products at certain placements have a conceptual resulting in inferred value. Customers use several decision strategies from which they infer value, and the placement of products can be one such inference point (Buchanan *et al.*, 1999). For instance, it has been observed that verticality is used to infer value. Meier and Robinson (2004) showed that objects that are high in the visual space are perceived as good, whereas objects that are low in the visual space are perceived as bad. Valenzuela and Raghubir (2010) showed that customers make value inferences based on shelf verticality, as products on the bottom were assumed to be priced lower than products on the top shelf. Hence, previous research indicates that value can be inferred from vertical object positioning.

In the following two studies, we describe how eye-tracking technology can reveal new insights pertaining to which factors may influence customers when they stand in front of the shelf.

In the study, "The influence of shelf space position on consumer decision-making: A process tracing study of consumer visual attention" (Shams, 2013), we explored this question in depth to get deeper insight into how perception of shelf space allocation influences product search during decision making. Specifically, the paper explores (1) how beliefs about spatial positioning influence the visual search for alternatives, and (2) how incongruence between actual spatial positioning and beliefs about spatial positioning influences visual search. These factors were tested by switching the shelf locations of the top and bottom sections of products and giving participants instructions to purchase premium or value products while measuring their eye movements using the Tobii remote eye-tracking system. After the eye-tracking calibration procedure, we showed the participants two shelves and asked them to choose premium or value products, depending on their random assignment into one of four groups with the combination of shelf congruency (congruent or incongruent) and task (premium or value).

Two separate lab experiments with 256 participants showed that spatial positioning beliefs influence visual attention, as customers looked at the expected positions rather than the actual positions. Hence, customer beliefs about spatial positioning not only influence judgment, but fundamentally influence customers' decision-making process at the point of purchase. Spatial positioning was related to value perception; customers' visual attention was influenced by beliefs about the inherent value of different positions on the shelf. An incongruence between customers' beliefs and actual positioning disturbed the decision-making process and increased the search effort during choice. Customers' vertical positioning beliefs were applied early in decision making and presumably used to simplify the decision by reducing the search effort. Hence, we believe that verticality guides the search for information in the decision-making process similar to a heuristic process. The results clarify the role of the product shelf structure as a touchpoint in the customer journey. Customer expectations are based on previous experiences that influence the decision process. When the expectations are not met, the customer becomes confused, and the cognitive effort in the process increases.

Our article, "Vision (im) possible: The effects of in-store signage on customers' visual attention" (Otterbring *et al.*, 2014) was, to our knowledge, among the first to investigate customers' visual attention by means of eye-tracking methodology in the real retail servicescape. Specifically, using the Tobii Glasses, we examined how customers use in-store signage during navigation and decision making, and how exposure to signage material influences their subsequent visual attention when standing in front of a supermarket shelf. In one of the studies (Otterbring *et al.*, 2014; Experiment 2), a total of 74 customers volunteered to participate in an in-store experiment to investigate customers' visual attention and choice behavior. After calibrating the eye-tracking equipment, we started recording customers' visual attention, and a research assistant asked each customer, incidentally, whether he or she could see an in-store sign featuring a cereal product, while pointing in the direction of the sign. The assistant then explained that the shelves behind the sign were filled with cereals, and the customer's task was to select one of the cereal products he or she could consider buying that day and pick it up.

Depending on the randomly assigned experimental condition, some customers viewed an in-store sign featuring one cereal product, while other customers viewed an in-store sign featuring another similar cereal product of the same brand and size, with a similar price. Both these products were also available on the shelves behind the in-store sign, and the primary purpose was to examine whether the specific product that customers had been perceptually primed by the in-store sign and if this could influence how quickly and frequently they looked at this particular product when later standing in front of the shelves, compared to the non-primed reference product.

The results revealed that, regardless of which specific product was used to prime the customer, customers detected the priming product significantly more quickly than the comparable reference product. In fact, customers having their first eye fixation on the priming product, before the reference product, was almost twice as likely compared to the other way around. Moreover, customers also had a significantly larger number of observations of the priming product relative to the reference product, meaning that both detection and the total amount of visual attention were positively influenced by the signage content. In addition, customers generally looked at an extremely limited number of all the products available on the shelves. Even in the case of the primed products, the average number of observations was just above one, thus clearly indicating that (1) customers only look at a narrow subset of products on a supermarket shelf, and (2) the inclusion of products in this subset can be effectively influenced by what the customers are previously exposed to in the retail servicescape.

Store

The structure of the store and use of information elements within it has the capability to influence behavior radically. The store environment can either hinder goal fulfillment or assist in the journey depending on how the environment is structured, and thus the store layout interplays with the customer's current and previous experiences, such as familiarity with a particular store setting and needs and shopping goals.

Customers can have planned goals that they bring to the store, but there are also goals that are activated during the shopping trip. Planned purchases are the result of shopping goals that stem from needs that are recognized before a visit to the store (Bucklin and Lattin, 1991), whereas unplanned purchases are the result of shopping goals that stem from needs that were unrecognized before the shopping event (Park *et al.*, 1989). The store environment has different functions in assisting the customer, depending on if the goals are planned or unplanned. If customers know what they are looking for before entering the store, the goal is to search for a specific target, or something recognized as a solution to a current need. This should be easier than the more complex problem-solving process of setting goals and evaluating possible solutions at the same time.

In the following studies, we look at two important aspects of this journey: first, the bulk of the journey, which consists of navigation, and further, how the point of purchase relates to customers' shopping goals.

The impact of customers' predefined shopping goals and in-store experiences on their shopping behavior is the topic of our paper, "Heuristics and resource depletion: Eye-tracking customers' *in situ* gaze behavior in the field" (Wästlund *et al.*, 2015). In three different contexts, we investigated how customers' goals when entering a store influenced their gaze behavior during the store visit.

We investigated first the effect of shopping goals on the number of products observed and second how completion of the first goal influenced the number of products observed during subsequent choices. All in all, 354 ordinary customers at three different stores used mobile eye trackers during a store visit. In the first study, we asked customers filling up their cars' gas tanks if they were about to enter the gas station to buy something and, if so, whether they would be willing to wear the mobile eye-tracking equipment while shopping in the gas-station store. Customers who paid by card at the pump were thus excluded from the study. We then compared the gaze patterns between customers with different levels of preplanned goals. The results showed a clear effect of level of planning on customers' gaze patterns, where customers with a specific goal observed much less of the store stimuli compared to customers with more abstract goals.

In the following two experiments, which were conducted in a grocery store and a sporting goods store, we again compared how shopping goals could impact gaze patterns while choosing products at a shelf and how such shopping goals, in turn, could influence customers' gaze patterns during subsequent choices. This was done by giving customers different purchasing goals that they were asked to complete as if the goals were their own. Again, the results showed that the level of goal complexity influenced the distribution of visual attention. Complexity of the first shopping task also affected the subsequent shopping task. Our interpretation of this effect is that the level of complexity of a goal leads to different degrees of resource depletion (Bruyneel *et al.*, 2006), with depleted customers being more inclined to use simpler heuristics during subsequent decision making (Gigerenzer and Gaissmaier, 2011).

Overall, these field experiments show that (1) the complexity of the shopping goal influences the distribution of visual attention, and (2) higher levels of complexity of the initial goal deplete resources, which, in turn, diminishes visual attention during subsequent choices. From a service experience perspective, these results highlight the importance of creating a servicescape that facilitates the customer's completion of shopping goals.

Another in-store activity that can be more or less depleting is locating the various products one is looking for. Our article, "Eye-tracking customers' visual attention in the wild: Dynamic gaze behavior moderates the effect of store familiarity on navigational fluency" (Otterbring *et al.*, 2016), was an attempt to study which factors influence customers' navigational ease while in a store. More precisely, we investigated whether customers can compensate for lacking store familiarity by adopting a more widely distributed viewing pattern, and hence examined if dynamic gaze behavior would influence customers' navigational ease differently, depending on their familiarity with the particular store.

A total of 100 customers participated in the study, which was conducted in a grocery store using a quasi-experimental design. The customers received a shopping list, identical for all customers, and were asked to pick up the products on the list as a fill-in shopping trip for these items (for example, bread, tomatoes). This shopping list procedure was used to increase the likelihood that participants would take roughly the same path around the store. After calibrating the head-mounted eye-tracking system (Tobii Glasses), we started recording the customers' visual attention and instructed them to start their shopping trip for the list items. During this task, participants might pass 16 digital signs located close to the products on the list, and their visual attention toward the digital signs was used as a proxy for dynamic gaze behavior, since customers tend to rely on signage material to form initial impressions of the retail servicescape and facilitate navigation (Bitner, 1992; O'Neill, 1991; Otterbring *et al.*, 2016). After completing the shopping task, the customers completed a brief survey with measures of the navigational ease of the store and their level of familiarity with the store.

The results showed that both store familiarity and dynamic gaze behavior positively influenced customers' navigational ease; however, the effect that store familiarity had on navigational ease was moderated by customers' levels of dynamic gaze behavior. Among customers who were unfamiliar with the store, a higher level of dynamic gaze behavior had a significant positive effect on navigational ease. Customers who were familiar with the store found it equally easy to navigate, regardless of their levels of dynamic gaze behavior. From a practical point of view, these findings indicate that retail managers should strive to enhance in-store navigation in the retail servicescape, as such facilitated navigational efforts may not only induce higher levels of liking and lead to more favorable in-store evaluations but may also have downstream effects on customers' actual purchase behavior (reviewed in Otterbring *et al.*, 2016).

Despite this seemingly self-evident claim, that enhanced in-store navigation should produce positive customer outcomes, consultants sometimes recommend that retail managers complicate the navigational aspects of the customer journey by forcing customers to look at a larger number of products in their search process, under the assumption that this will increase impulse purchases. However, in light of research demonstrating that difficulties associated with in-store navigation have costly consequences ranging from confusion, irritation, and frustration to stress, dissatisfaction, and patronage withdrawal (reviewed in Otterbring *et al.*, 2016), our conclusion is that enhanced in-store navigation should reasonably be regarded more as pleasure than pain, both from the customer's and the retailer's viewpoints.

Conclusion

In this chapter, we have taken a retrospective look at our research and summarized it from a customer experience and value creation point of view in order to unveil the hidden aspects of service innovation. In our 3S model, we lay the foundation of understanding customer experience at three distinct levels of analysis by means of novel technology: we show how eye tracking, and a focus on the decision-making process at the Stock, Shelf, and Store levels, can be used as a method to increase understanding of the customer journey from a process perspective, while simultaneously providing retail managers with advice as how to develop a store environment that facilitates and simplifies customers' value creation.

As pointed out by Lemon and Verhoef (2016), the customer journey and the service experience begin before the customer enters the store. In line with this assumption, our findings show that customers' pre-defined shopping goals and store familiarity influence their gaze behavior during the store visit. By means of mobile eye tracking, we have seen how customers with specific goals hone in on their targets while ignoring as much as possible of the remaining surroundings. This is true for both shelves containing non-target products and in-store marketing materials. However, it is noteworthy that customers who do not know the location of their target products utilize in-store marketing material as navigational cues. From a Store level perspective, it is thus necessary to facilitate customers' swift in-store navigation and ability to easily complete their goals. Successful design of the retail servicescape will enable customers to achieve their goals with minimal effort. Failing to do so will leave customers more cognitively depleted as they complete their shopping tasks.

In addition to pre-defined goals, customers enter the store with a pre-conceived set of beliefs regarding product placement and pricing on the Shelf level. In our lab-based eye-tracking studies, we have seen that by utilizing these preconceived beliefs as shortcuts, customers try to simplify the search and consideration phases while choosing products from a shelf. A shelf layout organized according to these beliefs facilitates the product search. However, a shelf layout organized in a less congruent fashion impedes the product search. Another factor influencing gaze behavior at the Shelf level is point-of-purchase marketing material. Successfully promoted products receive more attention at the Shelf level.

Given that the vast majority of purchase decisions are made at the shelves (POPAI, 1996), it is important to note that even though attracting the attention of customers is a pre-condition for sales, attention is, in itself, not enough to create conversion. By investigating customers gaze patterns while they are actually making a product choice, eye tracking allows us to understand how various design elements influence customers' decision-making processes at the Stock level of the retail service experience. The results highlight the importance of the placement of packaging design elements in order to convey the intended message to customers considering various options, as well as to make it easy to find the product for those customers who know what they are looking for.

Our retrospective journey shows that in order to harness the power of service innovation in the retail servicescape, it is paramount to pay attention to all three levels of analysis of the 3S model. By doing so, it is possible to create a servicescape that increases customers' possibilities to easily achieve their goals and thus enhances the customer experience and value creation.

References

Baker, J., Parasuraman, A., Grewal, D., and Voss, G. B. (2002). The influence of multiple store environment cues on perceived merchandise value and patronage intentions. *Journal of Marketing*, **66**(2), 120–141.

Berkowitz, M. (1987). Product shape as a design innovation strategy. *Journal of Product Innovation Management*, **4**, 274–283.

Bettman, J. R., Luce, M. F., and Payne, J. W. (1998). Constructive consumer choice processes. *Journal of Consumer Research*, **25**(3), 187–217.

Bitner, M. J. (1992). Servicescapes: The impact of physical surroundings on customers and employees. *The Journal of Marketing*, **56**, 57–71.

Bloch, P. H. (1995). Seeking the ideal form: Product design and consumer response. *Journal of Marketing*, **59**, 16–29.

Bolton, R., Gustafsson, A., McColl-Kennedy, J., Sirianni, N. J., and Tse, D. K. (2014). Small details that make big differences: A radical approach to consumption experience as a firm's differentiating strategy. *Journal of Service Management*, **25**(2), 253–274.

Bruyneel, S., Dewitte, S., Vohs, D. K., and Warlop, L. (2006). Repeated choosing increases susceptibility to affective product features. *International Journal of Research in Marketing*, **32**(2), 215–225.

Buchanan, L., Simmons, C. J., and Bickart, B. A. (1999). Brand equity dilution: Retailer display and context brand effects. *Journal of Marketing Research (JMR)*, **36**(3), 345–355.

Bucklin, R. E. and Lattin, J. M. (1991). A two-state model of purchase incidence and brand choice. *Marketing Science*, **10**(1), 24–39.

Chandon, P. J., Hutchinson, W. J., Bradlow, E. T., and Young, S. H. (2008). Measuring the value of point-of-purchase marketing with commercial eye-tracking-data. In M. Wedel and R. Pieters (eds.), *Visual Marketing: From Attention to Action*, Chapter 10, (pp. 225–258). New York: Lawrence Erlbaum Associates.

Childers, T. L. and Houston, M. J. (1984). Conditions for a picture-superiority effect on consumer memory. *Journal of Consumer Research*, **11**(2), 643–654.

Clement, J. (2007). Visual influence on in-store buying decisions: An eye-track experiment on the visual influence of packaging design. *Journal of Marketing Management*, **23**(9), 917–928.

Deng, X. and Kahn, B. E. (2009). Is your product on the right side? The "location effect" on perceived product heaviness and package evaluation. *Journal of Marketing Research*, **46**(6), 725–738.

Dréze, X., Hoch, S. J., and Purk, M. E. (1994). Shelf management and space elasticity. *Journal of Retailing*, **70**(4), 301–326.

Evans, J. S. B. (2008). Dual-processing accounts of reasoning, judgment, and social cognition. *Annuual Review Psychology*, **59**, 255–278.

Foulsham, T. and Underwood, G. (2008). What can saliency models predict about eye movements? Spatial and sequential aspects of fixations during encoding and recognition. *Journal of Vision*, **8**(2), 1–17.

Gigerenzer, G. and Gaissmaier, W. (2011). Heuristic decision making. *Annual Review of Psychology*, **62**, 451–482.

Goldberg, J. H. and Kotval, X. P. (1999). Computer interface evaluation using eye movements: Methods and constructs. *International Journal of Industrial Ergonomics*, **24**(6), 631–645.

Grönroos, C. (1998). Marketing services: The case of a missing product. *Journal of Business and Industrial Marketing*, **13**(4/5), 322–338.

Henderson, J. M., Weeks, P. A., and Hollingworth, A. (1999). The effects of semantic consistency on eye movements during complex scene viewing.

Journal of Experimental Psychology: Human Perception and Performance, **25**(1), 210–228.

Holmqvist, K., Nyström, M., Andersson, R., Dewhurst, R., Jorodzka, H., and van de Weijer, J. (2011). *Eye Tracking: A Comprehensive Guide to Methods and Measures*. New York: Oxford University Press.

Huber, J. and McCann, J. (1982). The impact of inferential beliefs on product evaluations. *Journal of Marketing Research*, **19**(3), 324–333.

Lam, S. Y. (2001). The effects of store environment on shopping behaviors: A critical review. *Advances in Consumer Research*, **28**(1).

Lemon, K. N. and Verhoef, P. C. (2016). Understanding customer experience throughout the customer journey. *Journal of Marketing*, **80**(6), 69–96.

Levy, J. (1976). Lateral dominance and aesthetic preference. *Neuropsychologia*, **14**, 431–445.

Lohse, G. L. and Johnson, E. J. (1996). A comparison of two process tracing methods for choice tasks. *Organizational Behavior and Human Decision Processes*, **68**(1), 28–43.

Martin, D., Gustafsson, A., and Choi, S. (2016). Service innovation, renewal, and adoption/rejection in dynamic global contexts. *Journal of Business Research*, **69**(7), 2397–2400.

Meier, B. P. and Robinson, M. D. (2004). Why the sunny side is up — associations between affect and vertical position. *Psychological Science*, **15**(4), 243–247.

Nedungadi, P., Chattopadhyay, A., and Muthukrishnan, A. V. (2001). Category structure, brand recall, and choice. *International Journal of Research in Marketing*, **18**(3), 191–202.

Novemsky, N., Dhar, R., Schwarz, N., and Simonson, I. (2007). Preference fluency in choice. *Journal of Marketing Research*, **44**(3), 347–356.

O'Neill, M. J. (1991). Effects of signage and floor plan configuration on way-finding accuracy. *Environment and Behavior*, **23**(5), 553–574.

Otterbring, T., Shams, P., Wästlund, E., and Gustafsson, A. (2013). Left isn't always right: Placement of pictorial and textual package elements. *British Food Journal*, **115**(8), 1211–1225.

Otterbring, T., Wästlund, E., Gustafsson, A., and Shams, P. (2014). Vision (im)possible? The effects of in-store signage on customers' visual attention. *Journal of Retailing and Consumer Services*, **21**(5), 676–684.

Otterbring, T., Wästlund, E., and Gustafsson, A. (2016). Eye-tracking customers' visual attention in the wild: Dynamic gaze behavior moderates the effect of store familiarity on navigational fluency. *Journal of Retailing and Consumer Services*, **28**, 165–170.

Page, C. and Hen, P. M. (2002). An investigation of the processes by which product design and brand strength interact to determine initial affect and quality judgments. *Journal of Consumer Psychology*, **12**(2), 133–147.

Park, C. W., Iyer, E. S., and Smith, D. C. (1989). The effects of situational factors on in-store grocery shopping behavior: The role of store environment and time available for shopping. *Journal of Consumer Research*, **15**, 422–433.

Parkhurst, D., Law, K., and Niebur, E. (2002). Modeling the role of salience in the allocation of overt visual attention. *Vision Research*, **42**(1), 107–123.

Payne, J. W., Bettman, J. R., Coupey, E., and Johnson, E. J. (1992). A constructive process view of decision making: Multiple strategies in judgment and choice. *Acta Psychologica*, **80**(1–3), 107–141.

Payne, J. W. (1976). Task complexity and contingent processing in decision making: An information search and protocol analysis. *Organizational Behavior and Human Performance*, **16**(2), 366–387.

Pieters, R. and Wedel, M. (2004). Attention capture and transfer in advertising: Brand, pictorial, and text-size effects. *Journal of Marketing*, **68**(2), 36–50.

Pilditch, J. (1961). Packaging for profits: A perfectly sound product idea can be sidelined by attractive but impractical packaging. *American Demographics*, **33**.

Pilditch, J. (1973). *The Silent Salesman: How to Develop Packaging That Sells*. London: Business Books.

POPAI. (1996). Popai study: In-store decisions rule. *Discount Merchandiser*, **36**(3), 19.

Rayner, K. and Castelhano, M. S. (2008). Eye movements during reading, scene perception, visual search, and while looking at print advertisements. In M. Wedel and R. Pieters (eds.), *Visual Marketing: From Attention to Action*, Chapter 2, (pp. 9–42). New York: Lawrence Erlbaum Associates.

Rettie, R. and Brewer, C. (2000). The verbal and visual components of package design. *Journal of Product & Brand Management*, **9**(1), 56–70.

Russo, E. J. (2011). Eye fixations as a process trace. In M. Schulte-Mecklenbeck, A. Kühberger, & R. Ranyard (Eds.), *A Handbook of Process Tracing Methods for Decision Research: A Critical Review and User's Guide* (pp. 43–64). New York: Psychology Press.

Schmitt, B. H. (2003). *Customer Experience Management: A Revolutionary Approach to Connecting with Your Customers*. New York: The Free Press.

Shams, P. (2013). *What Does It Take to Get Your Attention? The Influence of In-Store and Out-Of-Store Factors on Visual Attention and Decision Making for Fast-Moving Consumer Goods.* Dissertation, Faculty of Economic Sciences, Communication, and IT, Karlstad University. Karlstad, Sweden: Karlstad University Studies 2013:5.

Silayoi, P. and Speece, M. (2004). Packaging and purchase decisions: An exploratory study on the impact of involvement level and time pressure. *British Food Journal*, **106**(8), 607–628.

Silayoi, P. and Speece, M. (2007). The importance of packaging attributes: A conjoint analysis approach. *European Journal of Marketing*, **41**(11–12), 1495–1517.

Simon, H. A. (1955). A behavioral model of rational choice. *The Quarterly Journal of Economics*, **69**(1), 99–118.

Sorensen, H. (2009). *Inside the Mind of the Shopper: The Science of Retailing.* New Jersey: Prentice Hall.

Svenson, O. (1996). Decision making and the search for fundamental psychological regularities: What can be learned from a process perspective? *Organizational Behavior and Human Decision Processes*, **65**(3), 252–267.

Underwood, R. L. and Klein, N. M. (2002). Packaging as brand communication: Effects of product pictures on consumer responses to the package and brand. *Journal of Marketing Theory and Practice*, **10**(4), 58–68.

Underwood, R. L., Klein, N. M., and Burke, R. R. (2001). Packaging communication: Attentional effects of product imagery. *Journal of Product & Brand Management*, **10**(7), 403–422.

Valenzuela, A. and Raghubir, P. (2010). Are consumers aware of top-bottom but not of left-right inferences? Implications for shelf space positions. Working Paper, Baruch College, City University of New York.

Verhoef, P. C., Lemon, K. N., Parasuraman, A., Roggeveen, A., Tsiros, M., and Schlesinger, L. A. (2009). Customer experience creation: Determinants, dynamics and management strategies. *Journal of Retailing*, **85**(1), 31–41.

Wästlund, E., Shams, P., Löfgren, M., Witell, L., and Gustafsson, A. (2010). Consumer perception at point of purchase: Evaluating proposed package designs in an eye-tracking lab. *Journal of Business and Retail Management Research*, **5**(1), 42–51.

Wästlund, E., Shams, P., and Otterbring, T. (2018). Unsold is unseen… or is it? Examining the role of peripheral vision in the consumer choice process using eye-tracking methodology. *Appetite*, **120**, 49–56.

Wästlund, E., Otterbring, T., Gustafsson, A., and Shams, P. (2015). Heuristics and resource depletion: Eye-tracking customers' *in situ* gaze behavior in the field. *Journal of Business Research*, **68**(1), 95–101.

Wedel, M. and Pieters, R. (2008). Introduction to visual marketing. In M. Wedel & R. Pieters (Eds.), *Visual Marketing: From Attention to Action*, Chapter 1, (pp. 1–8). New York: Lawrence Erlbaum Associates.

Winkielman, P., Schwarz, N., Fazendeiro, T., and Reber, R. (2003). The hedonic marking of processing fluency: Implications for evaluative judgment. In, Musch, J., and Klauer, K. C., The psychology of evaluation: Affective processes in cognition and emotion. Chapter 8, (pp. 189–217). Psychology Press.

Yang, S., Lu, Y., Gupta, S., Cao, Y., and Zhang, R. (2012). Mobile payment services adoption across time: An empirical study of the effects of behavioral beliefs, social influences, and personal traits. *Computers in Human Behavior*, **28**(1), 129–142.

Chapter 11

Values-Driven Service Innovation for Transformational Change

Samuel Petros Sebhatu and Bo Enquist

Service Research Center — CTF, Karlstad University, Sweden

Key takeaways

1. In this chapter, we addressed the idea of a values-driven service innovation through sustainable business practices and service research for transformation, value co-creation, and sustainability/CSR practice to provide "sustainable service business" a broader meaning. There is a new reality for business and society.
2. This chapter builds upon the latest service and transformative change management research both theoretically and conceptually. It uses service research labeled as value creation through service, where service innovation and resource integration are two key elements, to interact with sustainable business practices, to find a broader meaning and to meet transformative change in the new globalized business landscape.
3. The chapter provides a new sustainable business practice described as "next practice" for value co-creation through service, which is

consistent with interactive research for business and managerial implications. It introduces values-driven service innovation, in which broader transformative and sustainability thinking brings ethical, social, and/or environmental dimensions into service innovation research.

4. The chapter fits the transformation agenda and the concepts of sustainability service innovation through sustainable business practices (BoP 3.0) to a more general model of next practice business to visualize this conceptual and empirical study. It is an interesting opportunity to make a link between transformative service research and sustainability/CSR in service research.

"Sustainable business" is a fuzzy term that implies that business is in some way sustainable, but in what way? Edvardsson and Enquist (2009) addressed values-based service for sustainable business and used IKEA for contextual understanding to study a values-based, driven global enterprise as a sustainable business. In this chapter, we use the concept of a sustainable business to assess and understand situations where sustainability is the key driver for innovation and transformation, embedded in the core values of the organization. The objective is built upon the latest service and transformative change management research, both theoretically and conceptually. We are using service research labeled as value creation through service, where service innovation and resource integration are two key elements, to interact with sustainable business practices and find a broader meaning, and to understand transformative change in the new globalized business landscape. The study presented in this chapter was also driven by innovation based on an organization's transformation agenda to co-create value and networking, and to secure engagement and the foundational values of the sustainable business. Nidumolu *et al.* (2009) has shown in an explorative way why sustainability can be seen as a key driver of innovation.

Base of the pyramid (BoP) was originally a way of thinking about and doing business with the poor. The most recent generation of BoP was presented in *Base of the Pyramid 3.0 — Sustainable Development through Innovation and Entrepreneurship* (Casado Cañeque and Hart, 2015), which addressed a shift from the first idea of selling to the poor to BoP 2.0 engaging the poor as stakeholders to 3.0 through a change of mindset, open innovation, an innovation ecosystem, cross-sector partnership, and sustainable development. Inspired by the aforementioned three stages of BoP, we suggest, in this chapter, an analogy with values-based thinking for the development of sustainable service innovation. The main aim is to assess and more deeply understand the values-driven service innovation of a sustainable service business, and which environmental and societal perspectives contribute to the innovation process in the supply chain with new thinking.

This chapter is explorative. It is built around four concepts: (1) values, (2) service innovation, (3) value co-creation, and (4) transformative service embedded in societal and environmental perspectives. The chapter will illustrate these concepts with a case study of an enterprise that reconfigured their engagement at the BoP by innovating to aid future entrepreneurs — the coffee company Löfbergs. Löfbergs' business model is embedded with the concept of "next practice" and innovative opportunities of sustainability and transformation. This chapter explores both the contextual and managerial sides of Löfbergs, where Löfbergs is seen as a values-driven family business (Enquist *et al.*, 2015) driven by practicing goodwill (Ericson, 2018) and by the climate change challenge, which is a driver for sustainability service innovation solutions, leading to transformational change in its business practices.

This chapter will contribute to developing managerial and social embeddedness in sustainability service innovation. Although several business models have already been designed for the general purpose of running a sustainable business, the "next practice" as a business model is not fully developed and studied. "Next practice" simply refers to a sustainable innovative future business model for cross-sector partnership by engaging entrepreneurs.

In this chapter, we assess this next practice concept by using the case of Löfbergs as a values-driven service innovation practice: (1) we explore Löfbergs' engagement with the next generation of coffee farmers, in sharing their daily problems both economic, social and ecological, which secures the future of the next generation of farmers and premium coffee and opposes the conventional relationship in the industry ("coffee as commodity"); and (2) we define a framework for how to work with sustainability service innovation by employing a multi-stakeholder approach.

Theoretical and Conceptual Framework

This study is driven by both the contextual and managerial sides of sustainable and innovative businesses, with the service research used as an open source for transdisciplinary research (Gustafsson *et al.*, 2016), where service innovation (Edvardsson and Enquist, 2011; Lusch and Vargo, 2014) and sustainability (Edvardsson and Enquist, 2009; Sebhatu, 2010, Enquist *et al.*, 2015; Casado Cañeque and Hart, 2015) will be the focus for transformation based on social and ecological challenges (Loorbach, 2010; Rockström and Klum, 2015; Enquist, 2016) in a dialectic way (Enquist *et al.*, 2015) based on a broader theoretical and conceptual framework, to meet a transformation agenda in practice and to explore and interpret a new meaning (Alvesson and Sköldberg, 2010; Nahser, 2013). It is important to reconceptualize and integrate these concepts in a holistic way to change the mindset (Loorbach, 2010; Rockström and Klum, 2015; Casado Cañeque and Hart, 2015) and better interact in the business landscape. Early on, Stiglitz (2006) described a need for transformation to handle the economic, social, and environmental challenges of globalization. Rockström and Klum (2015) argued that there is a window for transformation for prosperity growth, but this transformation has to be handled within planetary boundaries. These discussions and arguments outline a new partnership for innovation and transformation and a path for the transformation (Loorbach, 2010), which includes both the global society and the biosphere (Rockström and Klum, 2015).

In the article by Akaka and Vargo (2015), the context of service obtained a broader meaning by viewing encounter and service escapes from an ecosystem perspective: "It put service at the forefront of social and economic research because all exchange is essentially service driven" (Akaka and Vargo, 2015, p. 460). The ecosystem view is also related to innovation and value creation; researchers have stated that "value is created through multiple levels of interactions: micro (e.g., service encounter), meso (e.g., organizations, "industries," and brands communities), macro (e.g., societal)" (Vargo *et al.*, 2015, p. 67). The open source of the service dominant logic provides us with an appropriate platform for addressing co-creation and innovation; however, this logic is less developed for multi-governance, ethical, societal, and environmental issues.

The service ecosystem is based on systemic beliefs. Vargo and Lusch (2014) utilize an actor-to-actor approach. We will use the service ecosystem as a tool for interpreting a real context; however, we must further develop the service ecosystem idea for our purpose. The idea of transcendence for business logics addresses the social and environmental perspectives and governance issues (Enquist *et al.*, 2015). With shared institutions, we seek to determine how to cooperate in service ecosystems based on shared values and shared meanings; this behavior enables this activity to be part of a more stakeholder- and values-based orientation (Edvardsson and Enquist, 2009). We will generate certain ideas to expand the service ecosystem in that direction from three different sources to meet the managerial challenges:

- Ecosystem and business strategy
- Innovation ecosystem in the context of BoP
- Ecosystem in an analogy with the natural ecosystem

The original BoP concept (BoP 1.0) was as a new way of thinking about and doing business with the poor (Prahalad and Hart, 2002; Prahalad, 2005). BoP 1.0 was later considered a failed business model (Karnani, 2007a,b). Sebhatu (2008) suggested the field of social responsibility BoP for a broader view of BoP combined with a service logic. Businesses deliver economic and social benefits to the poor (Margolis and Walsh, 2003; Prahalad, 2005; Karnani, 2007a) and engage with local stakeholders (Hart, 2010); the many avenues of BoP for alleviating poverty through social business (Yunus, 2008) can be described as BoP 2.0. Most studies agree that, in order to succeed in market initiatives with the poor, partnerships are crucial: "the correct partnership is everything" (Weiser *et al.*, 2006, p. 6). Casado Cañeque and Hart (2015) give a roadmap for a more inclusive BoP business opportunity in what they call "Base of the Pyramid 3.0," in which sustainable development through innovation and entrepreneurship gives new meaning to BoP as a corporate social responsibility (CSR) business practice.

This sustainable way of thinking also has to be part of creating a value network as a strategy that provides the input to deal with the transformation process as part of the well-being of the customers and stakeholders

(Anderson *et al.*, 2012) by integrating sustainability into new infrastructural changes. BoP 3.0 is the way, we believe, that these ideas for building an innovative ecosystem can be used in other contexts. One chapter of Casado Cañeque and Hart's 2015 book is more specifically about ecosystems: Dagsputa and Hart's chapter, "Creating an innovation ecosystem for inclusive and sustainable business." The authors state that it is important to build an innovation ecosystem for inclusive and sustainable business for the successful development and scaling of a BoP enterprise everywhere in the world (p. 108). The aim is to build such a system as a sustainable business practice though the following (pp. 100–101):

- An integrated model (build the model around the challenges)
- Next practice (an action-based model embedded in the context for transformation)
- Co-creation (build a spirit of co-creation for different stakeholders into the institute by design)
- Local embeddedness (integrated experience locally); local and global thinking (locally embedded institutions that are also globally connected)
- Walk the talk (cooperation between not-for-profit entrepreneurship and for-profit entities based on a triple bottom line and win–win solutions)

To have a broader view of service innovation and value creation through service, as we label sustainability service innovation where ethical, social, and environmental issues are of importance, transformation must have the same importance as other factors, such as value co-creation. We need to expand our research more toward sustainable business practices (Loorbach, 2010, 2014; Rockström and Klum, 2015; Bragdon, 2016).

These discussions and arguments open up the potential for a new partnership between innovation and transformation (Loorbach, 2010, 2014) that includes the global society (the big world) and the biosphere (the small planet). Abundance within planetary boundaries requires a deep mind-shift (Rockström and Klum, 2015). This is indicated in an article written by Nidumolu, Prahalad, and Rangaswami that shows in an explorative way why sustainability can be seen as a key driver of innovation (Nidumolu *et al.*, 2009). What is driving what? In this chapter, we introduce sustainability service innovation, an integration of sustainable business practice with service innovation.

Service innovation relates to value co-creation, in which the innovation is in identifying novel ways to co-create value (Lusch and Vargo, 2014). Edvardsson and Enquist (2011) have identified some criteria for service innovation that differ from criteria for product innovation. One of those criteria is that a service system is embedded in a social context and because of that has social movements and norms that impact the value-creation processes (Edvardsson and Enquist, 2011).

In the service research, Enquist and Sebhatu (forthcoming) argue for sustainable service business 3.0 that includes the concepts of value co-creation, sustainability/CSR practice, and transformation interacting with service innovation, thus meeting challenges in the new business landscape.

This argument is related to the argument of Rockström and Klum (2015), that humanity has an incredible ability to overcome even the most daunting of challenges. That is how innovation works. By defining thresholds and a maximum allowable use of resources, biological ecosystems, and the climate, we can trigger a new wave of sustainable technological inventions thanks to an abundance of ideas and solutions for human prosperity and planetary stability (p. 25). Rockström and Klum address this challenge as follows: "A transition to sustainability can only attained by combining technology with deep system innovations and lifestyle changes" (p. 133).

An actual global transformation agenda in practice is the United Nations Global Sustainable Development Goals from November 2015, the 2030 Agenda for Sustainable Development (United Nations, 2015). This agenda is a plan of action for people, planet, prosperity, and partnership. Agenda 2030 outlines actions for nations, cities, companies, and civil society to transform the world to be sustainable. Many companies and cities have started to outline their own transformation agendas to meet the Agenda 2030 challenges. A positive aspect of Agenda 2030 is that it can be used as a platform for both environmental and societal perspectives to meet global sustainability goals and challenges. But "the devil is in implementation" (von Weizsäcker and Wijkman, 2018, p. 38). If the 11 social and economic goals (Goals 1–11) are reached using conventional growth policies, the three environmental goals (Goals 13–15) cannot be reached. There must be a balance among the goals.

There is a window of transformation for prosperity growth, but it has to be handled within planetary boundaries (Rockström and Klum, 2015). Bragdon (2016) shows how transformation is taking root in the corporate world, where priority is given to a more eco-centric transition based on living asset stewardship related to people and nature. In the traditional model of the firm with a capital-centered mindset, employees are seen as replaceable factors of production and the biosphere and society are treated as "externalities". With a more organic model of the firm, people and nature are more important than capital assets, and companies live in harmony with life. Examples of two global actors that have built their business models in this organic way are Unilever and Novo Nordisk (Bragdon, 2016).

Research Methodology

As our methodological approach, to create a new meaning in the dialectic between the theoretical framework and a real context, we use American pragmatic thinking with the help of Peirce's three principles: (1) inquiry, for a deeper understanding of the main stakeholders' point of view; (2) abductive reasoning, for interpretation; and (3) seeing a new meaning in the transformation process (Nahser, 2013) from a methodological understanding beyond objectivism and relativism (Bernstein, 1983). We suggest obtaining inspiration from Peirce's three principles when using a service logic for "strategic thinking". This approach can be used in a normative manner for change that, as depicted by Lusch and Vargo (2014), is not prescriptive but strategic and abductive. The abductive approach is also related to our use of the Qualitative Research in Reflexive Methodology (Alvesson and Sköldberg, 2010). Abduction is about inter-pretation, and we see a new interpretative meaning when we attempt to read the signs in the transformative change process in the cases (inductive) in light of our theoretical and conceptual frame (deductive).

Our case study was developed over a three-year period of time. The data was collected between 2015 and 2018 in combination with informative field data (Alvesson and Sköldberg, 2010), such as interviews, interview transcripts, observations, round-table discussions, and transformation lab (T-lab) discussions (as part of a focus group approach) and documents. Our data access was unique (Gummesson, 2017) and well-triangulated (Yin, 2003). We sampled a company with strong sustainability reporting and specific engagement in sustainability service innovation, with good commitment to Agenda 2030 (Strauss and Corbin, 1990). Following Bowen's (2008) argument that it is insufficient to simply state that sampling concluded when we reached saturation, we adopted specific guidelines. The primary data was collected through interviews with leaders and management of the company; observation and T-lab sessions occurred at a distinct place in an innovation park as follows:

- We followed Löfbergs for more than 3 years. We met key individuals at the executive and management levels (the chairman of the board and the sustainability director), we read open and internal documents from the organization, and we have scientific articles and memos from our research following the company.
- We conducted new interviews with a broader point of view during spring 2016 at Löfbergs's headquarters in Karlstad, Sweden.
- We also arranged a joint T-lab session in autumn 2016 together with the chairman (representing the family owner) and the sustainability director. At the same session were one designer and one project manager from the global design and supplier chaincompany of IKEA, two professors in business ethics and CSR from two distinguished American universities, and three leaders of an innovation park. We met at a neutral location — an innovation park in a service innovation lab. We sought to discern the transformation agenda for meeting sustainability challenges for the two values-driven enterprises — IKEA and Löfbergs — to engender a more general discussion about stewardship, hyper norms, and sustainability service innovation.
- We have chosen to observe the T-lab session as a source of primary data because it provided sufficient, highly informative data research materials as a "context of discovery" (Hunt, 1991) with high validity

(Krueger, 1988), as argued in focus group discussions. The T-lab focuses on understanding the complexity of governance issues and societal challenges (Loorbach, 2010; Grin *et al.*, 2011; Loorbach, 2014; Bragdon, 2016). It chooses as the transformation research from different stakeholders including policy makers, citizens, businessman, and activists (Grin *et al.*, 2011).

The collected materials were analyzed through a case analysis (Eisenhardt, 1989). The case is analyzed based on the description, understanding, and interpretation of the research material.

Empirical Study

The Anders Löfbergs Group is regarded as the most sustainable coffee group in Europe, that with passion, strong brands, and the best tasting coffee delivers increased value for its customers and owners. Löfbergs is a values-driven family business founded in 1906 and is today one of the largest family-owned coffee roasters in the Nordic Countries. What drives Löfbergs? Our values are our compass, our vision helps us aim high and our strategies make us goal-oriented (Löfbergs, 2018). Löfbergs is one of the largest importers of organic and fair trade certified coffee in the world. The company operates in more than 10 markets and is one of the eight founding members of the global initiative Coffee & Climate.

Certifications are extremely important to ensure access to coffee for the future without having a negative impact on people and the environment. They are one of the most important tools in sustainability efforts. Certifications give the farmers more knowledge and better prospects for growing coffee sustainably. But Löfbergs is not satisfied with external certifications alone. Löfbergs also has its own code of conduct (C&C) and a thorough system for evaluating its suppliers so that they meet C&C requirements for sustainable farming.

Certification is important, but taste means even more; flavor always comes first. Certification doesn't tell anything about the quality of the coffee. When purchasing coffee, Löfbergs has quality requirements the coffee must meet first, and then it must be certified.

The coffee sector is particularly affected by climate change. As a key export commodity, coffee is cultivated in more than 70 countries. With processing and retailing, the industry employs more than 100 million people worldwide. Coffee is the second most valuable commodity exported by developing countries. Smallholder family farmers constitute 70% of producers, with a major contribution from women who often provide the majority of the labor. A total of 90% is produced in developing countries. Climate change has already negatively impacted coffee production. Löfbergs systematically invests and makes commitments in its value chain, which has a social responsibility impact from bean to cup (from coffee farming to transport, production, distribution, and consumption), showing the commitment throughout the value chain (Figure 1).

In Löfbergs' long-term strategy, one open question is, "What are we doing to secure the coffee of the future?" One answer is the Next

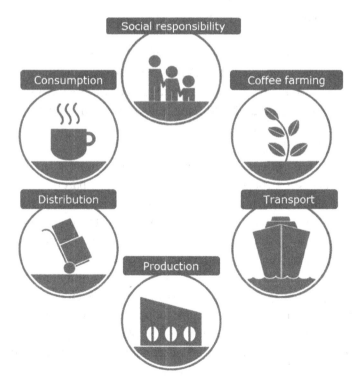

Figure 1. Löfbergs' value chain built on "Responsibility from Bean to Cup".

Generation Coffee initiative. A message from the chairman and CEO of Löfbergs explains: "We are supporting the young coffee farmers who will give us the coffee of the future. We call this initiative Next Generation Coffee. Through education and financial support in the form of quality supplements, premiums and direct trading, we are improving development opportunities for the next generation of coffee farmers in Tanzania and Colombia. We are doing this so they can build better lives for themselves and their families, and so they will see a future in coffee farming." Next Generation Coffee is a new program started by the family owners of Löfbergs because the greatest challenges in securing coffee for the future are climate change and the next generation of coffee farmers. The chairman continues to explain, "In our meetings with coffee farmers, we have noticed a desire and a drive among the young farmers who are part of this initiative, and we are already seeing that our cooperation is improving knowledge about how climate change can be addressed. In order to deal with climate change and give a new generation of coffee farmers a reasonable chance to support themselves, demand for sustainable coffee must increase" (Löfbergs, 2018). Next Generation Coffee is a developing program for next generation smallholders about entrepreneurship, sustainable and efficient farming methods, and selling directly to secure a sustainable living by coffee farming. The program is also a way for Löfbergs to secure a supply of premium coffee.

The Coffee & Climate initiative to mitigate climate change from the coffee sector has voluntary members representing more than 50% of the sector. Löfbergs is a founding member and an active part of this transformation program. The initiative is associated with the United Nations Sustainable Development Goals. "Today, a greater proportion of the coffee bought by restaurants, cafés and public bodies is organic. Many players are leading the way by serving only coffee that is both organic and Fairtrade. We want all buyers to start taking responsibility and buy coffee that is truly sustainable. There are no longer any excuses for choosing anything else. Consumers should also stop and ask themselves how their coffee is produced. Your choice of coffee plays an important role, and together we can contribute toward sustainable coffee production and a sustainable future. In this way, we can secure access to really good coffee in the future" (Löfbergs, 2018).

The Anders Löfbergs Group stands behind Agenda 2030, the United Nations' Global Goals for Sustainable Development. Löfbergs is convinced that industry plays a decisive role in the work to achieve these goals, not least when it comes to dealing with climate change and reaching the two-degree goal. The goals act as guidance for all decisions, whether they relate to work in producing countries, business development, product development, or day-to-day operations.

The main sustainability goals Löfbergs plans to reach by 2020 are having a 100% certified assortment, 100% renewable energy, 40% less climate impact, and 40% female managers.

Discussion

In this chapter, we address values-driven service innovation as a key driver for innovation and transformation embedded in the core values of the organization. In service research, service innovation and resource integration are two key elements that interact with sustainable business practices for a broader meaning: transformative change in the new globalized business landscape, labeled as value-creation through service.

The empirical study showed that Löfbergs is a values-driven service business (Enquist *et al.*, 2015). Ericson (2018) sees Löfbergs as a family business driven by practicing goodwill. Goodwill practicing has societal implications, and the case study of Löfbergs in this chapter gives the practice of goodwill a deeper meaning, showing Löfbergs in a proactive way tackling the Agenda 2030 goals. Löfbergs has used the climate change challenge as a driver for sustainability service innovation solutions for transformational change in its business practices. Inspired by the Dasgputa and Hart's (2015) ecosystem thinking for sustainable business practice, we built an analyzing and interpreting matrix (see Table 1). The columns represent the commitment of Löfbergs's value chain — "from bean to cup" — while the rows represent Dasgputa and Hart's template for sustainable business practice.

The integrated model of Löfbergs' "from bean to cup" is about tackling climate change challenges as part of a sustainable business practice embedded in transformation: transformation to handle the economic, social, and environmental challenges of globalization (Stiglitz, 2006) for

Table 1.   The sustainable business practices (left column) of Löfbergs's "bean to cup" value chain (top row).

	Coffee farming	Transport, production, and distribution	Consumption and social responsibility
Integrated model (build the model around the challenges)	Climate change	Climate change	Climate change
Next practice (an action-based model embedded in the context for transformation)	Next Generation Coffee; Climate & Coffee	Fossil free	Quality and sustainably grown coffee
Co-creation (build a spirit of co-creation for different stakeholders into the institute by design)	Engaging in supporting sustainable farming methods and conditions	Smart packaging and effective responsible logistic solutions	Interactive communication to improve the sustainability performance of customers and meet the demands of health and sustainability trends; #Caffeslatte initiative
Local embeddedness (integrated experience locally; *local and global thinking* (locally embedded institutions that are also globally connected)	A drive among the young farmers; improved opportunities for farmer self-support	Renewable energy: minimizing emissions from processing and transport	Certified coffee for better taste and experience: organic and fair trade, investments and commitments to social responsibility
Walk to talk (cooperation between not-for-profit entrepreneurship and for-profit entities based on a triple bottom line and win–win solutions)	Co-founded Coffee & Climate, which helps small-scale coffee farmers to deal with climate change; launched "Next Generation Coffee"	Haga Initiative business network; Fossilfritt Sverige; Agenda 2030 Initiative implemented with various actors	Haga Initiative business network; Fossilfritt Sverige; CSR Sweden; Agenda 2030 Initiative implemented with various actors

prosperity growth within planetary boundaries (Rockström and Klum, 2015). This Löfbergs approach follows Agenda 2030 and its implementation. The company outlines its own transformation agendas to meet the Agenda 2030 challenges. Agenda 2030 can be used as a platform for both environmental and societal perspectives to meet global sustainability goals and challenges. Löfbergs has followed Agenda 2030 through its Next Generation Coffee initiative. Löfbergs is also a proactive member of the Coffee & Climate initiative, together with other leading global coffee companies.

The next practice infrastructure of Löfbergs for transport, production, and distribution (Table 1, row 2, column 2) is part of the key driver for challenge-driven innovation transformation: having a fossil free footprint from the different processes. The next practice about consumption and social responsibility from the customer's side (row 2, column 3) has the key driver of quality and sustainably grown coffee, which has to be tackled in different ways in the vendor and retail markets.

One important part of next practice is the design of co-creation of value (Table 1, row 3) for different stakeholders of Löfbergs. The next generation BoP is about sustainable development through innovation and entrepreneurship (Casado *et al.*, 2015), which addresses a shift from BoP 2.0 to 3.0 through a change in mindset, open innovation, innovation ecosystems, cross-sector partnerships, and sustainable development. In coffee farming, co-creation of value means supporting sustainable farming methods and conditions. In operations, the challenge-driven innovation for the co-creation of value currently concentrates on smart packaging and effective, responsible logistic solutions. In consumption and social responsibility, part of the co-creation of value with customers and others in society is about interactive communication contributing to improving the sustainability performance of the customers and also meeting the demands of health and sustainability trends. Certified coffee has to be treated as a premium coffee, creating a healthy and sustainable lifestyle. One example launched in January 2018 is the #Caffeslatte initiative, where the interactive communication is about using all coffee beans for drinking and not for waste. This initiative is a way to tell the market that coffee is for drinking not to waste the extra brewed down the drain.

Locally embedded and globally connected (Table 1, row 4) is, for coffee farming, a drive among the young farmers to support the next generation and improved opportunities for farmer self-support. In operations, it is about renewable energy minimizing emissions from processing and transport. In consumption and social responsibility, it is mainly about organic and fair trade certified coffee for better taste and experience, and challenge-driven innovative investments and commitments for social responsibility.

The last row, walk to talk, is about the implementation of Agenda 2030 by taking action in cooperation with not-for-profit entrepreneurs and for-profit entities based on a triple bottom line and win-win solutions. Tackling the need for continued coffee farming, Löfbergs cofounded Coffee & Climate, which helps small-scale coffee farmers deal with climate change, and launched the Next Generation Coffee initiative. To improve operations and for customers and social responsibility, Löfbers implemented the Agenda 2030 initiative with various actors including CSR Sweden. A main actor is the Haga Initiative business network; another is Fossiltfritt Sverige. For the well-being of the customers and stakeholders, this sustainable way of thinking also has to be part of creating a value network as a strategy that provides the input to deal with the transformation process (Anderson *et al.*, 2012) by integrating sustainability into new infrastructural changes.

Conclusion and Implications

In this chapter, we addressed the idea of a values-driven service innovation through sustainable business practices and service research for transformation, value co-creation, and sustainability/CSR practice to provide "sustainable service business" a broader meaning. There is a new reality for business and society. This chapter prioritizes innovation and transformation that includes the global society and the biosphere. Integral to the approach is the insight that abundance or prosperity growth within planetary boundaries requires a deep mind-shift. Thus, this chapter makes the following contributions:

The chapter describes a new practice — managerial insights as next practice value co-creation through service, meeting sustainable business practices (see Table 1), which is consistent with interactive research for business and managerial implications.

The chapter introduces values-driven service innovation, in which broader transformative and sustainability thinking brings ethical, social, and/or environmental dimensions into the service innovation research.

The chapter gives sustainable business practices a new meaning to "next practice" business, and a change of mindset in which sustainability is used as a driving force for transformation and innovation (it addresses transformation, co-creation, and sustainability/CSR practice).

The chapter demonstrates adherence to a transformation agenda for transformative change in real contexts via the case of Löfbergs as part of the global Coffee & Climate initiative — for a values-based or vision-driven transformation to break old boundaries. The transformation agenda follows Agenda 2030.

Finally, the chapter fits the transformation agenda and the concepts of sustainability service innovation through sustainable business practices (BoP 3.0) to a more general model of next practice business to visualize this conceptual and empirical study. It is an interesting opportunity to make a link between transformative service research and sustainability/ CSR in service research. The societal perspective of prosperity meets well-being and sustainability/CSR in a dynamic service ecosystem for transformative change in which both people and nature matter.

The managerial and societal implications of this chapter focus on the ecological and societal challenges in the micro, meso, and macro land-scapes, and provide the insight that business and ethics cannot be sepa-rated. Agenda 2030 is used as a plan of action for people, planet, prosperity, and partnership to meet real challenges to outline a values-driven transformation agenda for transformative change in real contexts.

References

Akaka, M. A. and Vargo, S. L. (2015). Extending the context of service: From encounters to ecosystems. *Journal of Service Marketing*, **29**(6/7), 453–462.

Alvesson, M. and Sköldberg, K. (2010). *Reflexive Methodology: New Vistas for Qualitative Research* (2nd edn.), London: SAGE Publications.

Anderson, L, Ostrom, A. L., Corus, C., Fisk, R. P., Gallan, A. S., Giraldo, M., Mende, M., Mulder, M., Rayburn, S. W., Rosenbaum, M. S., Shirahada, K., and Williams, J. D. (2012). Transformative service research: An agenda for the future, *Journal of Business Research*, **66**(8), 1203–1210.

Bernstein, R. J. (1983). *Beyond Objectivism and Relativism*. Philadelphia: University of Pennsylvania Press.

Bowen, G. A. (2008). Naturalistic inquiry and the saturation concept: A research note. *Qualitative Research*, **8**(1), 137–152.

Bragdon, J. H. (2016). *Companies that Mimic Life — Leaders of the Emerging Corporate Renaissance*. Saltaire, UK: Greenleaf Publishing.

Casado Cañeque, F. and Hart, S. L. (eds.), (2015). *Base of the Pyramid 3.0, Sustainable Development through Innovation & Entrepreneurship*. Sheffield, UK: Greenleaf Publishing.

Dasgupta, P. and Hart, S. L. (2015). Creating an innovation ecosystem for inclusive and sustainable business. In Casado Cañeque, F. and Hart, S. L. (eds.), *Base of the Pyramid 3.0*. Sheffield, UK: Greenleaf Publishing. Chapter 6, 96–108.

Edvardsson, B. and Enquist, B. (2011). The service excellence and innovation model: Lesson from IKEA and other service frontiers. *Total Quality Management and Business Excellence*, **22**(5), 535–551.

Edvardsson, B. and Enquist, B. (2009). *Values-Based Service for Sustainable Business: Lessons from IKEA*, London: Routledge.

Eisenhardt, K. M. (1989). Building theories from case study research. *Academy of Management Review*, **14**(4), 532–550.

Enquist, B. (2016). *Public Transport as Transformative Driver for Living and Sustainability Cityregions*. Karlstad University Studies, 2016:19, Karlstad, Sweden (in Swedish).

Enquist, B. and Sebhatu, S. (forthcoming). Values Based Service Innovation for Sustainable Business 3.0 — Lessons about Transformation Agenda in Practice.

Enquist, B., Sebhatu, S., and Johnson, M. (2015). Transcendence for business logics in value networks for sustainable service business. *Journal of Service Theory and Practice*, **25**(2), 181–197.

Ericson, M. (2018). *Moral Human Agency in Business — A Missing Dimension in Strategy as Practice*. Cambridge, UK: Cambridge University Press.

Grin, J., Rotmans, J., and Schot, J. eds.), (2011). *Transitions to Sustainable Development — New Directions in the Study of Long Term Transformative Change* (paperback edition), London: Routledge.

Gummesson, E. (2017). *Case Theory in Business and Management: Reinventing Case Study Research*. London: SAGE Publications.

Gustafsson, A., Kristensson, P., Schirr, G. R., and Witell, L. (2016). *Service Innovation*. New York: Business Expert Press.

Hart, S. L. (2010). *Capitalism at the Crossroads*: *Next Generation Business Strategies for a Post-Crisis World* (3rd edn.). Upper Saddle River, NJ: Wharton School Publishing.

Hunt, S. D. (1991). *Modern Marketing Theory*: *Critical Issues in the Philosophy of Marketing Science*. Cincinnati, OH: South-Western Publishing.

Karnani, A. (2007a). Fortune at the Bottom of the Pyramid: A mirage. *California Management Review*, **29**(4), 90–111.

Karnani, A. (2007b). Employment, not micro credit, is the solution. *Stanford Social Innovation Review*, **5**(3), 34–40.

Krueger, R. A. (1988). *Focus Groups*. Newbury Park, CA: SAGE Publications.

Loorbach, D. (2010). Transition management for sustainable development: A prescriptive, complexity-based governance framework. *Governance: An International Journal of Policy, Administration, and Institutions*, **23**(1), 161–183.

Loorbach, D. (2014). *To Transition! Governance Panarchy in the New Transformation*. Rotterdam: Dutch Research Institute for Transitions, Erasmus University.

Lusch, R. F. and Vargo, S. L. (2014). *Service Dominant Logic — Premises, Perspectives, Possibilities*. Cambridge, UK: Cambridge University Press.

Löfbergs (2018). *Our Sustainability Report, 2016/17*. Karlstad: AB Anders Löfberg.

Löfbergs (2017). *Our Sustainability Report, 2015/16*. Karlstad: AB Anders Löfberg.

Margolis, J. D. and Walsh, J. P. (2003). Misery loves companies: Rethinking social initiatives by business. *Administrative Science Quarterly*, **48**, 268–305.

Nahser, F. B. (2013). *Learning to Read the Signs. Reclaiming Pragmatism for the Practice of Sustainable Management* (2nd edn.). Sheffield, UK: Greenleaf Publishing.

Nidumolu, R., Prahalad, C. K., and Rangaswami, M. R. (2009). Why sustainability is now the key driver of innovation. *Harvard Business Review*, **87**(9), 56–64, September.

Prahalad C. K. (2005). *The Fortune at The Bottom of The Pyramid*: *Eradicating Poverty Through Profits*. New Jersey: Wharton School Publishing, London: Pearson Education.

Prahalad, C. K. and Hart, S. L. (2002). The fortune at the bottom of the Pyramid. *Strategy + Business,* **26**, 54–67.

Rockström, J. and Klum, M. (2015). *Big World Small Planet — Abundance Within Planetary Boundaries*. Stockholm: Max Ström Publishing.

Sebhatu, S. P. (2010). *Corporate Social Responsibility for Sustainable Service Dominant Logic*. Karlstad University Studies, Karlstad, Sweden.

Sebhatu, S. P. (2008). The challenges and opportunities of creating sustainable shared value at the base of the pyramid: Cases from sub-Saharan Africa. In Kandachar, P. and Halme, M. (eds.), *Sustainability Challenged and Solutions at the Base of the Pyramid*. Sheffield, UK: Greenleaf Publishing, Chapter 8, 146–161.

Stiglitz, J. E. (2006). *Making Globalization Work*. New York: W.W. Norton.

Strauss, A. and Corbin, J. (1990). *Basics of Qualitative Research: Grounded Theory Procedures and Techniques*. Newbury Park, CA: SAGE Publications.

United Nations Sustainable Development (2015). *Transforming Our World: The 2030 Agenda for Sustainable Development*. United Nations Sustainable Development Agenda 20130, A/RES/70/1.

Vargo, S. L. and Lusch, R. F. (2014). Inversions of service-dominant logic. *Marketing Theory,* **14**(3), 239–248.

Vargo, S. L., Wieland, H., and Akaka, M. A. (2015). Institutions in innovation: A service ecosystems perspective. *Industrial Marketing Management,* **44**(1), 63–72.

von Weizsäcker, E. and Wijkman, A. (2018). *Come On! Capitalism, Short-termism, Population and the Destruction of the Planet*. New York: Springer-Verlag.

Weiser, J., Kahane, M., Rochlin, S., and Landis, J. (2006). *Untapped: Creating Value in Underserved Markets*. San Francisco, CA: Berrett-Koehler Publishers, Inc.

Yin, R. K. (2003). *Case Study Research: Design and Methods* (3rd edn.). Thousand Oaks, CA: SAGE Publications.

Yunus, M. (2007). Credit for the poor, *Harvard International Review,* **29**(3), 20–24.

Interviews and Discussions

1. Kathrine Löfberg, Chairman of the Board, and Eva Eriksson, Director of Sustainability, April 2016, AB Anders Löfbergs Head Office, Karlstad.

2. Kathrine Löfberg, Chairman of the Board, and Eva Eriksson, Director of Sustainability, October 2016, Karlstad Innovation Park, Service Innovation Lab — T-lab discussions.
3. Kathrine Löfberg, Chairman of the Board, and Eva Eriksson, Director of Sustainability, April 2017, AB Anders Löfbergs Head Office, Karlstad.
4. Eva Eriksson, Director of Sustainability, February 2018, AB Anders Löfbergs Head Office, Karlstad.

Chapter 12

Bridging the Gap — From Great Ideas to Realized Innovations

Linda Bergkvist and Jenny Karlsson

Karlstad University, Sweden

Key takeaways

1. Many firms and organizations experience challenges in implementing their innovative ideas.
2. This chapter extends existing implementation research by integrating a service innovation process perspective. It suggests how implementation of service innovation could be managed in relation to conditions present at the environmental, organizational, managerial, and individual levels in order to realize ideas.
3. To bridge the gap between great ideas and realized innovations, conditions at different levels need to be managed.

   Conditions for realizing service innovation may serve as enablers and/or inhibitors.

   Challenges for service innovation implementation are related to the specific context in which the service innovation process takes place, accompanied social and cultural change processes, and tensions in actors' value creating processes.

Implementation of service innovation regards not only the service innovation itself, but also how the innovation is used, accepted, and institutionalized.

Frontline employee and user involvement can be accomplished through innovation groups.

4. This chapter illustrates conditions for implementation of service innovation ideas in the context of primary care.
5. Those interested in this chapter may also find Chapters 4 and 9 interesting.

Background

Even though service innovation has become a key to survival and success in a competitive business landscape (Carlborg *et al.*, 2014), firms today experience challenges in implementing their innovative ideas (Cadwallader *et al.*, 2010). In this chapter, implementation refers to realization of service innovation as it deals with aspects and conditions for realizing service innovation ideas. Innovation challenges depend on environmental, organizational, and managerial factors as well as the actions of frontline employees and other actors (Cadwallader *et al.*, 2010), but also on the different combinations of influential factors and the specific context (Garpenby, 2011). In our study, which is conducted within the context of primary care, 180 ideas for service innovations were generated of only a few became implemented.

Deficiencies in implementation research in a healthcare context has been illuminated already in previous research (Garpenby, 2011), and there has been calls for practice-related methods and strategies for implementation (Grol, 2001). Implementation is crucial for ideas to be translated into innovation and innovation into organizational practice, yet many meaningful interventions fail (Damschroder *et al.*, 2009) and the implementation of new methods, guidelines, or tools is a slow and unpredictable process (Carlfjord *et al.*, 2010). Deficiencies in implementing research-generated knowledge into healthcare practices may lead to an inability to offer the best possible care — a problem for both the individual patient and society as a whole (Grol, 2001). Therefore, practice-related methods and strategies for implementation that respond to such deficiencies are needed. Practice-based research that involves employees and users is a prerequisite for service innovation as these actors, based on their knowledge and experience of healthcare practices and daily interactions, open up for implementation (Karlsson and Skålén, 2015) and use of the research-generated knowledge. Even though there are growing pressures on the public sector to be more innovative, considerable disagreement exists on how to achieve this (Hartley *et al.*, 2013).

In the context of healthcare, innovation has mainly been studied from a biomedical perspective, while the service innovation perspective is still in its infancy (Groene *et al.*, 2009). When comparing the innovation of traditional physical products with service innovation, the former tends to focus on the output of internal, structured, and sequential innovation processes. The latter rather focuses on creating prerequisites for value creation where the process tends to be open and iterative with several actors involved (Vargo and Lusch, 2008). Recent innovation research recognizes service innovation as unintended and informal processes (Fuglsang and Sørensen, 2011) and that innovation may originate from many different types of activities (Toivonen and Tuominen, 2009). This reasoning also implies challenges for service innovation implementation more generally. To be successful in innovating services, there is a growing need for organizations, employees, and other actors to adopt a new mindset and new tools (Kindström and Kowalkowski, 2014). Drawing on the above discussion, this chapter illuminates that service innovation implementation in healthcare is in need of further research. Grounded in the sparse research in service innovation implementation in general and the critical role of implementation in healthcare, the present chapter aims to identify conditions for the implementation of ideas in service innovation.

The chapter draws on a qualitative case study within primary care with extensive involvement of frontline employees and patients, and to some extent also with managers on different levels of the organization. Grounded in the service innovation literature as well as implementation research, this chapter contributes to increase the understanding of service innovation implementation, both in general and within a healthcare context. The chapter reviews and develops existing research by illuminating how conditions may function as enablers and/or inhibitors and suggests previous implementation frameworks to be extended with a frontline employee and user perspective.

Service Innovation in a Healthcare Context

Even though service innovation plays a pivotal role in healthcare, healthcare organizations tend to face major difficulties when it comes to diffusion and implementation of innovations (Barnett *et al.*, 2011). As healthcare might influence patients' well-being and quality of life significantly (Mu *et al.*, 2018; Ostrom *et al.*, 2015), it is important that this sector is active when it comes to service innovation. The concept of service innovation has been widely used and broadly defined (Witell *et al.*, 2016). For example, service innovations have been described by Barcet (2010) as a benefit or solution obtained by users and the focal firm. Vargo and Lusch (2008, p. 5) argue that "innovation is not defined by what firms produce as output, but how firms can better serve," which focuses on the value the service can offer to the user instead of only having a focus on efficiency gains and effectiveness. A service innovation can be seen as a new service or a renewal of an existing service that is put into practice (Toivonen and Tuominen, 2009). In addition, to be an innovation the renewal should be new not only to its developer, but in a broader context, and it must involve some element that can be repeated in new situations, thus being reproduced, spread, or institutionalized in the organization (Fuglsang and Sørensen, 2011). In a healthcare context, such novelties imply improving both internal working processes and healthcare practices (Karlsson *et al.*, 2014), as well as patients' experiences and value creation related to the healthcare service (Skålén *et al.*, 2018).

Implementation Research

When reviewing the general implementation science literature, a large variety of definitions of the implementation concept can be found; it seems a uniform and generally accepted definition is missing. In everyday life, implementation is often associated with realization of ideas (cf. Nilsen and Roback, 2011), but it can also be defined as "a specified set of activities designed to put into practice an activity or program of known dimensions" (NIRN, 2018). Implementation is often mixed up with the concepts of diffusion and dissemination. The term diffusion implies that the innovation is adopted "from outside" the organization and into the organizational practice (Rogers, 1962). Adoption is the organizational process that is initiated as the organization becomes aware of the innovation, whereas implementation means the introduction of innovation into an organization. Implementation according to diffusion theory could be explained as an untargeted and passive spread of the innovation (cf. Greenhalgh *et al.*, 2004; Nilsen, 2015).

The term dissemination on the other hand concerns people's attempt to use an innovation in practice (Tabak *et al.*, 2012). This includes learning about the innovation and an attempt to integrate it in ordinary work. Dissemination thus refers to active and planned efforts to persuade target groups to adopt an innovation (Greenhalgh *et al.*, 2004; Nilsen, 2015). Diffusion and dissemination efforts are necessary, but not sufficient, for the actual use of an innovation and realization of promised results in practice. Simplified, diffusion and dissemination focus more on the innovation itself, while implementation also focuses on the use of the innovation to achieve expected results in a given practical setting (NIRN, 2018), for example, by integrating new practices and making it a part of the organization's existing routines (Greenhalgh *et al.*, 2004; Nilsen, 2015). Yet, the importance of context makes it difficult to provide general advice on how to conduct implementation in specific cases. Initially, representatives of the implementation science sought to generalize knowledge about which factors lead to effective implementation, but more recent research suggests that different factors affect how implementation occurs in different combinations in different contexts (Garpenby, 2011).

Even though the challenge of innovation implementation has been illuminated in previous innovation research (cf. Klein and Sorra, 1996), such challenges have not been extensively focused upon in service innovation research. Furthermore, implementation research has focused on implementation of existing innovations to a high degree, implying that the organization adopts the innovation. However, research that more specifically focuses on implementation of ideas for service innovation that has been generated from within the organization, or in relation to customers and other users, is sparse (Cadwallader *et al.*, 2010).

Service Innovation Implementation

From a service innovation perspective, implementation can be regarded as a part of a service innovation process. As introduced in the background of this chapter, service innovation processes have often been described as sequential processes with several phases (Alam, 2006; Scheuing and Johnson, 1989), often divided with the main phases of idea generation, development, and implementation (see e.g., Sundbo, 2008). The idea phase mainly deals with the "fuzzy front end" and contains idea generation activities, and the development phase is where the idea is designed and tested; these areas have been extensively focused upon in previous research. Implementation can be understood as the process to translate ideas into an innovation that is a part of the organizational practice (Cadwallader *et al.*, 2010) or accepted at the market or in society (Fuglsang, 2010). The actions that take place in the implementation phase play a pivotal role in realizing ideas for future value creation (Damschroder *et al.*, 2009) as the value of an idea is first realized when the idea is implemented (Engen and Magnusson, 2015). Yet, a bulk of the existing service innovation literature has a limited focus on this part of the service innovation process. This chapter recognizes service innovation processes as dynamic, interactive, and iterative processes through which a new service or a renewal of an existing service is achieved (Toivonen and Tuominen, 2009), with a specific focus on service innovation implementation.

Actors' Roles in Service Innovation Implementation

Klein and Sorra (1996) suggest that innovation implementation within an organization is the process of gaining targeted employees' appropriate and committed use of an innovation. This also implies a change in the behavior of the organizations' members. In examples from the context of healthcare, implementation can be regarded as social change processes that affect and are affected by actors and factors at different levels — individual, management/leadership, organization, and surrounding society (Nilsen and Roback, 2011). From a social change perspective, implementation can be considered as "dissemination and utilization of knowledge" in order to achieve change. The changes can be described as an ongoing learning process at different system levels (individual, group, organization). Based on a learning perspective on implementation, two innovation processes can be described: top–down implementation of innovations and bottom–up development of local innovations (see also Engen, 2016). Top–down occurs, for example, through decisions, guidelines, and policies, while bottom–up is a consequence of learning in the daily work. In bottom–up, the practitioner is seen as an important and active creator and mediator of knowledge, and learning can give rise to new ideas, products and working methods. A challenge lies in organizing and supporting the bottom–up perspective in order to utilize the knowledge and ideas of users and frontline employees (Engen, 2016; Garpenby, 2011; Karlsson, 2018).

Users

Patient involvement in the process of innovating healthcare services to improve, for example, safety and quality has received increased attention, even though the improvements to practice remain slow and variable and the research about patient involvement is still limited (Hardyman *et al.*, 2015). The involvement of users in the service innovation process has previously been acknowledged as vital for success (Magnusson *et al.*, 2003), as users often have a high understanding about how the service could generate customer value (Magnusson, 2009). This often results in users generating more creative ideas with a higher user value than, for example, professional innovators (Magnusson, 2009). Hence, it could be expected that patients, based on the problems they have encountered during interaction with healthcare, would bring necessary knowledge into the service innovation process. Patients that have been involved early in the service development process have contributed with ideas and insights on how to improve work processes, but also provided solutions and thoughts on how these could be implemented (Engström and Snyder, 2014). Yet, there is a lack of knowledge regarding how to involve patients in the service innovation process (Grol, 2001; Snyder and Engström, 2016), and the contextual and relational inhibitors and enablers to patient involvement have previously been ignored (Renedo *et al.*, 2015). Furthermore, users' understanding of what is organizationally possible to implement is limited; therefore employee involvement in service innovation is also key for innovating successful services.

Frontline Employees

The important role of frontline employees in service innovation implementation has been previously recognized by Karlsson and Skålén (2015, see also Cadwallader *et al.*, 2010), suggesting that their involvement facilitates implementation of a new service. As frontline employees with regular customer contact are able to contribute customer knowledge, practice knowledge, and product knowledge, when becoming involved in service innovation, Karlsson and Skålén (2015) argue for early and active involvement of frontline employees. If frontline employees are involved already in the beginning of the service innovation process, implementation can take place simultaneously as the service is innovated. This is because frontline employees become "one with the service" and create an understanding for the service offering and how it can create value for customers. If actors' requirements for future value creation are unmet, there is even a risk that the process might end before the implementation stage (Sundström *et al.*, 2017). Engaging employees in innovation work creates conditions for realizable innovations that suit both the customers and the business, but also for an improved innovation climate and a smoother implementation process (Ordanini and Parasuraman, 2011).

Frameworks for Service Innovation Implementation

As previously introduced, scholars (see e.g., Grol, 2001; Damschroder *et al.*, 2009; Garpenby, 2011) call for practice-related methods and strategies for implementation of innovations. Examples can be collected from the healthcare context. Even though many interventions have been found meaningful for patients, there is a challenge in realizing them. For the purpose of responding to such challenges, and to bridge the gap between theory and practice, implementation frameworks have been developed (see e.g., Meyers *et al.*, 2012; NIRN, 2018). These frameworks address the importance of what needs to be done, how to establish what needs to be done in practice, and by whom, and the specific context (NIRN, 2018) as well as the necessary action-oriented steps to succeed with implementation (Meyers *et al.*, 2012).

One of the most comprehensive frameworks for studying implementation in the field of healthcare is the Consolidated Framework for Implementation Research, abbreviated CFIR (Damschroder *et al.*, 2009). The framework is a meta-framework synthesizing implementation theories and conditions needed for successful implementation that can be used as guidance to increase the understanding of what works, where, and why, across different contexts. The framework is composed of five major dimensions: intervention characteristics, outer setting, inner setting, characteristics of the individuals involved, and the process of implementation, and related key conditions. The framework has been used as guidance in several implementation studies (for example, Damschroder and Lowery, 2013; Kirk *et al.*, 2016) as well as tested in various healthcare settings (for example, Breimaier *et al.*, 2015; Damschroder and Hagedorn, 2011), and been found fruitful to guide an implementation process. However, weaknesses have been reported (Breimaier *et al.*, 2015). These include for example that the CFIR lacks a focus on different stakeholders' aims and needs during the planning phase of an implementation process. In the long run, this may negatively affect stakeholders' acceptance and usage of the innovation and at the same time decrease understanding of inhibitors and enablers for innovation implementation. Other deficiencies reported include that the framework does not regard the pre-existing work practices, structures, and change strategies, which may influence the innovation implementation strategy in a negative manner (Breimaier *et al.*, 2015).

Going through the service innovation literature, frameworks for service innovation implementation are to a great extent missing, and just a few studies on idea implementation have been identified (for example, Baer, 2012). However, these do not focus on idea implementation in a service innovation process, but merely relate to product innovation. Besides the CFIR, which regards both internally and externally developed innovations, implementation frameworks tend to have in common that they draw on an adoption perspective; that is, they focus on the implementation of existing innovations, whereas implementation of ideas for service innovation is dismissed. Further they do not focus on how the implementation is conducted with regard to actors and their value creation.

A Study of Primary Care

The present chapter is based on a study of five primary care units within a Swedish county council. In order to identify conditions for the implementation of ideas in service innovation, we decided to use a qualitative approach, an approach that is useful to create an understanding of dynamic and complex processes (Denzin and Lincoln, 2011) with many actors involved. The project was directed toward conducting research on service innovation with extensive frontline employee and patient involvement through innovation groups. A project implementation group was formed with representatives from all units, area managers, and representatives from the development department at the county council. The selection of frontline employees and patients to the innovation groups was conducted by using a convenience sample. The patients were invited either by information signs and reply coupons or by personal invitation in the waiting rooms, whereas frontline employees were invited directly by the unit managers. The final age range of members was between 23 and 83 although it was skewed toward older people on the patient side, representing the age of users of primary care. Reflecting the uneven gender balance among frontline employees in primary care, the final selection was skewed toward women. The frontline employees represented a range of different professions including nurses, doctors, certified nursing assistants, receptionists, chiropodists, and physiotherapists.

The data was collected between 2014 and 2017 by observing six innovation groups and conducting interviews. The innovation groups consisted of patients (2 groups), frontline employees (2 groups), or a mix of patients and frontline employees (2 groups). As frontline employees and users are both important actors in the service innovation process, our point of departure was to include both types of actors in the innovation groups. In the innovation groups, the members co-created and discussed ideas and how these ideas could be realized.

Before the project started, each member was given an "idea book" — a notebook with questions to help in structuring their ideas (see Figure 1 below). The members were instructed to record ideas that emerged from their actual experiences of the healthcare service, but also to present a possible solution and how the solution could be realized (question 4 in Figure 1 below).

This helped the members focus not on complaints but rather on finding creative solutions to problems they experienced. Communication between different actors plays an important role in the implementation of innovation in healthcare (Damschroder *et al.*, 2009), yet no such

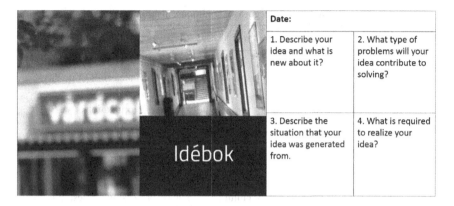

Figure 1. Idea book.

mechanism or method for communication between patients and employees existed at the primary care units prior to the initiation of this project.

The study focused on bottom–up driven service innovation where conditions for service innovation implementation have been studied; that is, from a frontline employee and patient perspective rather than from a top–down driven service innovation perspective. Focusing on innovating *with* the patient, rather than *for* the patient, enhanced the development of new, realizable ideas offering a promise of customers' value creation (Skålén *et al.*, 2018). However, this chapter also considers the managers' viewpoint, as they played an important role in identifying conditions for implementing the ideas generated in the innovation groups, thus realizing the service innovations. In total, 23 meetings were observed in which the groups generated 180 ideas for service innovations, only a few of which were implemented.

Twenty individual follow-up interviews were conducted with members of the service innovation groups. Five interviews were also held with unit managers and area managers to better understand the conditions for implementation of ideas in healthcare. All meetings and interviews were recorded and transcribed verbatim. The transcribed material was coded and analyzed, resulting in conditions for service innovation implementation. Inspired by Cadwallader *et al.* (2010, see also Nilsen and Roback, 2011), the conditions were related to the categories of environment, organization, middle managers, and frontline employees and users. The identified codes, conditions, and categories are summarized in Table 1 below.

Table 1.   Categories, conditions, and codes.

Categories	Conditions	Codes (examples)
Environment	Governance	Available resources, allocation of resource, measures of quality, political conditions, policies, needs, prioritization
Organization	Organizational structure	Top-down, bottom-up, transaction-oriented, problem identification, overview is missing, knowledge sharing
	Organizational culture	Power, professional roles, mindset, control, values, traditions
	Structure for innovation implementation	Method, implementation support, coordination, intra- and inter-organizational knowledge transfer, patient involvement, structure
	Authority	Ownership, responsibility
Middle managers	Commitment	Target, need of change, motivation, attitude, engagement, shared vision, common goals, degree of innovative idea
Frontline employees and users	Management support	Encouragement of idea, openness, support, understanding, leadership, user and employee involvement, insight in day-to-day work
	Resistance	Change fatigue, threat, anchoring, workload, realized benefits

Conditions for Service Innovation Implementation in Healthcare

Eight conditions have been identified, which alone or in combination serve as enablers or inhibitors of the implementation of service innovation. These conditions can be explained as more or less relating to environment, organization, middle managers, or frontline employees and users, and are presented according to these findings.

Environment

At the environmental level, issues related to the condition of *governance* were addressed as both enabling and inhibiting service innovation implementation.

Governance concerns issues that relate to availability of resources, allocation of resources, and how resources are distributed dependent on prioritized needs. It further relates to political conditions such as policies and rules. Lack of resources was seen as a notable inhibitor for realizing ideas, an inhibitor confirmed by both unit managers and area managers. A common situation for unit managers was to have insufficient resources, in the form of personnel, time, and/or money, to be able to work with the ideas and their implementation. Consequently, ideas that involved more radical, overarching changes, were often lower prioritized. However, some ideas requiring quite few resources were also not implemented due to restricted economic support. Further, unforeseen economic restrictions, resulting in an urgent need to manage the day-to-day practice, left little time to implement new ideas.

Ideas that were in line with political initiatives, such as increasing the number of online-booked patient visits, were prioritized and supported by providing the necessary resources. When a change is supported by a political decision, implementation of the specific services seems to be less challenging. However, in the example of the implementation of online booking, the change was not welcomed by all the different medical professionals, nor by the patients.

Among the innovation group members, issues related to political interests, such as providing resources to improve primary care, were considered inhibitors to service innovation. Members also reflected upon how existing measures of quality, policies, and rules enable or inhibit service innovation in healthcare in general. The innovation group members had also experienced the inertia in change processes within the county council, which is illuminated in the following statement:

> The county council is a colossus on clay feet, [...] hard to change, hard to move. It has clay feet and with great effort it manages to go forward without really knowing where to stay and what to do. It is

grateful for all ideas, but then it stops. [...]. It is difficult to engage a county council. (Patient, mixed innovation group)

Organization

Four organizational conditions were identified, presented in the following sections: *organizational structure, organizational culture, structure for innovation implementation* and *authority*.

Organizational structure

The organizational structure is characterized by how decisions are made, top–down or bottom–up, and the organizational perspective; that is, whether a transaction-oriented or relation-oriented perspective dominates. The analysis shows that to realize service innovation, some ideas are better performed as top–down initiatives whereas others as bottom–up. Ideas that will influence work processes need to engage employees early in the process. This is illuminated in the following quote by one of the area managers:

> Some things need to be managed and controlled from the top whereas some changes must be based on very strong participation from [employees]. [...] An example is, [...] a change concerning that many of today's doctoral visits should be relocated to other professions. It is very important that such work is driven from below, or with a strong participation from below, to be part of how this change is going to be realized. If you come from above and say that this is how you should work, it will never succeed. [...] From top-down, perhaps organizational values, this have to be set from above, this is how it should be. [...] Sometimes you have to set the direction, the goal which we should aim for. [...] you need to look at it from a broader perspective, societal development and people's needs. (Area manager, implementation group)

Further, the analysis suggests that the transaction-oriented perspective, characterized in the data as a focus on professions and work tasks rather than on patients and patients' needs over time, dominates primary care, which has had some consequences. These consequences are expressed as relating to identification and understanding of existing problems in the healthcare context, and how these problems emerged. Deficiencies in sharing knowledge and experiences internally but also among different primary care units are further consequences of this perspective. Sometimes innovative ideas are presented without information about the exact problem or need that led to it, which in the long run may influence to what degree the solution is accepted and used by employees, as well as by patients. Another issue raised by unit managers relates to managing the daily practice with temporary staff. Personnel turnover influenced the work environment negatively, which in turn hindered the implementation of ideas; the focus needed to be on managing the ordinary everyday practice, rather than implementing ideas.

Organizational culture

The organizational culture at the primary care units is to a high degree characterized by existing traditions, professional roles, attitudes, and values, and may inhibit service innovation. How things are done is rooted in traditions, and what is expected of each other is strongly related to the professional role. As innovation includes changes to existing structures, practices, and norms, it challenges the accepted roles and the responsibility and control associated with each role. Professional roles are also associated with degree of power. Strong power combined with negative attitudes has consequences for realizing service innovation, as illuminated in the following quotation:

> The profession of medicine has in some way the final word when some routines are to be implemented or when ways of working should be changed. So I think if you do not manage to engage the profession of medicine, it will affect a lot. But certainly there is an increase in positive attitudes towards changes in other staff groups. (Unit manager, implementation group)

To accomplish service innovation, one of the area managers pointed out the need of a disrupted mindset, where managers and employees share values regarding development and innovative work.

Structure for innovation implementation

The findings show the need of an organizational structure that supports service innovation processes, enabling service innovation implementation. Both managers and frontline employees argue that support for innovation work is needed, which is discussed in terms of an organizational unit that provides resources in the form of personnel, methods, best practices, and tools for transforming great ideas into realized service innovations. The need of a structured method for the selection, invitation, and involvement of patients in innovation projects is one example:

> We partly regard the patient perspective through our contact with user organizations. [...] But I think that we need to broaden the perspective and consider how we can involve patients in a better way and it would have been great if we had a model for that. [...] However, it also requires resources for it and perhaps someone should be dedicated the assignment to integrate the patient perspective in change processes. (Area manager, implementation group)

Another challenge is the transfer of knowledge among primary care units; it is further recommended that this organizational, supporting unit should support knowledge diffusion as well as coordinate ongoing innovation projects. The findings show that without a structure for innovation implementation, implementation is more or less dependent on key persons, persons with positive attitudes toward changes and who have the strength and patience to accomplish the realization of the innovative ideas.

Authority

To succeed with implementing innovative ideas, dedicated authorities are key. With authority follows ownership and responsibility, also acknowledged as enablers of idea implementation. However, for authority to function as an enabler, the idea must be organizationally connected, and responsibility for the implementation work must be explicitly expressed. A patient articulates as follows:

> I think it is important to dedicate work tasks to persons, [...] "now I would like to know who can engage in this, and take responsibility".

[…] "Who takes responsibility" is an invaluable expression. (Patient, mixed innovation group)

When an innovative idea includes changes outside the primary care unit, it falls outside of the unit manager's authority, inhibiting implementation. This occurs even though the unit managers are the main actors responsible for realizing innovative work at the primary care unit. In situations where authority is missing, implementation becomes more complex. Implementation thus requires the involvement of more people and coordination within the county council. Consequently, innovation may take longer and could be hampered due to unclear ownership and management.

Middle managers

One condition identified as related to middle managers is *commitment*. The findings show that having a shared vision and goal, as well as the innovation level of the idea, influences to what degree managers are committed to idea implementation.

One reason why so few ideas were implemented in the service innovation process in the study seems to be the lack of a shared vision and common goals. When addressing if a shared goal existed, one of the area managers responded:

Perhaps we did not share the same goal in the project. […] Perhaps some were more focused on generating great ideas and realizing them while some were more interested in finding a method for how to come up with great ideas. (Area manager, implementation group)

A unit manager also commented the innovation level of ideas:

This [referring to an idea suggesting increased telephone availability at the primary care unit] is not an innovation but more a repeated complaint that we actually are struggling with since many years. I can understand that patients want to be able to get in contact [with their primary care unit] throughout the day and without being placed in line, but this has little to do with innovation. Things like this contribute to the fact that it may not be the greatest commitment. (Unit manager, implementation group)

The absence of a shared vision and goal is here interpreted as negatively influencing to what degree the members in the implementation group were committed to the project, as well as its progress. Besides a shared vision and goal, middle managers' commitment and attitude seem to be influenced by the innovation level of the idea. When the managers' did not perceive the idea to be an innovative solution, but rather focusing a known problem in the primary care context, this seemed to negatively influence the middle managers' commitment; a possible explanation of why so few ideas were implemented.

Frontline employees and users

Two conditions have been identified as related to frontline employees and users: *management support* and *resistance*.

Management support

Management support concerns how employees perceive managers' engagement in changes that will influence work practices, as well as managers' willingness to create good work environments. To even consider involving employees in innovation work, frontline employees highlight the importance of supportive managers that encourage ideas and put value in openness and users' and employees' contributions. Further, managers that have insight into organizational work practices and professionals' day-to-day work have developed an understanding of how ideas will influence work practices, as illuminated in this quotation:

> [The unit manager] sort of get it all together, so that it will be the best for us even if there is something that comes from the top and which has to be done. Then the manager fixes it to make it as smooth as possible in the organization. [...] The manager listens to us, but it is also that the manager has worked in the organization. [...] The manager picks up ideas, and comes up with own ideas and somehow makes it easier [for us]. The manager wants us to have a good workplace. (Frontline employee, personnel innovation group)

When managers support and engage in frontline employees' work, such as making decisions that promote good conditions for the implementation of ideas, there are increased opportunities to succeed with service innovation. Middle managers seem, thus, to have a key role in promoting employees' commitment in innovation projects.

Resistance

Resistance is related to employees' feeling of change fatigue and employees' involvement in service innovation processes. The frontline employees expressed resistance toward working to make changes due to previous unrealized efforts. Discussions relating to things such as changes and strategies are time-consuming activities that very seldom turn into implemented changes. Hence, a state of change fatigue is present that negatively influences employees' willingness to participate in the work of making changes. One of the frontline employees illuminated this change fatigue:

> So, we have done a lot of things like planning days and such things, but it usually falls on the implementation. It just becomes something that you discuss but then nothing happens. This has happened a lot of times, this is how it usually goes. A few years ago we spent a lot of time discussing how the [primary care unit] should be rebuilt [...] but then nothing happened, and we had put a lot of energy and time and ideas, and when nothing happens you lose interest. (Frontline employee, personnel innovation group)

Additionally, when ideas are implemented without the involvement of employees, the employees feel threatened and changes are experienced as an added workload, increasing the employees' resistance to the change. One of the area managers, who has experienced this resistance, pointed out that a key to avoid this resistance among employees is to make sure that the work to make the change is anchored among the ones that will be influenced by the change. This should be driven by management and could be realized through, for example, an internal working group, including different professions.

The findings have described the identified conditions for service innovation implementation and illuminated how these conditions may function as enablers or inhibitors. Next these findings are related to previous research.

Challenges for Realizing Innovative Ideas

A challenge for implementing service innovation is the prevailing focus in the implementation research on the adoption of already existing innovations that have been developed outside an organization's practice. Current strategies and frameworks are primarily related to adoption, whereas this chapter recognizes the importance of acknowledging implementation as a part of a dynamic service innovation process that emphasizes the notion of value creation. There is also a tendency, both in research and practice, to focus on the idea generation phase of the service innovation process. However, many great ideas are not realized, an issue that is highlighted in this chapter, and none of the perspectives ensure the successful implementation of existing innovations or ideas. Without having methods and frameworks for implementation that include both the adoption and the process perspectives, and that take frontline employees and users into account, there is a risk of having great ideas but less realization, as shown in this chapter.

There are several conditions that enable and/or inhibit an innovation being put into practice in an organization. An organizational challenge is to create enabling conditions for realizing service innovations, related to the categories suggested by Cadwallader *et al.* (2010); that is, environment, organization, middle managers, and frontline employees and users. First of all, national policies and rules are something that every county council must relate to and act accordingly with. The findings showed that environmental conditions may restrict an organization's ability to innovate and realize innovations. Even though the public sector's primary goal is to create value for all citizens (Alford, 2016), restrictions and the allocation of resources due to governance decisions have been shown to affect the possibility to realize innovative ideas in the studied primary care units. However, when ideas are in line with political initiatives, the resources allocated to the county council function as an enabler.

Related to the overall resource allocation, the county council allocates resources within its organization, which every primary care unit is dependent on. This factor should be taken into consideration before starting up service innovation processes within healthcare (public) contexts. More radical ideas are dependent on the overall allocation of both financial and human resources by the county council, but also on the organizational structure, manager commitment, and support for handling idea and implementation processes. Unfortunately, this implies that radical and extraordinary ideas might not being taken up in the system by the managers, as these ideas demand a large amount of resources and might be seen as "too radical" by upper management. In contrast, ideas for incremental innovation that relates to small, day-to-day adjustments of the service are more likely to be realized, as the individual unit manager, and to some extent also the frontline employees, have the authority to control implementation.

Crosby *et al.* (2016) suggest that creating public value through collaborative innovation requires leaders to act as sponsors, champions, catalysts, and implementers. These roles include the channeling of resources, such as knowledge and competences; removing barriers to collaboration; being supportive; and convening, organizing, facilitating, and energizing the innovation process, as well as realizing the idea and making it work in practice. Since service innovation involves implementing new work processes, approaches, and structures, innovation often takes place as parallel processes: the development of a specific service, and a change of the actors' mindsets and the practices as the "ways of doing" healthcare service. The empirical findings, however, illustrate that even though middle managers are given the authority to implement innovation, other challenges and conditions for service innovation implementation exist. Mindsets, traditions, and norms in the organizations' culture, and power related to professional roles and hierarchy, enable or inhibit both idea generation and idea implementation. Therefore, this chapter suggests that service innovation should be accompanied by change processes, such as social and cultural (cf. Nilsen and Roback, 2011).

The empirical findings show that traditions and professional knowledge play a pivotal role in the healthcare context, where employees with different professions have different power. Power, professional status, competing perspectives on knowledge, and resistance within organizational cultures may influence the direction and outcomes of the involvement of patients (Hardyman *et al.*, 2015) and other actors in the service innovation process. When several types of actors are involved that have different levels of power to influence both the generation of ideas for service innovation and how these ideas are realized, it implies turbulence and negotiations in the process (Sundström *et al.*, 2017). Such tensions are identified in the present study, for example, as different actors value future service innovations differently; it is also easy to become trapped in traditions and different logics (Pache and Santos, 2010), which inhibits the desire to absorb and accept new innovations.

Managerial Implications and Future Research

The managerial implications drawn from this study relate to the context in which the service innovation process takes place, the role of managers, and the role of frontline employees and users.

This chapter confirms that how implementation occurs is dependent on the specific context, and the service innovation process is suggested to be understood in relation to the context in which the process takes place, which in our study relates to primary care. The service innovation process may be both enabled and inhibited by conditions at different levels. It is therefore essential for managers to adopt a system perspective, reflecting upon the different environmental, organizational, managerial, and individual conditions, and how they in combination set the agenda for realizing service innovation. Consequently, we suggest that future research focus on further reflecting on innovative ideas in relation to these four levels, both in the context of healthcare but also in other contexts. Furthermore, as the conditions within these levels are not isolated from each other, we suggest that future research focus on the levels' relationships and influence.

Furthermore, middle managers' role in engaging and motivating frontline employees participating in service innovation is key. Involvement of frontline employees and users in the process facilitates the possibility to learn from and utilize these actors' explicit and latent needs and practice-related knowledge. Early and active involvement of frontline employees has been shown to facilitate the implementation of the service (Karlsson and Skålén, 2015; Ordanini and Parasuraman, 2011). Even though resources need to be allocated toward "the fuzzy front-end of service innovation" (Alam, 2006, p. 468), we also suggest the importance of having resources related to the realization of ideas. For example, the involvement of frontline employees and users lowers the risk of problems when realizing the idea, as well as the risk of future unwanted services. This chapter extends the previous research on how to involve patients in the service innovation process by introducing innovation groups as a method for idea generation, a method shown to be successful at generating implementable ideas. However, without managerial support and organizational structures, implementation of ideas tends to be limited. We suggest that further research focus more specifically on how the roles of the frontline employees and users have to be taken into account when managing implementation.

Service innovation involves implementing new work processes, approaches, and structures. This is often challenged by present mindsets, traditions, norms, and professional power, implying that service innovation is accompanied by different change processes. In this case, change management plays a pivotal role, where managers acknowledge and manage these parallel processes, as well as the challenges that emerge. For further research, we therefore suggest focusing on the challenges of these parallel processes and the role of managers in mitigating these challenges.

Power, professional status, competing perspectives on knowledge, traditions, and different logics function as triggers for a turbulent service innovation process (sometimes referred to as a political process; Sundström *et al.*, 2017), recognized by negotiations and tensions in actors' value-creating processes. Previous research has suggested that if the new innovation does not meet the requirements and expectations of future value, the process might be terminated before the implementation stage (Sundström *et al.*, 2017), a conclusion confirmed in this study. Managers should be aware of these triggers, and how they may influence the service innovation process, for example, when innovation groups are set up. We suggest future research to create a deeper understanding of the political processes and their consequences for realizing service innovation implementation.

Conclusions

Anchored in service innovation and service implementation research, this chapter identifies conditions that may function as enablers or inhibitors of the implementation of ideas in service innovation. The findings imply that the following conditions may function as enablers or inhibitors in a primary care context: governance, organizational structure, organizational culture, structure for innovation implementation, authority, commitment, management support, and resistance. Several of the identified inhibitors function as an invisible barrier to service innovation implementation that has proven hard to break, a challenge met by frontline employees as well as managers.

The chapter contributes to existing implementation frameworks, such as CFIR (Damschroder *et al.*, 2009), by suggesting frontline employees and users to be included and suggesting ways they can be involved in the service innovation process by participation in innovation groups. The chapter broadens the scope from an adoption focus toward including the perspective of the implementation of ideas generated in a service innovation process that is directly related to the focal organization. The identified conditions are crucial for the implementation of ideas and thus for service innovation to be realized.

References

Alam, I. (2006). Removing fuzziness from the fuzzy front-end of service innovations through customer interactions. *Industrial Marketing Management*, 35(4), 468–480.

Alford, J. (2016). Co-production, interdependence and publicness: Extending public service-dominant logic. *Public Management Review*, 18(5), 673–691.

Baer, M. (2012). Putting creativity to work: The implementation of creative ideas in organizations. *Academy of Management Journal*, 55(5), 1102–1119.

Barcet, A. (2010). Innovation in services: a new paradigm and innovation model. In Gallouj, F. and Djellal. F. (eds.), *The Handbook of Innovation and Services*. Cheltenham: Edward Elgar. Chapter 2, pp. 49–67.

Barnett, J., Vasileiou, K., Djemil, F., Brooks, L., and Young, T. (2011). Understanding innovators' experiences of barriers and facilitators in implementation and diffusion of healthcare service innovations: A qualitative study. *BMC Health Services Research*, 11(1), 1–12.

Breimaier, H. E., Heckemann, B., Halfens, R. J. G., and Lohrmann, C. (2015). The consolidated framework for implementation research (CFIR): A useful theoretical framework for guiding and evaluating a guideline implementation process in a hospital-based nursing practice. *BMC Nursing*, **14**(1), 14–43.

Cadwallader, S., Jarvis, C., Bitner. M., and Ostrom, A. (2010). Frontline employee motivation to participate in service innovation implementation. *Journal of Academy of Marketing Science*, **38**(2), 219–239.

Carlborg, P., Kindström, D., and Kowalkowski, C. (2014). The evolution of service innovation research: A critical review and synthesis. *The Service Industries Journal*, **34**(5), 373–398.

Carlfjord, S., Lindberg, M., Bendtsen, P., Nilsen, P., and Andersson, A. (2010). Key factors influencing adoption of an innovation in primary health care: A qualitative study based on implementation theory. *BMC Family Practice*, **11**(1), 1–11.

Crosby, B. C., Hart, P., and Torfing, J. (2016). Public value creation through collaborative innovation. *Public Management Review,* **19**(5), 655–669.

Damschroder, L. J., Aron, D. C., Keith, R. E., Kirsh, S. R., Alexander, J. A., and Lowery, J. C. (2009). Fostering implementation of health services research findings into practice: a consolidated framework for advancing implementation science. *Implementation Science*, **4**(1), 1–15.

Damschroder, L. J. and Hagedorn, H. J. (2011). A guiding framework and approach for implementation research in substance use disorders treatment. *Psychology of Addictive Behaviors*, **25**(2), 194–205.

Damschroder, L. J. and Lowery, J. C. (2013). Evaluation of a large-scale weight management program using the consolidated framework for implementation research (CFIR). *Implementation Science*, **8**(1), 51–67.

Denzin, N. K. and Lincoln Y. S. (2011). Introduction: The discipline and practice of qualitative research. In Denzin, N. K. and Lincoln, Y. S. (eds.), *The Sage Handbook of Qualitative Research.* Thousand Oaks, CA: SAGE Publications. Chapter 1, pp. 1–19.

Engen, M. (2016). *Frontline Employees as Participants in Service Innovation Processes: Innovation by Weaving.* Dissertation, Lillehammer University College.

Engen, M. and Magnusson, P. (2015). Exploring the role of front-line employees as innovators. *The Service Industries Journal*, **35**(6), 303–324.

Engström, J. and Snyder, H. (2014). Patient involvement in healthcare service development — who to involve and why. *Paper presented at the 13th Symposium on Service in Management (QUIS)*, Karlstad, 2013.

Fuglsang, L. (2010). Bricolage and invisible innovation in public service innovation. *Journal of Innovation Economics & Management*, 1(5), 67–87.

Fuglsang, L. and Sørensen, F. (2011). The balance between bricolage and innovation: Management dilemmas in sustainable public innovation. *Service Industries Journal*, 31(4), 581–595.

Garpenby, P. (2011). Perspektiv på implementering. In Nilsen, P. (Red), *Implementering. Teori och tillämpning inom hälso- & sjukvård.* Lund: Studentlitteratur. (In Swedish).

Greenhalgh, T., Robert, G., Macfarlane, F., Bate, P., and Kyriakidou, O. (2004). Diffusion of innovations in service organizations: Systematic review and recommendations. *The Milbank Quarterly*, 82(4), 581–629.

Groene, O., Lombarts, M. J. M. H., Klazinga, N., Alonso, J., Thompson, A., and Suñol, R. (2009). Is patient-centredness in European hospitals related to existing quality improvement strategies? Analysis of a cross-sectional survey (marquis study). *Quality and Safety in Health Care*, 18(Suppl 1), i44–i50.

Grol, R. (2001). Successes and failures in the implementation of evidence-based guidelines for clinical practice. *Medical Care*, 39(8), 46–54.

Hardyman, W., Daunt, K. L., and Kitchener, M. (2015). Value co-creation through patient engagement in health care: A micro-level approach and research agenda. *Public Management Review*, 17(1), 90–107.

Hartley, J., Sørensen, E., and Torfing, J. (2013). Collaborative innovation: A viable alternative to market competition and organizational entrepreneurship. *Public Administration Review*, 73(6), 821–830.

Karlsson, J. (2018). *Frontline Employees' Role in Service Innovation and Value Creation.* Doctoral dissertation, Karlstad University.

Karlsson, J. and Skålén, P. (2015). Exploring front-line employee contributions to service innovation. *European Journal of Marketing,* 49(9/10), 1346–1365.

Karlsson, J., Skålén, P., and Sundström, E. (2014). How front-line employees nurture service innovation through co-creation with their customers: A case study of public health care. In Fuglsang, L., Rönning, R., and Enquist, B. (eds.), *Framing Innovation in Public Service Sectors.* London: Routledge, Chapter 2, pp. 18–40.

Kindström, D. and Kowalkowski, C. (2014). Service innovation in product-centric firms: A multidimensional business model perspective. *Journal of Business & Industrial Marketing*, 29(2), 96–111.

Kirk, M. A., Kelley, C., Yankey, N., Birken, S. A., Abadie, B., and Damschroder, L. (2016). A systematic review of the use of the consolidated framework for implementation research. *Implementation Science*, 11(1), 72–83.

Klein, K. J. and Sorra, J. S. (1996). The challenge of innovation implementation. *Academy of Management Review*, **21**(4), 1055–1080.

Magnusson, P. R., Matthing, J., and Kristensson, P. (2003). Managing user involvement in service innovation. *Journal of Service Research*, **6**(2), 111–124.

Magnusson, P. R. (2009). Exploring the contributions of involving ordinary users in ideation of technology-based services. *Journal of Product Innovation Management*, **26**(5), 578–593.

Meyers, D. C., Durlak, J. A., and Wandersman, A. (2012). The quality implementation framework: A synthesis of critical steps in the implementation process. *American Journal of Community Psychology*, **50**(3–4), 462–480.

Mu, Y., Bossink, B., and Vinig, T. (2018). Employee involvement in ideation and healthcare service innovation quality. *The Service Industries Journal*, **38**(1–2), 67–86.

Nilsen, P. (2015). Making sense of implementation theories, models and frameworks. *Implementation Science*, **10**(1), 53.

Nilsen and Roback (2011). Implementering, kunskap och lärande, In Nilsen, P. (Red), *Implementering. Teori och tillämpning inom hälso- & sjukvård*. Lund: Studentlitteratur. Chapter 3, pp. 51–69. (In Swedish).

NIRN (2018). *Implementation Defined*. Retrieved from: http://nirn.fpg.unc.edu/learn-implementation/implementation-defined.

Ordanini, A. and Parasuraman, A. (2011). Service innovation viewed through a service-dominant logic lens: A conceptual framework and empirical analysis. *Journal of Service Research*, **14**(1), 3–23.

Ostrom, A. L., Parasuraman, A., Bowen, D. E., Patrício, L., and Voss, C. A. (2015). Service research priorities in a rapidly changing context. *Journal of Service Research*, **18**(2), 127–159.

Pache, A. C. and Santos, F. (2010). When worlds collide: The internal dynamics of organizational responses to conflicting institutional demands. *Academy of Management Review*, **35**(3), 455–476.

Renedo, A., Marston, C. A., Spyridonidis, D., and Barlow, J. (2015). Patient and public involvement in healthcare quality improvement: How organizations can help patients and professionals to collaborate. *Public Management Review*, **17**(1), 17–34.

Rogers, E. M. (1962). *Diffusion of Innovations* (1st ed.). New York: Free Press.

Scheuing, E. E. and Johnson, E. M. (1989). A proposed model for new service development. *The Journal of Services Marketing*, **3**(2), 25–34.

Skålén, P., Karlsson, J., Engen, M., and Magnusson, P. R. (2018). Understanding public service innovation as resource integration and creation of value propositions. *Australian Journal of Public Administration*, **77**(4), 700–714.

Snyder, H. and Engström, J. (2016). The antecedents, forms and consequences of patient involvement: A narrative review of the literature. *International Journal of Nursing Studies*, **53**, 351–378.

Sundbo, J. (2008). Innovation and involvement in services. In Fuglsang, L. (Ed.), *Innovation and the Creative Process. Towards Innovation with Care.* Cheltenham, MA: Edward Elgar. Chapter 2, pp. 25–47.

Sundström, E., Karlsson, J., and Camén, C. (2017). Service innovation as a political process. *The Service Industries Journal*, **37**(5/6), 341–362.

Tabak, R. G., Khoong, E. C., Chambers, D. A., and Brownson, R. C. (2012). Bridging research and practice: Models for dissemination and implementation research. *American Journal of Preventive Medicine*, **43**(3), 337–350.

Toivonen, M. and Tuominen, T. (2009). Emergence of innovations in services. *The Service Industries Journal*, **29**, 887–902.

Vargo, S. and Lusch, R. (2008). Service-dominant logic: Continuing the evolution. *Journal of the Academy of Marketing Science,* **36**(1), 1–10.

Witell, L., Snyder, H., Gustafsson, A., Fombelle, P., and Kristensson, P. (2016). Defining service innovation: A review and synthesis. *Journal of Business Research*, **69**(8), 2863–2872.

Chapter 13

Exploring the Challenges of Servitization in Manufacturing Companies

Peter R. Magnusson*, Christiane Hipp† and Bo Edvardsson*

*Karlstad University, Sweden
† Brandenburg University of Technology at Cottbus, Germany

Key takeaways

1. Many manufacturing companies are becoming increasingly infused by service offerings, which often causes old business models to become obsolete. The transition from manufacturing to a service-oriented company has been reported to be troublesome, but has received little research attention.
2. The purpose of the chapter is to identify — on both a strategic and operational level — barriers that manufacturing companies can overcome and drivers they can utilize in order to successfully transform into innovative and service-oriented firms.
3. The chapter contributes with a reference model for servitization grounded in previous literature and adapted based on the empirical findings in two studies. Three major activities that hinder servitization

are identified: being stuck in a mindset, knowledge spillover, and pricing/charging. Managerial implications for handling the transition process are given.

4. The chapter is mainly applicable to manufacturing industries in a B2B context.

Embracing Services in Manufacturing

Many manufacturing companies are evolving their businesses to be more infused by service offerings in order to gain competitive advantage. Neu and Brown (2005) showed that manufacturing or goods-dominant firms can successfully become "solution providers" by adding services to their existing product portfolios. Examples of this can be found in several companies in different countries, such as Heidelberger Druckmaschinen, Trumpf, ABB, General Electric, Siemens, Schindler, and Otis.

Old business models often become obsolete when services are included in the offering. However, the transition from a product-oriented company to a service-oriented one has been reported to be troublesome (e.g., Matthyssens and Vandenbempt, 2008; Neu and Brown, 2005; Oliva and Kallenberg, 2003; Vargo and Lusch, 2008). Jacob and Ulaga (2008) contended that the research on transition from a product focus to a service focus in business markets is still at an early stage and called for more empirical research on the subject.

The aim of this chapter is to identify and analyze, both on a strategic level and an operational level, the transition process from a product orientation to a service orientation. The discussion involves the following topics:

1. The question of how manufacturing companies actually define services.
2. The triggers to become more service oriented; that is why the company started the process.
3. Critical factors for product-to-service transition; that is, barriers and drivers (enablers) that manufacturing companies need in order to successfully transform into service-oriented firms.

The chapter is based on two studies. Study 1 used an explorative inductive approach and was an in-depth case study from a large European manufacturing company. 28 in-depth interviews were conducted with managers, including top-project managers and managers from different departments including service development, business development, strategic development, financing, information management, patent office, and production. The interviews were also combined with archival data spanning back 12 years in time. Study 2 was used to further deepen the understanding of the critical transition-factors identified in Study 1 and was based on interviews with four different manufacturing companies that had, to varying extents, adopted service operations.

Distinction between Products and Services

Service innovations and their peculiarities have been increasingly pushed into the center of economic policy and innovation management research (Djellal and Gallouj, 2001; Drejer, 2004; Gebauer *et al.*, 2005, 2008; Gebauer and Friedli, 2005; Gershuny, 1978; Hauknes, 1998; Miles, 1994; Sundbo, 1997; Tidd and Hull, 2003). Furthermore, the question arises as to which differentiation criteria between products and services have been identified in the literature. This does not aim so much to find an unequivocal separation of products and services as to identify typical service characteristics that influence the way innovation processes *per se* are dealt with. Auernhammer and Stabe (2002) and Hipp (2008), have identified, summarized, and categorized a dozen different factors that distinguish services and manufacturing goods. Zeithaml *et al.* (1985) condensed the differences between products and services down to four characteristics, the frequently cited "IHIP": intangibility, heterogeneity, inseparability (of production and consumption), and perishability (cannot be stored/inventoried).

The most challenging and also quoted characteristic of services in the literature is the 'intangibility' of the service output (Hill, 1997). Even if the service affects physical transformations (for example, transport) or is embodied in a material medium (for instance, a DVD), the service product purchased will not embody a tangible object but will resemble the problem-solving process or result. It can be summarized that the absence of outputs, which are independent physical entities, is an important characteristic of most services (Tether and Metcalfe, 2004).

For services, intangibility creates difficulties in demonstrating the output, in advance, to potential clients (for an overview, see Fuchs, 1968; Hill, 1997; Quinn, 1986; Russel, 1973; Soete and Miozzo, 1989). This means that their qualities cannot easily be explained or assessed by the customer. Efforts to overcome this problem include guarantees, quality standards, and demonstration packages. The same issue hinders endeavors toward standardization. The intangible nature of most services inspires thoughts about strategies, which customize service outputs and adapt them to the needs of the users. Closely connected to the intangible nature of services are the problems concerning storage and, thus, the transportation and exportation of services. The inability to keep services in stock means that production and consumption cannot be separated, and the customer must be integrated into production and delivery.

This leads to an intriguing relationship between services and products, which has led to a new emerging perspective among service marketing scholars. Vargo and Lush (2004a,b) advocated that the difference or similarities between services are of minor interest; instead, the *value-in-use* for the customer should be deemed important. They argued for a 'service-dominant logic' where value is created when either physical products or services are used. Thus, service becomes a perspective on value creation focusing on the realized value for customers, and that value is assessed on the basis of value in use (Edvardsson *et al.*, 2005). In this view, the differences between services and products are suppressed, which is in opposition to traditional service research, and has given rise to criticism (e.g., Stauss, 2005).

In the present chapter, we define a product–service concept as a combination of physical products, services, and/or other resources/enablers offered by the seller to be combined with the customer's resources and capabilities in a specific way that forms the prerequisites for attractive, realized customer value.

Understanding Services in Manufacturing

The nature of manufacturing services

Services in manufacturing are associated, to varying degrees, with the core business of the enterprise whose core business consists of manufacturing and distributing products. Services in manufacturing can be classified and characterized in various forms. The list below shows a selection of various typological ways of classifying these services (Frambach *et al.*, 1997; Kotler and Armstrong, 1996).

1. Maintenance and repair services (for example, equipment repair, janitorial services), usually supplied under contract.
2. Business advisory services (such as legal, accounting, advertising, management consulting), typically new task-buying situations.
3. Pre-sales services are those that help the buyer make a purchase decision and stimulate adoption of an industrial product (for example, demonstrating the product and offering trial use of it).
4. Sale services are those that help the customer take the product into use; examples include installation and training.
5. After-sales service is designed to keep the customer satisfied with the purchase; for example, failure handling and regular maintenance inspections.

Other scholars who have elaborated on this issue include Boyt and Harvey (1997), who discussed different ways of classifying services for the purpose of easing segmentation. Mathieu (2001) discussed the differences between services supporting the product versus the customer. However, there is no unifying classification of services in manufacturing, which is not surprising considering the heterogeneous nature of manufacturing industries. However, a common dominator seems to be that the manufacturing services are rarely "stand-alone," but are in some way linked to some physical product.

Servitization a transformational process

Vandermerwe and Rada (1989) coined the concept of servitization to describe how business-to-business manufacturers develop new services complementing their product-based offerings to deliver additional functionality (Martinez *et al.*, 2010); this can produce a competitive advantage for manufacturers, leading to increased sales and profitability (Robinson *et al.*, 2002). On an aggregate level, servitization can be regarded a process. Oliva and Kallenberg (2003) presented this as a goods-to-service continuum covering: (A) consolidation of product-related services (services related to goods), (B) entering the installed base service market, (C) expanding to relationship-based services or to process-centered services, and (D) taking over end users' operation.

Position (A) implies that services are add-ons to goods, and position (D) suggests that goods are add-ons to service. Thus, the importance of goods decreases and the importance of services increases as the company moves along the continuum. Accordingly, servitization has been associated with a company's shift in the value chain, from product-centric to service-centric business models, and with new organizational structures (Brax and Visintin, 2017). In the present chapter, we have adopted a definition that summarizes servitization from Kowalkowski *et al.* (2017), who stated that servitization is defined as: "the transformational process of shifting from a product-centric business model and logic to a service-centric approach".

Viewing servitization as a transformational process implies a change of mental models, or the dominant logic (Prahalad, 2004), among all employees regarding how business should be run. This includes how resources could be used and reconfigured in new ways (e.g., Baines *et al.*, 2009), how the company's routines and processes needs to be updated, and what norms and values that need to permeate the company (Kindström and Kowalkowski, 2014).

An issue for debate has been whether firms should try and integrate the services into the core product offerings, as advocated by Oliva and Kallenberg (2003), or to separate service and product operations, as claimed by Neu and Brown (2005). More empirical studies at different companies and industries, as well as more transitions-oriented theoretical conceptualizations, are needed in order to answer this question.

Barriers for product-to-service transition

Although previous research has identified problems transiting from a product to a service provider, very few studies have examined these on micro level. However, some potentially general barriers have been identified. The short summary below builds upon the findings of Oliva and Kallenberg (2003), Neu and Brown (2005), and Matthyssen and Vandenbempt (2008).

A frequently mentioned issue is the need for a *cultural change* when moving from a pure physical output to something more intangible. There is a need for a mental shift from prioritizing product quality and process efficiency to understanding how to satisfy customer needs.

When tangibles become less important, this will require understanding, development, and implementation of *new business models*. Due to the limited experience among both customers and suppliers, a major problem seems to be how to price and charge for services.

Integrating service operations require skills, structures, and processes that are new to the manufacturing company. Thus, organizing for service operations demands more intra-communication in the company, where all employees understand their operations from a customer value-adding perspective.

However, past research has generated limited in-depth knowledge regarding the barriers and potential enablers for the transition process (Jacob and Ulaga, 2008), and the present study aims to help rectify this situation.

Method

This chapter is divided into two studies. *Study 1 — ECO-case* aimed to obtain in-depth knowledge regarding the transition process by studying different units within a manufacturing company that was transitioning from being a pure manufacturing firm to a more service-oriented organization. The intention was to better grasp and understand the cultural inertia that has previously been detected as one of the main hurdles for transition. *Study 2 — Triangulation of four organizations* aimed to validate and deepen the knowledge regarding the dimensions identified in Study 1 by investigating four companies. The two studies are described more in detail below.

Study 1 — ECO-case

Outline

The study investigated the main driving and hampering factors when transiting from pure product orientation to becoming more service-oriented; and also analyzed how barriers might be overcome. The case company was selected because it was in the midst of a transition from being a pure manufacturing firm to a more service-oriented one. First, six explorative interviews were conducted to plan for the rest of the study. The interviews revealed the existence of widely contrasting perspectives (or cultures) regarding the company's emerging service operations. This led us not only to restrict the interviews to the service division and top management, but also to investigate a wider scope of the company. We conducted 27 in-depth interviews with different managers, including top-project leaders at different functions/units within the studied firm; namely, the service development, business development, strategic development, financing department, information department, and patent department. The interviews lasted between 60 and 120 minutes and were conducted in accordance with a semi-structured interview guide that focused on the following issues: (a) defining services on a conceptual level, (b) the firm's current phase in the service transition process, (c) drivers for infusing services, (d) problems with transiting toward service operations, and (e) tools and methods, if any, used to ease the transition. Not all issues were necessarily dealt with by all respondents. Some of the respondents were contacted again after the interviews to supplement and clarify comments. All interviews were tape-recorded and transcribed for analysis.

During the visits and interviews, archival material was collected spanning a 12-year period, enabling a longitudinal analysis of the transition process. The archival material mainly consisted of two types of information: official information brochures aimed for potential customers; and all issues of the company's in-house magazine (aimed at all employees). In the latter, every issue had a column in which someone from the top management, including the CEO, wrote about an important and topical issue. Therefore, this column reflected top managements' prioritization and official point of view over more than a decade.

Investigated company

The case company is called ECO (Engine Components), which is a fictitious name in order to preserve the anonymity of the investigated firm. ECO is more than 70 years old and a subsidiary of a large multinational company. ECO specializes in four different areas; the one of interest for this study was the manufacture of hi-tech engine components. The industrial sector that makes this type of engine has undergone a restructuring process. Twenty years ago, most of these types of engines were normally designed, manufactured, and supported by single companies (OEMs) that utilized different subcontractors. However, due to an increased level of complexity, and development costs, all new engines are today developed in different consortia on a risk- and revenue-sharing basis. Each partner in a consortium is specialized and responsible for certain module(s) and, or component(s).

ECO had previously only manufactured on a subcontractor basis. At that time, the input for the process was a drawing and the output was a piece of hardware (the component); the process was known as *make to print*. To be able to become a consortium partner, ECO had, about 10 years before our study, also began to take on the design of some of the components. This entailed the input being a demand specification from which they produced a design (drawing) of the component that was then produced, known as *design make*. At the same time, they also began to take on the post-sale responsibility for their components, known as total care or product support. This transition had completely changed the type of knowledge resources that the company needed. Many more man-hours were now spent on activities that did not directly lead to the production of a piece of hardware. This had made the company realize that it was gradually becoming increasingly service-oriented; at least, this was the term used by the people in the service department who were responsible for developing the company's service operations. The aim of ECO's strategy was for an increasing part of the revenue to come from services. Also, the CEO of the parent company had explicitly stated that all subsidiaries should increase their services turnover to 50% in a number of years. However, no official change program was underway at ECO to activate the transformation into becoming more service-intensive.

Study 2 — Triangulation of four organizations

This was a complementary study that aimed to triangulate and deepen the understanding regarding the findings identified in Study 1. We chose four different firms that represented a range of various manufacturing industries and were therefore not competitors. All firms had a long tradition of traditional manufacturing before starting to develop service operations. In Table 3, an overview of the companies can be found. Based on the results in Study 1, semi-structured interviews with key individuals (people with deep insight in the product-to-service transition for the specific organization) were conducted. One interview per company was performed and the interviews focused on the issues identified in Study 1; that is, triggers, barriers, success factors, and tools. The interviews lasted for about one hour each. Notes were taken during the interview and were then transcribed into a clean copy and then fed back to the respondent for review.

Empirical Results and Reflections

Based on the main aspects of the questionnaire and the basic assumptions described above, four different areas of reflections are presented in this chapter: (a) defining services on a conceptual level, (b) the service transition process, (c) triggers for infusing services, and (d) critical factors with transiting toward service operations.

How do companies define manufacturing services?

The difficulty of defining services is shown not least by the plethora of efforts in the academic literature. It is definitely no easier for practitioners. One of the respondents at ECO, who had actually reflected quite a lot on the subject, expressed: "It's funny, we've talked about services, and when I'm explicitly asked 'what is a service?' it is actually hard to formulate an answer ... it's not self-evident, even for me..."

The puzzlement regarding how to define services on a conceptual level was common among most of the respondents in both studies. The most widespread approach was to define services by distinguishing them from products using certain characteristics, such as their intangibility, the customers' involvement and the co-production of services, and the indistinct ownership and IPR (intellectual property rights) of services compared with products. Thus, these distinguishing characteristics are quite similar to those mentioned in the traditional service literature. More specifically, many of the respondents also emphasized the high information (or knowledge) content in most of their services. The two most frequent characteristics mentioned (among all interviewees) were, first, that services call for a better understanding of the customers' processes; and second, that knowledge and competence formed the basis for their service offerings.

Interestingly, the respondents at ECO were asked to describe what they thought the company offered in terms of services today, and where it was heading in the future. Three different perspectives were discernible among the respondents, we have named them: *The Service Salvationists, The Service Pragmatists*, and *The Service Confusionists*. The latter group was the few respondents who were seemingly unaware that ECO was aiming to become more service-oriented. Since very few of the respondents displayed this unawareness, we will concentrate on the other two groups — the Salvationists and the Pragmatists.

The Service Salvationists were very much in favor of ECO becoming a service-oriented company. These people came mainly from the service development department, or had been the driving forces behind ECO opening itself up to service operations. For them, almost all activities could be seen as potential services, even manufacturing; thus, the business was a service business in which the service offered create customer value. However, they admitted that this perspective represented only a small part of the company. According to this group, service orientation would, in the future, probably render it unnecessary to have its own manufacturing — the firm could instead capitalize entirely on its knowledge resources by offering services. Many of the Service Salvationists were quite frustrated about the fact that so many at the company were stuck in, as they put it, "an old manufacturing culture". In the Salvationists' eyes, much of the company's output was actually services already, but they thought that people in general did not perceive that they were developing or producing services. One respondent even felt that the word 'service' had become "cursed" by many in the company so he had become reluctant to use it himself. The Service Salvationists could be considered a very homogenous group. They had developed a very clear framework regarding why service orientation was so important for the future of the company. There was also widespread frustration about the fact that the transition toward service orientation was taking so long and lacked the full support of upper management.

The Service Pragmatists, on the other hand, had accepted services as a *complement* to manufacturing operations. For them, however, the production of hardware was at the heart of the company and services were considered add-ons that can be used to support the sales of hardware. This was clearly illustrated by one of the respondents who, when asked what percentage of the company's profits emanated from services, responded: "Services are costs; it is the hardware that generates the revenue". When further asked if this "fact" was not mainly due to the calculation model used at the firm, the respondent's reply was immediate: "I consider that our calculation models *do reflect* the *reality*" [end of discussion]. The link between service and hardware makes it virtually impossible to separate manufacturing from the company, according to the Service Pragmatists. Several of the respondents in this group thought that "the talk about services had gone too far". Instead, what was important in their eyes was the ability to offer the customers something that brought them value; that is, good products. Compared to the Service Salvationists, the Service Pragmatists were more heterogeneous. Some of them had reflected on services quite a lot and had come to the conclusion that the foundation of the company was, and must remain, its manufacturing operations and competence. Others saw strong potential in services, but felt that services were quite complex and abstract and hard to fit into their business models. Pragmatists do not deny that services have some value, but only if connected with the physical products, thus basically a product-oriented logic.

Transiting toward services

Our findings indicate that the transition process from a product perspective to a service-oriented perspective is lengthy and rarely subject to a quick organizational change program. In all six cases, it took time for the manufacturing companies to unlearn the old product logic in favor of a service logic; that is, refocusing from the product to instead focusing on how to serve customers.

In our main case (ECO), the first signs of a new business logic could be found 10 years back when an employee was rewarded with 13,000 Euro for a proposal that reduced the firm's short-term revenues, but increased the value for the customer. In ECO's staff journal, a top manager commented that this was a turning point in the firm's policy. "Ten years ago, it would have been very unlikely that a suggestion which gives reduced revenue would have resulted in a reward. Today it is a different situation."

From Table 3, we can see that the firm Alfa, which has come the furthest toward a service perspective, started its transition 15 years ago and can still not be considered to have adopted a service logic. A common factor among all the cases is that the new services were initially built around the company's existing physical product offerings. This corresponds to what Mathieu (2001) defined as "a service supporting the supplier's product", (SSP). Inspired by the work of Oliva and Kallenberg (2003) we can, based on the study, discern five different phases that a manufacturing company can undertake during the servitization process. These are illustrated in Table 1. In the first phase, a company starts providing spare parts and repair services.

It is notable that, for each phase, the conceptualization of service changes over time as the firm moves from one phase to another. This can be illustrated by analyzing ECO's in-house magazine. The first time "service" is mentioned in ECO is eight years ago before our study, when one of the top-managers defined what a 'product' is for ECO: "A product can be both hardware and/or software, in other words both components and services". This was one of the first indications that the company's offerings do not necessarily have to be physical products; however, the service is vaguely defined. Three years later, one of the company's top project managers declared in an interview that: "… it is now a paradigm-shift away from the old product-oriented logic to the new where the process is the product". She clarified that, by "process" she meant services, repair work, maintenance, spare parts supply, technical support, and information systems. Thus, we can conclude that the conceptualization of service is something that is, and must be, adapted during the transition toward a more service-oriented firm. It should also be noted that several conceptualizations are normally active simultaneously.

Table 1.   Phases of servitization.

Phase	Conceptualization — Service is...
1st: Service and supply services	Providing spare parts and repairing after failure
2nd: On-site maintenance of products	Proactive and planned service before failure
3rd: Training to better utilize the products	Teaching customers to better utilize delivered products
4th: Production process consultancy to improve the effectiveness	Helping the customer to design/adapt the surrounding context of the delivered product
5th: Asset management (insourcing)	Taking care of a defined part of the customer's operations

Triggers for infusing services

Many of the respondents had the opinion that there were several interacting factors that drove evolution in the direction of more and more services. The interviewees identified a number of triggers for ECO to start its service operations. First, it comes from the customers. ECO's customers (the OEMs) wanted to outsource some of their operations to subcontractors or partners; in ECO's case, this was, for example, the construction and design of the components, but also total care commitment. The second trigger was that offering services was in line with the parent company's long-term strategy to increase its turnover from services. Third, services were considered a means of better capitalizing on the combined competence of the company. Fourth, the profit margins on services were expected to be higher than on hardware, as long as value-based pricing for services can be established. Fifth, services were regarded as harder to copy by competitors, because many of the value additions took place "in the heads" of the employees. Sixth, as services are interactions, they can be a means of strengthening relations with customers. No single trigger could be identified as being the most important.

Essentially the same triggers were found in Study 2 (see Table 3). For Alfa, it was a strategic decision from top management to differentiate its businesses to also include services. In the Beta case, it was a customer demand to initially have maintenance services that led the top management to initiate service operations. For Gamma, it was a large project where the customer required that the company should offer not only the physical product but also the start-up and operation. Based on the experiences from this project, the company could develop and extend its service offerings. Finally, Delta's interest in service operations came from a very limited group of people at middle management level. The company was (and is) very competitive in its field due to technical excellence; however, the technical performance could not be utilized by the customer as it was far beyond their actual needs. Thus, developing complementary services around the products was a way of gaining competitive advantage.

Critical factors for service transition

In this sub-section, we present three critical factors that either works as barriers or boosters for a service transition.

Stuck in a manufacturing mindset

A recurring factor on all cases was the cultural inertia. For ECO, it was the Service Salvationists who expressed this. In a way, they claimed they had "seen the light" and had understood that the future of the company lay in becoming increasingly service-oriented. Several of the respondents felt that many other employees were actually providing more services than they were aware of due to their "manufacturing mindset". "It's like selling drills when the customers are asking for holes", said one frustrated interviewee. The manufacturing culture of the company became evident during the interviews. The basic view among the Service Pragmatists — who, by definition, had a manufacturing mindset — was that the company *was, had always been*, and *would always be* a *manufacturing* company. The vision of becoming a service company was very alien, as illustrated by this quotation:

> *I think it's very important in our internal communication to express that we're NOT a service company, to avoid people doing the wrong things. We're a manufacturer and we deliver hardware … what's important is to be profitable.*

The same experiences were reported from the companies in Study 2. Several respondents expressed frustration regarding the unwillingness to take services "seriously". The status of working with service operations was initially low in all of the investigated companies. However, as time went by and the service operations could be expected to be profitable, the status increased. For Alfa, service operations had a relatively high status. Lack of status was also put forward as a barrier for adopting service operations.

As discussed, intangibility is probably the most important service characteristic and also the most problematic, especially in a manufacturing company that has always been able to relate to a physical outcome as the basis for its businesses. The intangibility introduces a main problem regarding how to communicate the content and benefits with its services both internally and externally; this, in turn, raises problems regarding pricing/charging for them, and even to capitalize on them. All of the investigated companies struggled with this problem.

Knowledge spillover and IPR

A main critical factor in ECO for developing services, at least knowledge-based ones, was the problem of protecting immaterial resources. Several respondents complained that too many of the employees had not realized that immaterial resources had to be protected. This was due to the old manufacturing logic; advanced concept design, calculations and analyses seemed to be extremely hard to capitalize on as the tradition among many of the engineers was to "give away" results to the customer for free as the profit was assumed to come from selling hardware. These employees did not realize that, for instance, knowledge was a resource that the company actually could, and should, earn money on. One frustrated project manager stated:

> *We surveyed the information flow in our work processes and then detected that many of our advanced analyses were sent directly to the customer for free ... we have a climate [at ECO] where it's virtually impossible to get any help from our engineers if you call them from inside. But if a customer calls, they'll do ANYTHING.*

There had been an occasion when the company had developed a new concept (drawings of new components) during a tendering process. Although the concept had been rejected, the tenderer had taken the concept to a competitor. As ECO had not claimed any proprietary rights on the concept, this was not considered illegal. The respondent argued that this mistake was due to having the mindset that you should make money on the hardware; the process (service) of designing the concept had no value.

Pricing and charging

In all of the investigated companies, pricing and charging of services was identified as difficult, especially if the services were knowledge-intensive. The customer accepts paying for 'time', but not for 'value'. This might have to do with the culture among the customers, who were used to paying for hard products, but receiving the services (such as support) for free. The following quote comes from one of the project managers at ECO:

> *In relation to customer X, it's possible to sell services, but you can't charge for the value of the service; you can only charge for the number of hours it takes to perform the service. For instance, if you do a smart analysis, you can only charge for the number of hours it takes Sven to run the analysis.*

This problem is mainly linked to the intangibility, which makes it hard for the customers to actually evaluate and appreciate their value. The dilemma is that you cannot make a knowledge-based service (such as analysis) too transparent because it will risk revealing the intellectual property. When selling manufactured goods, much of the knowledge has been embedded in the physical product and included in the price, making it even harder for the manufacturer to detach this and charge for it separately.

A recurring comment among the respondents in Study 2 was that their sellers often saw services as something they could "add for free" in order to get the deal. This was often considered a matter of educating the salespeople to understand that services needed new business models.

Concluding Discussion

A knowledge-based transition

If ECO and other manufacturing companies are to succeed in their efforts to become more service-oriented, there will be some crucial problems that they must deal with: the cultural gap, defining what services are, and how to gain profit from them (business model). These three issues are partially interdependent since the definition of services, or rather the lack of it, is one cause of the divergent perspectives.

The cultural gap between the Service Salvationists and the Service Pragmatists is not perhaps as wide for us as outsiders as it was perceived by the people involved. Both sides actually saw services as a means of increasing the competitiveness of the company. However, the Service Pragmatists have a traditional goods marketing perspective on services; services are means of satisfying customer needs. Services are add-ons and closely linked to the physical product. Instead, Service Salvationists perceived service operations as a strategic change for the company, which would imply new business models for the company. Related to Table 1, the two groups regard the company as being in two different phases; the Service Pragmatists describe its service operations in terms of the first two phases, whereas the Service Salvationists span more or less all the way to the fourth (and final) phase in the figure.

As long as there are two opposing perspectives on service operations, this will hamper the transition toward increased service orientation. Many of the differences in perspective between the groupings are due to knowledge asymmetry. Almost everyone who was classified as Service Salvationists was either among the pioneers introducing service orientation at the company or had been working with services for several years. They displayed greater knowledge regarding "text-book" knowledge of services (service theory). Furthermore, they had, over a number of years, developed a mental framework for understanding service operations better. On the other hand, The Service Pragmatists generally had less experience of service operations and regarded them more as a burden and something new that they had to understand.

There was a noticeable lack of commitment from the top management in ECO. The vision of becoming a service-oriented organization demands a totally revised business strategy for each of the companies. This can be a decisive factor affecting why the company had such divergent perspectives on services.

Linked to this, we could identify a gap in the current research literature. Although lots of typologies and characterizations of services exist, none focus on understanding the peculiarities of service innovation and the operations of manufacturing companies. From the present study, we can understand that the company offers general services (such as financing and logistics) on one hand, and services connected with their specific technological knowledge in the specific engine component industry, on the other. The technological knowledge enables them to design and offer product support, over and above manufacturing. The firm's core competence in the technology forms the basis for expanding new service offerings and the transition toward more service orientation, as vividly illustrated by one of the interviewees:

> *... I think the combination [between hardware & technology knowledge] is really good...if you have the knowledge to design and develop an engine component, then you will also have the basis for designing services around it. If you worked instead all day long in an office on the third floor of a skyscraper and had never ever been close to a manufacturing unit or an engineer, then it would be quite impossible.*

We agree with this observation. The core competence of the manufacturing company must be preserved and should be the basis for the transition into offering services. In all the cases, it is quite evident that the competence regarding their physical products was the basis for developing service offerings. Table 2 illustrates this evolution. The critical point is to move from phase three ("training to better utilize the products") to phase four ("production process consultancy to improve the effectiveness"). At this stage, the product knowledge must be complemented with a deeper understanding of the customer's specific context. *The competitive advantage is based on both knowing your products and understanding the customer's situation.*

Thus, understanding and implementing knowledge creation is a fundamental factor for creating customer value and succeeding with the product to service transition. Indeed, fundamentally new knowledge is

Table 2. Servitization — knowledge dependency and value creation.

Phase	Knowledge demand	Value for customer
1st: Service and supply services	Service and spare parts supply of existing products	Accessibility (reactive)
2nd: On-site maintenance of products	Knowledge of the functionality of own products	Accessibility (proactive)
3rd: Training to better utilize the products	Knowledge includes also a certain understanding of the customer's processes	Efficiency and effectiveness of the physical product
4th: Production process consultancy to improve the effectiveness	Knowledge includes a deep understanding of the customer's context and processes	Efficiency and effectiveness of the customer's processes
5th: Asset management (insourcing)	Knowledge to operate the delivered products in the customer's context	Risk reduction and effectiveness of the total company

required when services become a part of or the locus of the company's offerings. Focusing on merely producing physical products can be based on engineering competence. A service-oriented company must also understand the business in terms of how it creates value for its customers. Becoming more service-oriented should not be confused with unlearning old skills such as manufacturing competence. This brings us to the debate about whether services and products operations should be separated or integrated at a manufacturing company.

Separate or integrate — this is not the question

We contend that the service operations of a manufacturing company must be separated *and* integrated. On the one hand, services and products must be *separated* in order to enable people to reflect on and learn the peculiarities of services that actually exist, as with the service development group in the ECO case. On the other hand, services and products must be *integrated* in order to close the cultural gap that exists between product- and service-oriented activities. As previously noted, it is quite evident that most of the services are actually based on the firm's technology competence. Goldstein *et al.* (2002) argued that service activities and interactions that include people skills (customers and employees) and physical resources must be integrated in order to result in the intended service.

As previously mentioned, Vargo and Lusch (2004a) sought to remove the dichotomy between services and products by claiming that it is their (services' and/or products') 'value in use' that matters. We agree with Gummesson that "customers do not buy goods or services; they buy offerings which render service which create value" (1995:150). However, that is one side of the coin — the user's perspective. From the manufacturer's perspective, it is quite different to develop, produce, and sell services compared to physical products; otherwise, the transition toward integrating services into the company's offerings would not cause any problems for a manufacturing company. However, the transition of a manufacturing company toward becoming service-oriented is evidently a rather difficult change process, both regarding these cases and others in the literature. To succeed in this process, we must not ignore but instead acknowledge and consider the differences that exist between services and products. It is clear from our findings that services, from a producer perspective, have other characteristics that make them very different from the producer perspective, as this quotation from the head of service development illustrates:

> *It wouldn't be fruitful to say that everything is services — even if I think that is the case. Then people would just smile and continue doing what they're doing — we wouldn't have any changes if we didn't pinpoint the service peculiarities.*

It might not be crucial to differentiate between services or physical products from a customer perspective. However, from a provider perspective, the offering of services will create new challenges in the form of new processes, competencies, the initiation of new relationships, and a cultural transformation. This will demand an organized strategic and operational long-term change program.

Finally, we argue that the current separate or integrate debate is irrelevant. As long as we are lacking a conceptualization of services for

Table 3. Overview of companies in Study 2.

	ECO	Alfa	Beta	Gamma	Delta
Types of service					
Supply	●	●	●	●	●
On-site maintenance	●	●	●	●	●
Training	●	●		●	●
Consultancy (KIBS)	●	◉	◉	◉	●
Intasking/Insourcing	◉	◉	◉		○
Hurdles/problems					
Product (goods) logic (Culture)	◉	◉	●	●	●
Business model (service for free)	●		●	●	●
Pricing/charging	◉		●	●	●
IPR	◉	●		●	
Understanding and customer value		●	●	●	◉
Success factors					
Support from top management	◉	●			
Local presence to understand the customer	◉	●			○
Competence development	●	●			●
Internal co-operation	●	●			
Long-term commitment from top management to support service operations	●	●	●		

	Growth (end)	Mature	Growth	Growth (beginning)	Growth (beginning)
Pilot project	●				
Drivers of transition					
Customer demand	●		●	●	
Better margins			●	●	
Competitive advantage	●	●			●
Competence utilization					
Industry trend	●	●			
Tools for supporting the transition toward a service perspective					
Telemetry			◉		
Clarification	◉				
Visualization					
Simulation			●		
State of transition Initiation, Growth,					
Matureness (linked to state)	Growth (end)	Mature	Growth	Growth (beginning)	Growth (beginning)
Time	10 years	15 years	10 years	15 years	6 years
Locus of change	Middle management	Top management	Top management	Project	Middle management
Status of service operations in the org.		Relatively high and rising			Relatively low but rising

Notes: ● : Extensive; ◉ : To some extent; ○ : Very rare; — : Non existent.

manufacturing industries, it is not relevant to debate whether to integrate and separate product and service operations. What is needed is concepts that embrace both physical products and services; we call these product–service concepts. The literature is separated into product development and service development. The conceptualization of products (product concept) and services (service concept) is not in harmony. It is evident, for manufacturing companies at least, that the services developed are heavily linked to the physical products. This should accordingly be reflected in a service–product conceptualization. Furthermore, this conceptualization should reflect the different phases of the product-to-service transition.

References

Auernhammer, K. and Stabe, M. (2002). Product-service co-design scenario and state of the art in research. Final report to the European Commission under the Growth Programme, Contract Number: GRD1-CT-2002-00716. Stuttgart: Fraunhofer-IAT.

Baines, T. S., Lightfoot, H. W., Benedettini, O., and Kay, J. M. (2009). The servitization of manufacturing: A review of literature and reflection on future challenges. *Journal of Manufacturing Technology Management*, **20**(5), 547–567.

Boyt, T. and Harvey, M. (1997). Classification of industrial services: A model with strategic implications. *Industrial Marketing Management*, **26**(4), 291–300.

Brax, S. A. and Visintin, F. (2017). Meta-model of servitization: The integrative profiling approach. *Industrial Marketing Management*, **60**, 17–32.

Djellal, F. and Gallouj, F. (2001). Patterns of innovation organisation in service firms: Postal survey results and theoretical models. *Science and Public Policy*, **28**(1), 57–67.

Drejer, I. (2004). Identifying innovation in survey of services: A Schumpeterian perspective. *Research Policy*, **33**(3), 551–562.

Edvardsson, B., Gustafsson, A., and Roos, I. (2005). Service portraits in service research — A critical review. *International Journal of Service Industry Management*, **16**(1), 107–121.

Frambach, R. T., Wels-Lips, I., and Gtindlach, A. (1997). Proactive product service strategies — An application in the European health market. *Industrial Marketing Management*, **26**, 341–352.

Fuchs, V. R. (1968). *The Service Economy*. New York: National Bureau of Economic Research.

Gebauer, H., Fleisch, E., and Friedli, T. (2005). Overcoming the service paradox in manufacturing companies. *European Management Journal*, **23**(1), 14–26.

Gebauer, H. and Friedli, T. (2005). Behavioral implications of the transition process from products to services. *Journal of Business & Industrial Marketing*, **20**(2), 70–78.

Gebauer, H., Krempl, R., and Fleisch, E. (2008). Exploring the effect of cognitive biases on customer support services. *Creativity and Innovation Management*, **17**(1), 58–70.

Gershuny, J. (1978). *After Industrial Society: The Emerging Self-service Economy*. London: Macmillan.

Goldstein, S. M., Johnston, R., Duffy, J., and Rao, J. (2002). The service concept: The missing link in service design research. *Journal of Operations Management*, **20**(2), 121–134.

Gummesson, E. (1995). Relationship Marketing: Its Role in the Service Economy. In W. I. Glynn, & J. G. Barnes (Eds.), *Understanding Services Management*. Chapter 7. New York, USA: John Wiley & Sons.

Hauknes, J. (1998). Services in innovation – Innovation in services: SI4S final report (S14S Synthesis Papers S1). Oslo: STEP.

Hill, P. (1997). Tangibles, Intangibles and Services: A New Taxonomy for the Classification of Output. *Paper presented at the Paper for the CSLS Conference on Service Centre Productivity and the Productivity Paradox*, Ottawa, Canada.

Hipp, C. (2008). Service peculiarities and the specific role of technology in service innovation management. *International Journal of Services and Technology Management*, **9**(2), 154–173.

Jacob, F. and Ulaga, W. (2008). The transition from product to service in business markets: An agenda for academic inquiry. *Industrial Marketing Management*, **37**(3), 247–253.

Kindström, D. and Kowalkowski, C. (2014). Service innovation in product-centric firms: A multidimensional business model perspective. *Journal of Business & Industrial Marketing*, **29**(2), 96–111.

Kotler, P. and Armstrong, G. (1996). *Principles of Marketing*. (7th edn.). Englewood Cliffs N.J.: Prentice Hall.

Kowalkowski, C., Gebauer, H., Kamp, B., and Parry, G. (2017). Servitization and deservitization: Overview, concepts, and definitions. *Industrial Marketing Management*, **60**, 4–10.

Martinez, V., Bastl, M., Kingston, J., and Evans, S. (2010). Challenges in transforming manufacturing organisations into product-service providers. *Journal of manufacturing technology management*, **21**(4), 449–469.

Mathieu, V. (2001). Service strategies within the manufacturing sector: benefits, costs and partnership. *International Journal of Service Industry Management*, **12**(5), 451–475.

Matthyssens, P. and Vandenbempt, K. (2008). Moving from basic offerings to value-added solutions: Strategies, barriers and alignment. *Industrial Marketing Management*, **37**(3), 316–328.

Miles, I. (1994). Innovation in services. In M. Dodgson, and R. Rothwell (eds.), *The Handbook of Industrial Innovation*. Chapter 18, Aldershot: E. Elgar.

Neu, W. A. and Brown, S. W. (2005). Forming successful business-to-business services in goods-dominant firms. *Journal of Service Research*, **8**(1), 3–17.

Oliva, R. and Kallenberg, R. (2003). Managing the transition from products to services. *International Journal of Service Industry Management*, **14**(2), 160–172.

Prahalad, C. K. (2004). The blinders of dominant logic. *Long Range Planning*, **37**(2), 171–179.

Quinn, J. B. (1986). Technology adoption: The service industries. In R. Landau, & N. Rosenberg (Eds.), *The Positive Sum Strategy*, Chapter 20, pp. 357–371. Washington: National Academy Press.

Robinson, T., Clarke-Hill, C. M., and Clarkson, R. (2002). Differentiation through service: A perspective from the commodity chemicals sector. *Service Industries Journal*, **22**(3), 149–166.

Russel, L. (1973). *The New Service Society*. London: Longman.

Soete, L. and Miozzo, M. (1989). Trade and development in services: A technological perspective (Working Paper No. 89-031). Maastricht: MERIT.

Stauss, B. (2005). A Pyrrhic victory. The implications of an unlimited broadening of the concept of services. *Managing Service Quality*, **6**(4), 324–335.

Sundbo, J. (1997). Management of innovation in services. *The Service Industry Journal*, **17**(3), 432–455.

Tether, B. S. and Metcalfe, J. S. (2004). Systems of innovation in services. In F. Malerba (ed.), *Sectoral Systems of Innovation. Concepts, Issues and Analyses of Six Major Sectors in Europe*, Chapter 8, pp. 287–321. Cambridge, UK: Cambridge University Press.

Tidd, J. and Hull, F. M. (2003). *Service Innovation. Organizational Responses to Technological Opportunities & Market Imperatives*. London: Imperial College Press.

Vandermerwe, S. and Rada, J. (1989). Servitization of business: Adding value by adding services. *European Management Journal*, **6**(4), 314–324.

Vargo, S. L. and Lusch, R. F. (2004a). Evolving to a new dominant logic for marketing. *Journal of Marketing*, **68**(1), 1–17.

Vargo, S. L. and Lusch, R. F. (2004b). The four service marketing myths: Remnants of a goods-based, manufacturing model. *Journal of Service Research*, **6**(4), 324–335.

Vargo, S. L. and Lusch, R. F. (2008). From goods to service(s): Divergences and convergences of logics. *Industrial Marketing Management*, **37**(3), 254–259.

Zeithaml, V. A., Parasuraman, A., and Berry, L. L. (1985). Problems and strategies in services marketing. *Journal of Marketing*, **49**(2), 33–46.

Chapter 14

Value Creation in Service-Based States of Business Relationships

Lars Witell, Peter R. Magnusson, Bo Edvardsson
and Helen Beckman

Karlstad University and Linköping University
Karlstad University, Arla Foods

Key takeaways

1. The research concerns what happens in a business relationship when services are introduced by the supplier.
2. This chapter reports on how different value drivers contribute to value creation at various states of a long-term business relationship.
3. The shift from products to services can be described as a change from value creation through the product's efficiency alone to value co-creation through the product's efficiency and effectiveness within the customer's production process. A value driver that has a certain effect will over time loose this effect; to continue to co-create value, resources have to be committed to activate new value drivers in the business relationship.
4. This chapter concerns servitization in B2B manufacturing firms.
5. Those interested in this chapter may also find Chapters 7–9, and 13–15 particularly interesting.

Introduction

Scholars and business leaders alike have advocated the need for companies to shift from primarily manufacturing goods to offering services (see e.g., Gebauer, 2007; Ulaga and Eggert, 2006). Although existing research offers a number of guidelines that can help companies strengthen their market positions and increase their differentiation, these guidelines tend to focus on how to make the change from products to services rather than how to build and develop resources to sustain the differentiation over time. For business relationships based on machinery with long product life cycles, services and product upgrades often become the units of exchange. In such ongoing business relationships, the creation and introduction of value through service becomes the key to long-term survival and success (Gebauer *et al.*, 2011).

The reorientation of manufacturing firms from goods to services has manifested itself in the development of new conceptual frameworks such as service transition (Oliva and Kallenberg, 2003), the service-dominant logic (SDL; Vargo and Lusch, 2004, 2008) and the IMP view on business marketing (Matthyssens *et al.*, 2009). The present research builds on the concept of value and how it relates to resources and competencies (Zerbini *et al.*, 2007). It expands the existing research regarding the role of the business relationship as a source of value (Walter *et al.*, 2001; Lindgreen and Wynstra, 2005) in order to investigate the role of several categories of value (product, service, and relationship) throughout various states of a business relationship.

Value cannot be built into an offering; rather it is co-created with customers and assessed by the customers in their own context as it is used (Vargo and Lusch, 2004). Value is defined as the total benefits (of resources, goods, and services) in relation to the total burdens or sacrifices (price and other resources spent) throughout the life cycle of the offering (Eggert *et al.*, 2006; Ulaga and Eggert, 2006). While there is a long tradition of value assessment studies in business research, they tend to focus on the value of the physical product and neglect the service and relational categories. For suppliers of machinery, the product price is only a part of the total cost for the customer over the life cycle of the offering. In order to obtain a larger share of customer expenditures, suppliers must understand the drivers that create value for customers and how these drivers change over the life cycle of the offering.

This chapter reports on how different value drivers contribute to value creation at various states of a long-term business relationship. In particular, it seeks to (1) identify service-based states of business relationships, and (2) discover how the roles of value drivers change in each of these states. The study reported on in this chapter focuses on value (benefits and sacrifices) during co-creation and in particular the categories of value (product, service, and relationship; Lapierre, 2000). The empirical investigation is based on four case studies of business relationships between suppliers and their customers and includes 22 interviews conducted with key individuals.

Value and Value Drivers in a Relationship Context

Value

In a literature review, Woodruff and Flint (2006) identified four conceptual definitions of customer value: value added, the economic worth of a customer, the economic worth of a seller's product service offering, and value-in-use. Most authors agree, however, that value is, on some level, inherent or linked to the use of a product (Woodruff, 1997). From this perspective, value is created and experienced in a process in which both customers and suppliers play an active role. Value is therefore co-created with customers, which is a cornerstone in the SDL (Vargo and Lusch, 2004, 2008). "The locus of value creation, then, moves from the 'producer' to a collaborative process of co-creation between parties" (Vargo and Lusch, 2008). This perspective enables a new type of customer value that is embedded in the relationship (Lapierre, 2000; Ulaga, 2003).

Customers create value by combining their own resources with external resources (Ramirez, 1999; Mathieu, 2001). Vargo and Lusch (2004) argue that value varies from customer to customer (from relationship to relationship), is situational and contextual, and must therefore be defined for each business relationship. They suggest that interactions between "operand" resources (such as products, information, and other physical resources) and "operant" resources (knowledge, skills, and motivation linked to employees and customers) form the basis for value co-creation. Value is co-created when operant resources operate on operand resources. Operand resources are those upon which an operation is performed in order to produce an effect, which in the present frame of reference is a service. Customer value is achieved when the resulting effects from the operands, that is, the service, are experienced. From a provider's perspective, service should provide value-creating support to its customers' business, for example, by providing customers with growth and/or premium pricing opportunities and/or cost savings/cost control opportunities (Grönroos, 2008). This book chapter focuses on value drivers for customers, which form the basis for the provider's value capture (Witell and Löfgren, 2013).

To study and understand value creation through services in long-term business relationships, it is necessary to adopt a dynamic perspective (value-in-use over time) (Nilsson-Witell and Fundin, 2005). In other words, both realized and customer perceived value vary over time and throughout business relationships. First, because the improvement potential of a production process decreases with each improvement, a service that enhances the efficiency of that process loses value over time. Second, a supplier's knowledge about the context of its customer will improve over time, as will the potential to create value-in-use for the customer. Empirical studies have made a number of suggestions regarding the ways in which value is created in a long-term business relationship (Lapierre, 1997, 2000; Ulaga, 2003; Ulaga and Eggert, 2006; Walter *et al.*, 2003). Several scholars have used the concept of "value drivers" to explain how value is created or destroyed in B2B relations (Lapierre, 1997, 2000; Ulaga, 2003). However, these analyses have not used SDL, a view that value is co-created and assessed by customers based on value-in-use over time.

Value drivers

Value drivers are linked to the use of resources and have the potential to produce effects, that is, service, but in order to actually create value, the value driver must be mobilized by an operant resource (Vargo and Lusch, 2008). This operant can be a supplier and/or a customer using their knowledge, skills, and resources. The value created by a value driver depends on the operant's ability to perform on it; the same value driver may produce different effects at different times. The operant's capability, for instance, can be affected by absorbing knowledge about the operand, the customer context, and available resources. Accordingly, the value gained from a value driver is dynamic; some value drivers might become obsolete over time, while new ones might become relevant. In short, value drivers are defined here as the activities and interactions that occur when operant resources operate on operand resources. Value drivers denote the content, such as "product quality," that are achieved when a customer uses the product to create value in his or her business.

Service and relationships are important for value co-creation in long-term business relationships. Our operationalization of value builds on the frameworks put forward by Ulaga (2003) and Lapierre (2000), and uses the concept of domains, that is, benefits and sacrifices, to conceptualize value. Based on Lapierre (2000), the benefits are divided into three categories: products, services, and relationships. In their alternative models of value, Lapierre (2000), Ulaga (2003), and Walter *et al.* (2003) introduced specific value drivers. Lapierre's (2000) three categories were products (alternative solutions, product quality, and product customization), services (responsiveness, flexibility, reliability, and technical competence), and relationships (supplier's image, trust, and supplier solidarity with customers). The sacrifices were price, time/effort/energy, and conflict (monetary, resource, and relational/emotional). Ulaga's (2003) framework was based on six benefits (product quality, service support, delivery, supplier know-how, time-to-market, and personal interaction) and two sacrifices (direct product cost and process cost). Walter *et al.* (2003) focused on direct benefits such as cost reduction, quality, volume, and safeguards as well as indirect benefits such as market, scouts, innovation development, and social support. The present chapter argues that value drivers linked to operant resources should have two "sides" — positive and negative. "Trust," for example, is one of the benefit drivers, while a lack of trust ("no trust") creates a negative benefit.

States of business relationships

Batonda and Perry (2003) classified business relationship models into three categories: stages theory, states theory, and joining theory. The present study investigates relationships that were initiated more than 30 years ago for which there have been no new installations of machinery but for which some product upgrades have been performed. The basis of these relationships is repair and maintenance services providing value-in-use. These relationships are volatile; some years they experience no sales while in other years there are product upgrades. These relationships are reversible and complex, with a focus on services, so the empirical material could be described using states.

The states theory proposes that the process of change is an evolution of unpredictable states, with actors moving either backward or forward from one state to another (Edvardsson *et al.*, 2008; Rosson and Ford, 1982). This means that the state models do not portray relationship development as having to be orderly and sequential. They depict relationship development as being complex rather than evolving in the structured manner assumed by the stages models (Dwyer *et al.*, 1987). Accordingly, the transition from one state to another is not necessarily predictable, and it is also reversible; that is, a transition may revert to a previous state. The term "state" refers to the condition at a given point in time, while the phase in the development process is merely one of several possible conditions (Batonda and Perry, 2003, p. 1466). The states that take service as their point of origin must be identified in order to understand what takes place when a business relationship founded upon transactions of goods changes into one that is based on service.

Value drivers in different states of business relationships

Business relationships are dynamic in nature (Holmlund, 2004), which means that internal and external forces can cause both stability and change in a relationship. A company can change the nature of a business relationship by adopting a service-based strategy for value propositions (Vargo and Lusch, 2008) in order to form the basis for value co-creation. In a simulation study, Johnson and Selnes (2005) argued that suppliers can make acquaintances by providing parity value, make friends by providing differential value, and find partners by providing customized value. Cost increases are directly related to the delivery of customized services; in other words, relationship-specific investments occur when a firm seeks closer customer relationships (Bendapudi and Berry, 1997). In a similar manner, Eggert *et al.* (2006) focused on value creation through the product and concluded that suppliers must anticipate and respond to value changes in order to avoid dissatisfaction in an ongoing business relationship. To maintain successful partnerships, suppliers must consistently meet their customers' changing value demands. In an empirical investigation of 400 purchasing professionals at US manufacturing firms, Eggert *et al.* (2006) concluded that value perceptions depend on the relationship life cycle. Specifically, a supplier has the greatest opportunity to provide superior value creation in the customer's sourcing process in the early stages of the relationship life cycle. Throughout the relationship life cycle, however, there is an opportunity to create value at the customer operations level by transferring expertise and reducing the time-to-market.

Johnson and Selnes (2005) and Eggert *et al.* (2006) showed that value creation is state dependent and that higher levels of value are often delivered through service in a business relationship. The present study built on this research by clarifying the existence and role of different value drivers. First, value drivers were considered to be embedded in products, services, or the relationship (Lapierre, 2000). Second, the way in which the roles of different value drivers vary among states in business-to-business relationships was examined. Third, the study sought to identify the service-based states of a business relationship in a manufacturing context and the resources and competences needed in these states. Strength, direction of growth, and the role of service are seen as the defining characteristics of the business relationship states.

Methodology

Empirical context

The empirical investigation was conducted within the Swedish pulp and paper industry, with a specific focus on the business relationship between a supplier of machines and pulp and paper mills. The chosen supplier focuses on continuous cooking systems, which the participating customers had built during the 1960s and 1970s (see Table 1). The supplier has had ongoing business relationships with each customer for over 35 years. For the first 30 years, services were included in the price when a new production line was built, but a decision was made in 1999 to charge for goods and services separately. Services were initially offered individually, but the supplier soon started offering service agreements that consist of inspections, process studies, operation optimization, troubleshooting, and/ or training programs.

Table 1. An overview of four long-term business relationships.

Dimensions	R1	R2	R3	R4
Equipment was built	1967/1988	1968/1972/1988	1976	1974
Importance of equipment in the production line	Low	Low	Low	Low
Utilization of equipment	100%	123%	Just above 100%	150%
Ongoing service relationship initiated	2000	2000	2001	2003
Ongoing service relationship terminated	No	No	No	Yes (2004)
Categorization of service relationship	Revitalization	Revitalization	Regression	Regression
Duration of personal relationship (years)	15	7/3 (2 contact persons)	2	10
No. of changes of contact person (during the contract time)	0	1	1	0

Even though all of the participating customers had had business relationships with the supplier for over 35 years, they have experienced a new kind of service-based business relationship since 1999. Customers who required services had to start paying for them, but a formal business relationship based on services did not appear until the customer signed a contract for a service agreement. Of the four investigated business relationships (R1–R4), three are based on present service contracts, while one, after a termination of the service contract by the customer, is based on transactions.

Sample, data collection, and analysis

A case study methodology was used because of its suitability for understanding dynamics within a single setting (Eisenhardt, 1989). Interviews were conducted with representatives from both sides of the business relationship. A total of 22 interviews were conducted, of which seven were with the supplier and 15 with representatives from the customer side of the relationships. The interviewees included procurement managers, production managers, maintenance managers, production engineers, and maintenance engineers.

All interviews followed a semi-structured interview guide to examine critical service episodes in order to identify the value drivers (Flanagan, 1954). A critical episode occurs when at least one of the two actors requires special attention, either to his or her own needs or to emerging problems in the business relationship. The critical episode ends when the situation has been dealt with in a way that results in a stabilized relationship at the same level as it was before, a higher level, or a lower level, or a dissolved relationship.

Each of the interviews was transcribed, and the transcription was read through briefly to get a sense of the text as a whole. The transcribed interviews were then analyzed, and 99 critical service episodes were identified across the four long-term business relationships. For each of these episodes, the drivers that influenced the perception of value were sought. The conceptualizations by Lapierre (2000), Ulaga (2003), and Walter et al. (2003) served as the points of departure for the analysis of value. Two independent judges analyzed the 99 critical service episodes related to value co-creation and identified 164 value drivers. Before reaching a consensus about the codification, the inter-coder reliability was calculated for each interview; the mean value of the interviews was 75%.

Results

Identification of value drivers

Having analyzed the 164 identified value drivers, the study confirms that value drivers can be viewed within two domains (benefits and sacrifices) and three benefit categories (products, services, and relationship). Within the domains and categories, however, the identified value drivers differ to some extent from those identified in previous research. The identified value drivers in each domain or category are as follows: in "products" (product quality and process quality), "services" (performance, flexibility, responsiveness, and technical competence), "relationship" (image, trust, readiness to help, and knowledge sharing), and "sacrifices" (price, time/effort/energy, and conflict; see Figure 1). Definitions, examples of specific value drivers, and illustrations from the empirical investigation are presented in the Appendix.

The product category generally dealt with the product or the production process, which was then divided into "product quality" and

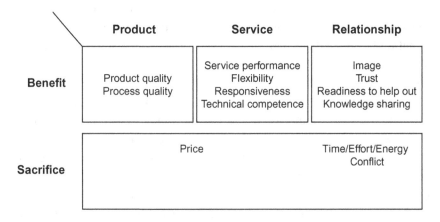

Figure 1.   An overview of value drivers.

"process quality". These value drivers were often described in terms of "their equipment is robust and works well" or "the service agreement creates operational benefits". Concerning the category of service, Lapierre's definition of "responsiveness" and "technical competence" was adopted. A new value driver, "performance," was introduced. A value driver, "flexibility" (Lapierre, 2000), was identified as having been defined too broadly in previous research. This meant that it could easily be confused with other value drivers (such as "readiness to help"), so its definition (see Appendix) was refined. "Reliability" was found to be somewhat vague, and it overlapped with other value drivers, such as "trust," "technical competence," and "performance". As a result, this value driver was not identified in the present study.

Regarding relationship-related value drivers, "image" and "trust" were identified as drivers of customer-perceived value. "Supplier solidarity to customer," however, was changed to "readiness to help" since the original name did not capture the customer-perceived value in this empirical context. In the process industry, most failures or problems in the production process are severe and costly, so the supplier can create value for the customer by showing a willingness and providing resources to help in such situations. A new value driver, "knowledge sharing" (linked to operant resources), is of interest to those customers that are not part of a larger group of paper mills and do not have the ability to discuss problems or share new information with other companies. Suppliers play an important role in such cases because of their knowledge of other paper mills. Finally, the three sacrifices mentioned by Lapierre (2000) — "price", "time/effort/energy", and "conflict" — were all identified by respondents.

The view on the role of the value drivers in the business relationship differs between the supplier and the customers. First, customers are more likely to reveal value drivers related to the relationship category and sacrifice domain. For the supplier, only the contact person responsible for relationship R3 is fully aware of the value of the relationship category. The other contact persons do not consider the relationship category as a key category for the customer. Second, when the supplier reveals those aspects that create value for the customer, almost all the value drivers can be found within the limits of the service agreement. The customer, meanwhile, looks at all the activities within the business relationship. For the supplier, 93% of the value drivers can be found within the service agreement, while the corresponding figure for the customers is 64% (see Table 2).

Identification of two service-based states of business relationships

The analysis of the four long-term business relationships in which services play a central part revealed two states of business relationships: *revitalization* and *regression*. In this context, "service-based state" refers to a state of a business relationship in which the core activities of value creation are performed through services. This means that most business contacts concern services, and that service personnel are the members of the supplier's staff who are in contact with the customer, often on a day-to-day basis. The identified service-based states provide a conceptualization of what can happen in an ongoing business relationship when there is a change in value co-creation activities.

The first state is revitalization, in which services become a trigger that reignites what was a stale relationship and expands the business relationship to include more service activities. In this state, the value drivers use resources that produce great effects in the customer operation. The second state is regression, in which a feeling of dependency leads the customer to reduce the size of the business relationship to such a point where it includes only a few core services. In this state, the produced effect of a service in the customer operation provides a diminishing return. The following section provides empirical illustrations of the two states of business relationships.

Two of the cases, R1 and R2, are in a state of revitalization. In these cases, the introduction of service agreements has served to renew business relationships and has had a positive impact on value creation. When services are introduced, the focus is on standardized services that can be offered to a wide range of customers, but due to the diminishing return of the standardized services, the manufacturer must eventually change from standardized to customized services. Cooperation between customers and manufacturers can be described as a shared process of value co-creation

Table 2. An overview of the identified value drivers within the different domains and categories over four long-term business relationships (the view of the supplier and the customer).

State	R1 Revitalization Supplier		R2 Revitalization Supplier		R3 Regression Supplier		R4 Regression Supplier	
	Positive	Negative	Positive	Negative	Positive	Negative	Positive	Negative
Product	4	0	1	0	2	2	2	0
Service	3	1	6	0	4	2	2	1
Relationship	0	0	5	0	0	0	0	0
Sacrifice	0	0	0	0	0	0	0	0

(Continued)

Table 2.   (*Continued*)

State	R1 Revitalization Customer		R2 Revitalization Customer		R3 Regression Customer		R4 Regression Customer	
	Positive	Negative	Positive	Negative	Positive	Negative	Positive	Negative
Product	6	0	5	0	5	0	5	0
Product Quality	0	0	0	0	0	0	4	0
Process Quality	6	0	5	0	5	0	1	0
Service	12	3	17	4	9	0	5	5
Performance	5	1	6	2	4	0	3	2
Flexibility	0	1	3	1	0	0	1	0
Responsiveness	3	1	5	1	4	0	0	1
Technical Competence	4	0	3	0	1	0	1	2
Relationship	8	0	13	1	2	0	4	4
Image	0	0	0	0	0	0	1	1
Trust	3	0	4	1	0	0	2	2
Readiness to help	3	0	3	0	1	0	0	0
Knowledge Sharing	2	0	6	0	1	0	1	1
Sacrifice	4	3	6	1	2	1	0	4
Price	1	1	1	0	0	1	0	1
Time/Effort/Energy	3	1	4	0	2	0	0	3
Conflict	0	1	1	1	0	0	0	0

built on trust and common responsibilities. Both parties actively work to find new areas of cooperation and identify value creation opportunities within the customer's core production and/or business processes. By using the customer's knowledge, skills, and motivation, it is possible to create a better understanding of the operand resources and introduce new value drivers into the business relationship. A manager described their role as a customer as follows:

> *"The service agreement must be alive and not be static from year to year, and it should be adjusted to the situation. That is the case in this business relationship, which also demands some resources from us. So it is a two-way arrangement. Sometimes we do not have the available resources needed and cannot be there."*

R3 and R4 are presently in a state of regression, with the service agreement shrinking in terms of the number of mobilized resources and performed activities. This means that there are fewer service encounters to revitalize or even maintain a business relationship between the two parties. Instead of co-creating value, the customer is using the service encounter to learn new competences, which it then uses to assume responsibility for some of the services specified in the service agreement. One of the managers in R3 described the role of the customer in the business relationship as follows:

> *"There are ideas, but there is also something that has a conserving effect in the organization. You have to remember that there must be a visionary in the business relationship, otherwise I doubt that there will be such a great development."*

The lack of co-creation in these two business relationships has limited the degree of renewal. The supplier has not been able to mobilize resources and let the suppliers or customers use them in new ways that would activate new value drivers. One manifestation of this is the failure of the supplier to shift from standardized to customized services. This arises as the result of a misconception that standardized services will continue to deliver improvements to the customer's operations.

Value drivers and service-based states of business relationships

The dynamics of the value drivers were investigated across the identified service-based states of business relationships. Five propositions have been developed for this chapter, based on empirical observations, that shed some light on the dynamics and the role of value drivers in different service-based states (see Table 2).

First, a number of value drivers are revealed by customers without any connection to the state of the service-based business relationship. The most important value drivers are service-related, and these are distributed evenly across the states of revitalization and regression. This means that the effects of the service-related value drivers — that is, performance, flexibility, responsiveness, and technical competence — are similar across the two service-based states.

Proposition 1: The service category is the main driver of value, regard-
less of the service-based state of the business relationship.

Dependence on the product-related value drivers is limited for the two business relationships that are in the state of revitalization. The relationship-related value drivers stand out in the value creation process, especially in those activities related to knowledge sharing, readiness to help, and trust. This can be seen in a comparison of the shares of identified value drivers belonging to the product and relationship categories between the two different states of business relationships. For those business relationships in the state of revitalization, 17% of the value drivers belong to the product category and 31% belong to the relationship category. In contrast, for business relationships in the state of regression, 26% of the value drivers belong to the product category and 24% belong to the relationship category.

Proposition 2: The product category drives value in the state of regres-
sion, while it is of minor importance in the state of revitalization.

The supplier has successfully reduced costs and increased productivity in the core processes of the customer (process quality). This value driver is dependent on the operant's ability to produce effects. When the production process starts to reach its maximum capacity, this limits value creation through this value driver. A customer from R1 made the following observation:

> *"Using information from the production process for trouble-shooting does not have that much potential when the availability of the production process is over 95 percent."*

The supplier must take action in relation to the diminishing role of the process quality over time. In the cases of R1 and R2, the supplier has been able to renew the service offering by introducing new services, widening the scope of the services, and providing knowledge-intensive services.

The value drivers in the product category are the main creators of value in the two cases in the state of regression. The supplier is known for its superior product quality, and this is what contributes to the customer-perceived value. Within the product category, value in the state of revitalization is created through process quality, while in the state of regression it primarily comes from product quality. The high quality of the supplier's goods leads the customer to continue buying the services even though they do not perceive the value-in-use as being high.

> *Proposition 3: The product category drives value through process quality in the state of revitalization, while product quality is the dominant source of value in the state of regression.*

The two business relationships in the regression state have experienced different paths. One of the customers (R4) has had virtually no negative experiences in its dealings with the supplier and few experiences related to the relationship category and sacrifice domain. In the case of R4, the data shows a high frequency of value drivers related to the relationship category. However, the high frequency of positive value drivers is counter-balanced by a high frequency of negative value drivers. When the business relationship involves a strong feeling of dependency, this can cause both actors to pay more attention to value drivers related to the relationship category (that is, view them more critically). The customer identifies negative value drivers related to the relationship category, while the supplier begins performing activities to strengthen the business relationship. The customer in this case had a deliberate strategy of learning more about the services the supplier provided and assessing the possibility of performing those services in-house. This limited the potential to co-create value, which led to the level of trust in the business relationship deteriorating. With fewer service encounters and the level of trust deteriorating, the activities of the supplier failed to provide energy and direction to strengthen the business relationship. The relationship had a low degree of renewal, and, in this particular case, the supplier was too late or was not able to renew the service offering.

Proposition 4: The relationship category drives value in the revitalization state and destroys value in the regression state.

When entering the state of revitalization, the supplier as an operant uses its knowledge, skills, and motivation better than the customer. In addition, it releases resources that can be better distributed. In the state of revitalization, the sacrifice domain seems to be important for minimizing conflicts, time, effort, and energy. The initiation of a service-based business relationship removes conflicts that may have hindered value creation for the customer due to its lack of resources. In the regression state, however, the cost of the service starts to have an important role. When the standardized services are delivered, customers often feel that although the value driver consumes the same amount of resources, it is less effective.

Proposition 5: The sacrifice domain drives value in the state of revitalization, while it also destroys value in the state of regression.

Conclusions

The contribution of this study should be seen in light of the transition that manufacturing firms are making from products to services (Fang *et al.*, 2008), a transition that offers a number of challenges specifically related to value co-creation (Cova and Salle, 2008). The present study has used the SDL to describe and analyze the value co-creation that occurs as a result of value drivers. The shift can be described as a change from value creation through the product's efficiency alone to value co-creation through the product's efficiency and effectiveness within the customer's production process.

This research has revealed that, in the regression and revitalization states of a business relationship, the role of both the two domains and the three categories of value drivers changes in terms of value co-creation with the customer. A value driver that has a certain effect will over time lose this effect, and to continue to co-create value, resources have to be committed to activate new value drivers in the business relationship. These different roles have been summarized in five propositions related to value creation in the two states of revitalization and regression. These propositions suggest that the categories, the individual value drivers, and the domains are all dynamic.

In contrast to Lapierre (2000), this research shows that both domains (benefits and sacrifices) can create and destroy value. Lapierre (2000) suggested that while the value drivers in the benefit domain can be perceived as both benefits (for example, flexibility) and sacrifices (inflexibility), the value drivers in the sacrifice domain can only be perceived as sacrifices (Ulaga, 2003). The present research, however, argues that the reduction of a sacrifice can create value, and that this value creation can be the main value creation activity for a specific supplier. Similarly, the failure of one value driver in the benefit domain can end a business relationship. This dual role of the value drivers requires the supplier to have in-depth knowledge about each individual customer's specific production and business process problems and challenges.

The drivers of value creation over time have been analyzed in this study within long-term business relationships. Unlike life cycle models (Vernon, 1966) and growth stages models (Dwyer *et al.*,1987; Wilson, 1995), which are based on products as the unit of exchange, our research suggests that a business relationship has different service-based states. The identified service-based states seem to follow a product-based state in which a business relationship has become stale. In the revitalization state, services act as a trigger for the expansion of the business relationship to include more service activities and for service to become the core of the value proposition and the unit of exchange. In the regression state, a feeling of dependency is a trigger that leads the customer to delimit the business relationship to include only a few services. Since it is not possible to improve the production-process quality further, value is created by the customer purchasing assurance from the supplier. Value-in-use is deteriorating because the supplier has not been able to introduce new means of value creation for the customer. Instead, the customer starts to summarize and focus on all the negative episodes of the business relationship and, as a result, decreases the size of the service offering.

What does this mean for managers?

First, the results of this study reveal that the effect of specific value drivers, or constellations of value drivers, can change over time in long-term business relationships. The more successful the supplier has been at improving the product's efficiency and effectiveness within the production process of the customer, the greater the extent to which realized customer value from the offered services will diminish over time. As the value-in-use decreases, so does the willingness of the customer to pay as much as it did previously. Therefore, the supplier must revitalize the relationship by continuously developing and adapting its service offerings based on what creates or contributes to value-in-use for the customer.

Second, the research shows that suppliers believe that activities within the service agreement create value. The customers, on the other hand, consider other activities outside the service agreement to be central to value creation. Over time, suppliers should try to identify these activities and include them in the service agreement. This helps the supplier to visualize the value co-created in the business relationship, and when these activities are put in the service agreement, it becomes possible to charge for them. Customers assess value based on value-in-use over time. If this is not understood properly, a supplier could end up in a situation in which, although they improve their service delivery in accordance with the service agreement, the customer experiences less value. The supplier could be performing activities for the customer for which they do not charge, but which the customer perceives as valuable. These activities could eventually be developed into services for inclusion in future service agreements. From the supplier's perspective, it is not only a question of value creation, but also a question of how to capture value over time.

Appendix: An Overview of the Conceptualization of Value Drivers

Domain or category	Value driver	Definition
Product	Product quality	Product quality signifies the value created in connection with a product's use; that is, the use of the supplier's equipment.
Product	Process quality	Process quality signifies the value created by improving the process. This could occur when the supplier rebuilds or improves the equipment, but the value is perceived as being the result of the improvement, not the improvement itself.
Service	Performance	Performance includes the overall performance of the service offering that the customer has ordered and bought and that is provided by the supplier and used by the customer.
Service	Flexibility	Flexibility signifies the way in which the supplier responds to the customer's requests and the ability to adjust its products and services to meet unforeseen customer needs (business and production needs). It is also the ability to handle change and to stand by and support the customer's value creation.
Service	Responsiveness	Responsiveness refers to the supplier's provision of timely answers and solutions to specific customer problems. It is about listening to and understanding the customer's problems. Responsiveness also includes the customer's relationship with the supplier and how easy it is to get in contact with the supplier.
Service	Technical competence	Technical competence includes the supplier's creativity and specialized expertise to solve problems and support the customer's value creation. It is also signified by the ability to demonstrate comprehensive process knowledge and the way in which the supplier uses new technology to generate customer-tailored solutions.

(Continued)

(Continued)

Domain or category	Value driver	Definition
Relation	Image	Image signifies the reputation and the credibility of the supplier in the eyes of the customer.
Relation	Trust	Trust signifies the customer's confidence in the supplier to stand by its side, support it by telling the truth, provide accurate information, and fulfill promises. It also includes the sincerity of the supplier to "be a partner" in developing the customer's production and business.
Relation	Readiness to help	Readiness to help includes the ability and willingness of the supplier to help the customer when unplanned incidents occur in the customer's production and/or business. These critical incidents demand timely assistance and dedication from the supplier.
Relation	Knowledge sharing	Knowledge sharing includes mutual learning and the information shared between the supplier and the customer as a result of value co-creation and their relationship.
Sacrifice	Price	Price includes the prices of the products and services, the impact that competition has on the prices paid, and the justification of the supplier for the prices it charges. It also includes most of the prices the customer pays in relation to the supplier's profitability and the fairness of most prices paid.
Sacrifice	Time/Effort/ Energy	Time, effort, and energy include the number of meetings between the customer and the supplier, the degree of bargaining with the supplier's staff required to reach an agreement, and the time and effort spent training a number of employees. This value driver also includes the time and effort that a customer spends developing a working business relationship with the supplier, and the energy it invests in the supplier.

(Continued)

(*Continued*)

Domain or category	Value driver	Definition
Sacrifice	Conflict	Conflict is signified by the frequency of disagreements between the customer and the supplier regarding business issues, controversial arguments between the parties, and disagreements about how the customer best can achieve its respective goals.

References

Batonda, G. and Perry, C. (2003). Approaches to relationship development processes in inter-firm networks. *European Journal of Marketing*, **37**(10), 1457–1484.

Bendapudi, N. and Berry, L. L. (1997). Customer's motivations for maintaining relationships with service providers. *Journal of Retailing*, **73**(1), 15–37.

Cova, B. and Salle, R. (2008). Marketing solutions in accordance with the S-D logic: Co-creating value with customer network actors. *Industrial Marketing Management*, **37**(3), 270–277.

Dwyer, F. R., Schurr, P. H., and Oh, S. (1987). Developing buyer-seller relationships. *Journal of Marketing*, **51**, 11–27.

Edvardsson, B., Holmlund, M., and Strandvik, T. (2008). Initiation of business relationships in service-dominant settings. *Industrial Marketing Management*, **37**(3), 339–350.

Eggert, A., Ulaga, W., and Schultz, F. (2006). Value creation in the relationship life cycle: A quasi-longitudinal analysis. *Industrial Marketing Management*, **35**(1), 20–27.

Eisenhardt, K. M. (1989). Building theories from case study research. *Academy of Management Review*, **14**(4), 532–550.

Fang, E., Palmatier, R. W., and Steenkamp, J.-B. E. M. (2008). Effect of service transition strategies on firm value. *Journal of Marketing*, **72**(5), 1–14.

Flanagan, J. C. (1954). The critical incident technique. *Psychology Bulletin*, **51**(4), 327–358.

Gebauer, H. (2007). An investigation of antecedents for the development of customer support services in manufacturing companies. *Journal of Business-to-Business Marketing*, **14**(3), 59–96.

Gebauer, H., Gustafsson, A., and Witell, L. (2011). Competitive advantage through service differentiation by manufacturing companies. *Journal of Business Research*, **64**(12), 1270–1280.

Grönroos, C. (2008). Service logic revisited: Who creates value? And who co-creates? *European Business Review*, **20**(4), 298–314.

Holmlund, M. (2004). Analyzing business relationships and distinguishing different interaction levels. *Industrial Marketing Management*, **33**(4), 279–287.

Johnson, M. D. and Selnes, F. (2005). Diversifying your customer portfolio. *Sloan Management Review*, **46**(3), 11–14.

Lapierre, J. (1997). What does value mean on business-to-business professional services? *International Journal of Service Industry Management*, **8**(5), 377–397.

Lapierre, J. (2000). Customer-perceived value in industrial contexts. *Journal of Business & Industrial Marketing*, **15**(2/3), 122–140.

Lindgreen, A. and Wynstra, F. (2005). Value in business markets. What do we know? Where are we going? *Industrial Marketing Management*, **34**(7), 732–748.

Mathieu, V. (2001). Service strategies within the manufacturing sector: Benefits, costs and partnership. *International Journal of Service Industry Management*, **12**(5), 451–475.

Matthyssens, P., Vandenbempt, K., and Weyns, S. (2009). Transitioning and co-evolving to upgrade value offerings: A competence-based marketing view. *Industrial Marketing Management*, **38**(5), 504–512.

Nilsson-Witell, L. and Fundin, A. (2005). Dynamics of service attributes: A test of Kano's theory of attractive quality. *International Journal of Service Industry Management*, **16**(2), 152–168.

Oliva, R. and Kallenberg, R. (2003). Managing the transition from products to services. *International Journal of Service Industry Management*, **14**(2), 160–172.

Ramirez, R. (1999). Value co-production: Intellectual origins and implications for practice and research. *Strategic Management Journal*, **20**(1), 49–65.

Rosson, P. J. and Ford, I. D. (1982). Manufacturer-overseas distributor relations and export performance. *Journal of International Business Studies*, **13**(2), 57–72.

Ulaga, W. (2003). Capturing value creation in business relationships: A customer perspective. *Industrial Marketing Management*, **32**, 667–693.

Ulaga, W. and Eggert, A. (2006). Value-based differentiation on business relationships: Gaining and sustaining supplier status. *Journal of Marketing*, **70**(1), 119–136.

Vargo, S. and Lusch, R. (2004). Evolving to a new dominant logic of marketing. *Journal of Marketing*, **68**(1), 1–17.

Vargo, S. L. and Lusch, R. F. (2008). From goods to service(s): Divergences and convergences of logics. *Industrial Marketing Management*, **37**(3), 254–259.

Vernon, R. (1966). International investment and international trade in the product cycle. *Quarterly Journal of Economics*, **80**, 190–207.

Walter, A., Muller, T. A., Helfert, G., and Ritter, T. (2003). Functions of industrial supplier relationships and their impact on relationship quality. *Industrial Marketing Management*, **32**(2), 159–169.

Walter, A., Ritter, T., and Gemüden, H. G. (2001). Value creation in buyer-seller relationships. *Industrial Marketing Management*, **30**(4), 365–377.

Wilson, D. T. (1995). An integrated model of buyer-seller relationships. *Journal of the Academy of Marketing Science*, **23**(4), 335–345.

Witell, L. and Löfgren, M. (2013). From service for free to service for fee: Business model innovation in manufacturing firms. *Journal of Service Management*, **24**(5), 520–533.

Woodruff, R. B. (1997). Customer value: The next source for competitive advantage. *Journal of the Academy of Marketing Science*, **25**, 139–153.

Woodruff, R. B. and Flint, D. J. (2006). Marketing's service-dominant logic and customer value, in *The Service-dominant Logic of Marketing: Dialog, Debate, and Directions*, R. F. Lusch and S. L. Vargo, (eds.), Chapter 14. Armonk, NY: M.E. Sharpe.

Zerbini, F., Golfetto, F., and Gibbert, M. (2007). Marketing of competence: Exploring the resource-based content of value-for-customers through a case study analysis. *Industrial Marketing Management*, **36**(6), 784–798.

Index

Printed in the United States
By Bookmasters